PELICAN BOOKS

A HISTORY OF MODERN FRANCE

VOLUME ONE

Alfred Cobban was born in 1901. He was educated at Latymer Upper School and Gonville and Caius College, Cambridge.

He was a lecturer in history at King's College, Newcastle upon Tyne, held a Rockefeller Fellowship for research in France, and was visiting Professor at the Universities of Chicago and Harvard.

He had been Professor of French History at University College, London, since 1953, and was head of the history department until 1966. He was also the editor of *History*.

Among his publications are *Burke and the Revolt against the Eighteenth Century*; *Rousseau and the Modern State*; *Dictatorship: Its History and Theory*; and *National Self-Determination*. More recently he has written *The Debate on the French Revolution*; *Ambassadors and Secret Agents: The Diplomacy of the First Earl of Malmesbury at the Hague*; the history of Vichy France in Toynbee's *Hitler's Europe*; *In Search of Humanity: The Role of the Enlightenment in Modern History*; *The Social Interpretation of the French Revolution*; and articles in the *English Historical Review*, *History*, *Political Science Quarterly*, *International Affairs*, and many other journals. The author died in 1968.

CONTENTS

Introduction

I. THE OLD RÉGIME   9

1. *The Death of the Grand Monarch*   9
2. *The Regent Fails to Put the Clock Back*   17
3. *Fleury and National Recovery*   28
4. *Prosperity and Poverty*   37
5. *Disorder at Home*   50
6. *Defeat Abroad*   68

II. THE AGE OF REFORM   82

1. *The Revolution in Ideas*   82
2. *Revival of Authority*   90
3. *Prelude to Reform*   99
4. *The Eve of Revolution*   112
5. *The Revolt of the Privileged Classes*   123
6. *Victory of the Third Estate*   136

III. THE DECADE OF REVOLUTION   152

1. *The Rising of the Masses*   152
2. *France under the Constituent Assembly*   162
3. *Fall of the Constitutional Monarchy*   185
4. *The Failure of the Brissotins*   200
5. *The Committee of Public Safety*   218
6. *Aftermath of Revolution*   241
7. *Balance-sheet of the Eighteenth Century*   259

Chronological Table   267
Further Reading   274
Index   285

MAPS

1. Généralités and Pays d'États 13
2. Internal Customs 57
3. Gabelles 59
4. Parlements and Conseils Souverains 66
5. Revolutionary Paris 160
6. Provinces and Départements 170
7. Eastern Frontier of France during the Revolution 206

INTRODUCTION

THE first object of the introduction is to explain what this history of modern France is not. It is not a strict narrative history, following the course of events year by year. Hence tables of dates have been added to assist the reader. It is not intended to be a text-book giving the facts, all the facts, and nothing but the facts necessary for passing an examination in French history. I have not attempted to spread the history evenly if thinly over the whole period. On the contrary I have concentrated attention where events are densest and most significant, and passed more rapidly over those periods and aspects which seem of less interest, even if this has meant neglecting much repetitive political manoeuvring. Again, the details of foreign relations, in peace and war, are passed over rather slightly. Of course, not all omissions are necessarily deliberate. In some cases they are the result of lack of information. This is particularly so in respect of economic history, for the results of research in this field are still hardly adequate even for a broad picture.

Such gaps constitute one of the major difficulties in compiling the appendices on Further Reading. These are not intended as anything more ambitious than their title suggests: they represent a rather arbitrary choice and obviously exclude many important works. At least some of my debts are reflected in these lists. There should be added an acknowledgement of what I have learned in supervising the work of those students who have researched on subjects from this period for their doctoral theses in my seminar during recent years. The justification for my treatment of the Girondins can now be found in Michael Sydenham's *The Girondins* (Athlone Press, 1961). An analysis of the membership and motivation of the revolutionary mobs, which has finally eliminated the picture drawn by Taine, is given by George Rudé in *The Crowd in the French Revolution* (Clarendon Press, 1959). The lack of influence of Rousseau's political writings before 1789, and their ambivalence after, is shown by Joan Macdonald in a study now being prepared for the press of their influence during the Constituent Assembly. An analysis of the application of the Civil Constitution of the Clergy in the diocese of Lisieux by Winifred Edington, part of which has been published in French periodicals, revealed, among other things, the acute financial problems it

involved. J. P. McLaughlin traced the growth of French an-
nexationist policy from the beginning of the Revolution, and
J. F. Murley completed the first detailed account of the circumstances out of which the Revolutionary War between France and
Great Britain arose. The counter-revolution has always been a
neglected field of study, at least by serious historians. J. A. Johnson,
writing a revealing study of the role of Calonne in the counter-
revolution, found the origin of its cleavages in the ministerial
rivalries of the *ancien régime*; N. F. Richards traced the attitude
of the British government in respect of the French monarchy
from 1789 to 1802; and the researches of Harvey Mitchell on
the counter-revolutionaries, which have partly been published in
journals, revealed the actual connexion of the comte d'Antraigues
with the famous and mysterious Dropmore Bulletins, and also
showed how near the Republic came to being overthrown at the
time of Fructidor. Turning back to the *ancien régime*, the struggle of
the factions for the succession to Fleury, which was only known
in general terms, has been subjected to a valuable examination by
Evelyn Cruickshanks. G. J. de C. Mead's analysis and survey of
the intendants of eighteenth-century France and J. Bosher's
account of the efforts to eliminate the internal customs dues will
both, I believe, when they are published, add considerably to our
knowledge of French administration in the eighteenth century; as,
in a different field, will a study by Nora Temple of the government
of French towns in the eighteenth century, with special reference
to Auxerre and Avalon; and one by Olwen Hufton of the social
structure of the town of Bayeux on the eve of the revolution.
Echoes from most of these theses, on the points mentioned, will
be found in Volume 1.

The second volume originally covered the whole period from
1799 to the Second World War. Inevitably the history of the
period after 1871 was much abridged, in particular the twentieth
century receiving a much briefer treatment than the earlier years.
In this new edition I have taken advantage of the expansion of the
history into three volumes to remedy this lack of proportion. The
second volume, which now ends in 1871, has a new concluding
section and the third volume, treating the history of France since
1871, has been greatly expanded and largely rewritten. It now
carries the history down to the present day, tracing the slow
growth, temporary overthrow, but ultimate survival, of the
republic.

The need to write a third volume in this history of modern

Introduction

France has provided a stimulus to reflection on the slow struggle of republican France to escape from its history. For a thousand years France was a monarchy; it has been a republic for less than a hundred. Monarchial traditions necessarily went deep in French society, and the establishment and consolidation of the republic was bound to be a long drawn out and uncertain struggle against them. When the trials of two world wars are added, it may well seem surprising that the republic, even in a series of numerical metamorphoses, should have survived. The work of those who founded and consolidated it, between 1871 and the beginning of the age of wars in 1914, must have been sounder than their critics, or perhaps even they themselves, knew. Monarchy and empire have attracted more attention and far more admiration from historians than the republic. But if the former had their moments of glory, the latter now begins to be seen as more truly an age of greatness. But it was marred by a social pattern of economic conservatism and class rigidity inherited from *ancien régime*, revolution and empire, which produced intense political conflicts and governmental instability.

There was a time when the history of republican France seemed a tiresome story of repetitious failure, the history of a régime too weak and governments too ephemeral to master circumstances, and of would-be rebels too futile and merely negative to take their place. If this were all, there would be little justification for the production of yet another account of how one Radical Socialist replaced another Radical Socialist on the banks of the Seine and the Rhône. But in history the past gains significance from the future, and the Fourth and Fifth Republics have given a posthumous justification to the Third by the achievement of social and international aims which had seemed doomed to perpetual frustration. A merely political history of the French republics is bound to seem trivial and superficial; but envisaged in terms of the evolution of a society, the history of modern France acquires a deeper dimension. As such it has a significance which as an account of the vagaries of day-to-day, or even year-to-year politics it was bound to lack. Social history has also to be seen on a longer time scale than political. The history of each age throws light on those that preceded and those that followed it. In writing a third volume on France of the Republics I have constantly found myself referred back by echoes of earlier régimes, and sometimes sent forward by anticipations of the latest one. The Fifth Republic seems to draw the threads of modern French history together. It has already concluded much hitherto unfinished business. But if it provides a suitable terminus for this history, it is not so much because it represents an end, as because it also represents a beginning.

I have taken advantage of the opportunity offered by this new edition to add a series of outline maps and to introduce some material derived from research published in the last year or two. I have also corrected a number of slips and am grateful to those reviewers and other readers who have drawn my attention to them. Another debt which I must express is to Mrs Audrey Munro for coping so efficiently and patiently with my handwriting in this and other books she has typed for me.

University College, London   A. COBBAN
June 1964

I

THE OLD RÉGIME

I. THE DEATH OF THE GRAND MONARCH

'THE years go by one after the other; time slips past us without our being aware of it; we grow old like ordinary men and we shall end like them': thus Louis XIV in his declining years, conscious of ineluctable mortality. He had seen all his great servants and a whole generation of his subjects pass away. Within a few months, in 1711–12, his son, grandson, and elder great-grandson died, leaving only an ailing baby to bear the hopes of the Bourbon dynasty. 'This time of desolation left so deep a mark,' wrote Voltaire, 'that I have met those who, long after, could not speak of it without tears.' The Sun King's day closed not in splendour but amid dark clouds of domestic sorrow, nation-wide discontent, and foreign defeat. When he had first appeared above the horizon, a boy king, riding on an Isabella barb amidst a glittering cavalcade to the ceremony that was to mark the formal ending of his minority, he had seemed to John Evelyn, watching the procession from the window of his friend, the philosopher Hobbes, a young Apollo. 'He went almost the whole way with his hat in hand, saluting the ladies and acclamators, who had filled the windows with their beauty, and the air with *Vive le Roi*. He seemed a prince of a grave yet sweet countenance.' This was in 1651. Sixty-four years later the body of the old king was laid to rest in the last of his royal garments at Saint Denis, beside the relics of his ancestors for a thousand years; within a century with them to be exhumed as indecently as the Jansenist remains he had ordered to be scrabbled up at Port Royal and scattered to the winds, while petty attorneys and minor officials exercised more arbitrary and terrible powers of life

9

and death than ever the chancellors and ministers of state of the greatest of the Bourbons had wielded, and a jumped-up lieutenant from a wild island, not even in the domains of the Grand Monarch, led the armies of France, under a flag the Bourbons did not know and were never to acknowledge, to conquer and perish in African deserts and Russian steppes.

Louis XIV reigned for seventy-three years and ruled for fifty-five. By 1715 the French monarchy was approaching the end of its long history, but in 1661, when the young king swiftly and ruthlessly hurled Fouquet, all-powerful Super-intendent of Finances and heir-expectant to Richelieu and Mazarin, from the pride of place and the magnificence of Vaux-le-Vicomte, newest and loveliest of châteaux, to per-petual prison, it seemed only a beginning. France had been a millennium in the making, now at last she was made. The great nobles, whose ambitions and rivalries had so often ravaged the country and let in the invader, had sunk from the mighty struggles of Burgundian and Armagnac, of Bourbon, Guise, and Montmorency, to the salon politics and mob violence of the Fronde, and from that to the role of mere appurtenances of majesty. After the death of Mazarin and the overthrow of Fouquet the courtiers questioned, anxiously or hopefully, who would be the new favourite and govern France for the king. Their speculations were wasted. Henceforth there was to be no first minister. The king him-self was to rule.

Louis never forgot the flight from Paris or the humiliation inflicted on his childhood by the Fronde. Saint-Simon said that he often spoke of those times with bitterness, though the story that he had been neglected by Mazarin and arrived at the throne untrained and unprepared seems to be the reverse of the truth. The lesson Louis drew from the Fronde was that the king must be absolute. To the older principle of divine right, Bodin, a century earlier, in the Religious Wars, had added the more modern idea of sover-eignty, and the royal lawyers, under the cardinals, the theory and practice of *raison d'état*. The idea and the fact of Bourbon absolutism reached their apogee together and found their embodiment in Louis XIV. Never did any prince, said Saint-Simon, possess the art of kingship to such a high degree. No king ever conferred his gifts with better grace, or was more able to make his words, his smile, his very glance, precious to those on whom they were bestowed. He personified majesty, yet nothing seemed to be studied and all was perfectly natural. If the pen of Saint-Simon, more often dipped in vitriol, could say this, we may believe it.

The rigid etiquette that Louis imposed on his court should be judged as the expression not of pettiness of mind but rather of political calculation. The object was to provide the necessary setting for a monarch who was to be the centre of the nation's life with all eyes turned on him. The court was a permanent spectacle for the people: the life of the king passed from birth to death in public. Louis XIV would as soon have neglected his council as the *grand couvert*, at which he dined in the presence of his subjects. Ill and able to do no more than sip a little moisture, he forced himself to the ceremony for the last time on 24 August 1715. He died on 1 September. A rigorous etiquette was needed if the impression was to be one of majesty and not of confusion. Given this, and a king like Louis XIV to play the principal part, and the court became the scene of a perpetual ballet performed before an audience of twenty million. A more classic background was needed for this than the ramshackle royal quarters in Paris. Although other reasons have been given why Louis left Paris for Versailles – the aversion from his capital induced by the troubles of the Fronde, his love of walking and hunting, the desire to relieve the royal mistresses of the embarrassment of life in a large city – not the least was the need to provide a glorious setting for the court. Versailles was described later by Voltaire as a great caravanserai filled with human discomfort and misery – he himself had been honoured for a time with a little room in the palace just above the privies – but the misery was not on view and the grandeur was.

The court, with its etiquette and ceremony, state dignitaries and royal mistresses, was the ornamental framework of monarchy. It brought the high nobles to Versailles where, away from the sources of their strength in the provinces, instead of civil wars they devoted themselves to palace intrigues and fought for the honour of holding the king's shirt when he rose in the morning, while their ladies quarrelled over the right of sitting on a small stool in the queen's presence. It must not be supposed that the whole nobility of France flocked to Versailles, or it would have needed to be a town larger than Paris. The important fact was that, bereft of the leadership of the greater families, the provincial nobles sank into political insignificance. Versailles was the source of more than honour, it was the fountain of favour; court life was a perpetual struggle for jobs, above all for the sinecures and pensions with which the acquiescence of the *noblesse* in its loss of power was bought. On only one member of the old *noblesse* did Louis XIV ever confer ministerial office: during his reign the royal bureaucracy, which had been so many centuries in the making, took over the government of France. The great feudatories and lesser seigneurs were eliminated from the administrative order and the country was divided up into *généralités* under royal *intendants*. These were *commissaires départis,* clothed with all the authority of the king, sent out from the royal council and returning to it in due course. Nothing that happened in their *généralités* was too great or too small for their attention. Through their correspondence the whole life of France passed in review like a great and unending panorama before the king's council, sitting in its various divisions day after day.

Acton described Louis XIV as the greatest man born in modern times on the steps of a throne. An unkinder verdict is that he was the greatest postmaster-general: he had a passion for detail – the arms, manoeuvres, discipline, uniform of his troops, and his buildings and household establishment above all. He found an ideal instrument for the more serious tasks of government in the person of Colbert. Son of a royal official beginning his career as a clerk in a banker's office, rising under Mazarin to the rank of his chief

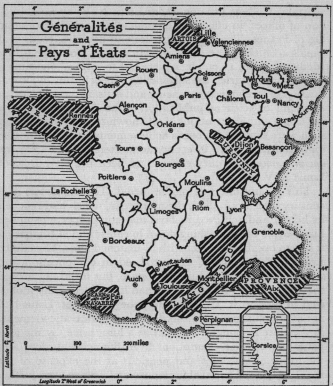

The généralités varied slightly in number during the century. In 1789 there were 33. Except for the pays d'états they were named after the town which was the seat of the intendant. It will be seen how often this is inconveniently placed in one corner of the généralité, far removed from much of the area it administered. When the Constituent Assembly decided that no part of a département should be more than a day's ride away from the *chef-lieu*, it cannot have been uninfluenced by the experience of the *ancien régime*.

The provincial états that survived in the eighteenth century had varying and restricted powers, mostly in matters of finance. One difficulty of writing the administrative history of France is illustrated by the fact that hardly any two of the better-known books in this field agree on what were the actual pays d'états in the eighteenth century.

assistant, Colbert became under Louis XIV, by a cumulation of offices, in effect the dictator of the whole economic life of France. Trading companies and colonies, roads and canals – on the great canal du Midi, from Toulouse to the Mediterranean, 12,000 men were put to work at one time – royal manufacturies, the subsidizing of new industries, introduction of foreign entrepreneurs and artisans, creation of an Academy of Sciences, publication of the *Encyclopedia of Arts and Crafts* with illustrations of all known types of machinery: such were some of Colbert's achievements. It should not be forgotten that what, in economic matters, was in 1789 the *ancien régime*, a century earlier had been the New Deal of Louis XIV and Colbert.

This is only one side of the medal. Three-quarters of a century after Louis died, the monarchy, which had reached its height and achieved its final majestic proportions under him, was to come crashing down in ruins; and in this case it is just to tax the architect with ill-matched aims. The edifice Louis had constructed far surpassed in complication and size that of any other European state, but it did not exceed the resources of France if these had been adequately mobilized to support it. Unfortunately they were not. Louis had not so much suppressed the declining aristocratic elements in the state as bought them off at a high price, by the perpetuation of their exemptions from financial burdens and the grant of sinecures and pensions at the expense of the royal revenue. The taxable resources of France were further reduced by the creation and sale of a host of venal offices, carrying with them financial privileges, from which the royal treasury lost far more in the long run than it gained immediately. During Louis' reign the expense of his buildings strained and that of his wars ruined royal finances, and the concentration of taxes on the poorer part of the nation drove it to desperate rebellion. In the following two reigns every war brought a financial crisis, until the last one, culminating in political upheaval and coinciding with a famine, turned into a revolution.

French finances were not reformed and French economy

did not prosper under Louis XIV, despite the indefatigable labours of Colbert. The trading companies faded into inanition, the state industries – Gobelins tapestry and the like – catered only for a luxury and, therefore, limited market. This was a period of declining prices and of contraction in the economic life of Europe. Great famines devastated France in 1693–4 and 1709–10. The population declined from war, starvation, and disease. The Grand Monarch even made war on his own subjects. When the persecution of the Huguenots reached its climax with the revocation of the edict of Nantes in 1685, *le grand Bossuet* called down benedictions on the King's head. 'Proclaim the miracle of our times. Send up to heaven your praises, and say to this new Constantine, this new Theodosius, this new Charlemagne: it is the worthy achievement of your reign. By you heresy no longer exists. God alone could accomplish this marvel.' Saint-Simon, in the pages of his secret diary, expressed a different opinion. 'The revocation of the edict of Nantes,' he wrote, 'without the least pretext or any necessity, depopulated a quarter of the kingdom, ruined its commerce and weakened it in all parts.' It has been estimated that in spite of efforts to close the frontiers to those flying from persecution, hundreds of thousands of Huguenots, including many of the industrial, commercial, and maritime classes, escaped abroad, while those who remained in France, in the wild country between Gard and Lozère, broke out in the terrible and prolonged revolt of the Camisards. In the cause of religion, Sorel writes, Louis XIV had lost more than he could have gained by the most victorious war, or than could have been demanded by his enemies as the price of the most disastrous peace.

Even in diplomacy and war, which were the essential *métier de roi*, Louis outlived his good fortune. The success of France under the cardinals had been founded on '*la modération dans la force*', the classic French foreign policy. Louis XIV, in the words of Sorel, '*le dénatura*', because he pushed his ambitions to the point at which they brought about the creation of a hostile coalition powerful enough to defeat even France.

Failure and disaster did not weaken the resolution of the Grand Monarch. Absolutism and bureaucracy kept the country in a frozen grip, apparently immobile. Underneath, new currents were stirring, but they were only to appear on the surface in a new reign. In the midst of defeat and discontent the old king, with his magnificent physique and supreme confidence in divine sanction and the performance of his kingly duty, stood unshaken. In his last years the firmness of the king's character upheld him still and he was perhaps not undeserving of the title 'great'. Brought to sue for peace from the victorious allies, he rejected the humiliation of himself turning his grandson, Philip V, off the Spanish throne. The heart – or was it the artistic conscience? – of Saint-Simon was melted by the sight of the old king struggling with misfortune:

Overwhelmed externally by the enemies he had provoked, who rejoiced in his powerlessness, envisaged him as resourceless, and mocked his past glory, he found himself without succour, without ministers, without generals, through having raised and upheld them by favour and whim and by the fatal vainglory of wishing and believing he could create them at will. Anguished at heart by the most personal and poignant losses, with consolation from no one, a prey to his own weakness, reduced to struggle alone against horrors a thousand times more frightful than his most perceptible ills, incessantly reminded of them by those left to him who were dearest and most intimate, who openly and unrestrainedly took advantage of the subjection into which he had fallen, and from which he could not, and did not even wish to relieve himself, though he felt all its burden; incapable moreover, because of an invincible ruling passion and a habit which had become second nature, of casting any reflection on the interest and behaviour of his jailers; in the midst of these domestic bonds, that constancy, that firmness of soul, that appearance of equanimity, that never-changing determination to remain at the helm of state so long as he was able, that hope against all hope, which came from courage and discretion, not from infatuation, that preservation of appearances in everything, of all this, few men could have been capable, and this is what truly entitled him to the description *great*, which had been so prematurely conferred on him. It was this which won for him the true admiration of the whole of Europe and that of those of his subjects who witnessed it, and which brought back to him so many hearts alienated by so long and harsh a reign.

At Denain, in 1712, Villars took advantage of the disruption of the hostile Grand Alliance to end the war with a victory; Torcy conducted the peace negotiations with ability; and France emerged at the Treaties of Utrecht and Rastadt with far less loss than at one time had seemed possible. The last of the agreements was signed in November 1715, but the king of France had died at Versailles on 1 September, at the age of seventy-seven and in the fifty-sixth year of his personal rule.

2. THE REGENT FAILS TO PUT THE CLOCK BACK

THE heir to the throne after Louis XIV was a child of five. A regency was inevitable and – the king of Spain being excluded by the peace treaties – it was also inevitable that the regent should be the prince of the blood nearest to the throne. This was Philip of Orleans, nephew to Louis XIV and the hope of all those whose discontent and rancour had been growing beneath the appearance of conformity imposed by absolute rule. That Orleans was the enemy of all he held dearest, Louis XIV well knew, and to political distrust was added personal detestation of him as a rake and unbeliever. Though Orleans had to be regent, the dead king, who aspired to rule France even after his death, had done his best to safeguard his system. He bequeathed effective authority to the royal bastards, begotten of that dazzling, proud, and bad-tempered beauty, the marquise de Montespan, and legitimized in 1714, to the indignation of the old nobility. The duc du Maine, pious and honourable, was appointed by the King's testament guardian of the young Louis XV and commander of the royal guard; he was to be succeeded if he died by his brother Toulouse. Orleans was allowed to be president of a council of regency, but the membership of the council was laid down in the will and was not to be susceptible of alteration during the minority. Decisions were to be by majority vote, '*sans que le duc dorleans chef du conseil puisse seul et par son auctorité particulière rien déterminer*'. If the vote were equal a fresh vote was to be taken, and only after this, if the council were still equally divided, did the regent have the casting vote. This was to reduce him to a nullity. Louis' testament was an attempt to do what no king could do. It was a flagrant contradiction of his own absolutist principles. On the death of a king his successor was automatically endowed with sovereignty in all plenitude and could be bound neither in law nor in fact by the will of his predecessor. The first act of the regent, in the name of Louis XV, was to emancipate himself from bondage to the dead hand of the great king.

Orleans had behind him the nobles, jealous of the bureaucracy and the royal bastards, the parlements, hoping to regain some of their lost influence, the Jansenists and all who resented the ecclesiastical domination of Mme de Maintenon and the Jesuits. Those who had been discontented by the centralized despotism of Louis XIV looked to him to bring back what were regarded by some sort of historical fantasy as the good old days before the cardinals began the destruction of aristocratic liberties. The parlements were used to quash the will of Louis XIV with due formality, and Saint-Simon has made a dramatic, though hardly historically accurate, story out of it, building up the scene at the parlement from the magnificent entry of the royal bastards, swollen with pride and confidence, to their humiliating deflation and crestfallen departure. It was really a foregone conclusion. The parlements had their right of remonstrance recognized in return for the part they played, though to attribute the trouble they subsequently caused to this episode is to read too much into it. The regent emerged with full powers of royal absolutism but with the intention of using them to bring that absolutism to an end.

Philip of Orleans was a man of culture and natural ability. A good general, he had been kept in the background by Louis XIV's hostility. This was not without cause.

Drunken and dissipated, Orleans' reputation was so bad that he was even suspected of poisoning his way to the throne, though without any justification. Living perpetually in the company of loose women and those whom the slang of the regency called *roués*, fit only to be broken on the wheel, he was habituated to debauchery, spiced with outrageous impiety, to the point of being unable to do without it and only able to amuse himself in rowdy orgies. It is said that he was one of those who can take no wine without drunkenness. Perhaps the truth is that he was bored with himself from birth and could only find distraction in wine and women.

Society followed the model set by the regent. The sanctimoniousness and dullness of the later years of Louis XIV were thrown off, like the stiff dresses and sombre hues which Mme de Maintenon had made fashionable. Gay colours, light fabrics, and swinging hoops and paniers, copied from the robes of *bourgeoises* and coquettes, brought lighter modes and manners along with a franker indifference to morals into high society. This was the age of Watteau, by royal appointment *peintre des fêtes galantes*. There was a general embarkment for Cythera, though the ephemeral moments of love in sun and shade that are seized by Watteau's brush immortalize a generation better characterized by the regent's little suppers. Not, indeed, that it is correct to identify either the good art or the bad morals too closely with the regency. Because political events constitute our basic historical calendar, we tend too easily to assume that other chronological divisions correspond to them. In fact, Watteau's art was already blossoming in the last years of Louis XIV, to open out under the regency and be cut off in full bloom with the painter's death in 1721. Before the seventeenth century had ended, Perrault's *La Belle au bois dormante, Cendrillon, Chaperon rouge* and other stories, published in 1696 and 1697, seemed to announce a spirit of simplicity and lightness. The darker side, too, of a new age, that world of rogues and adventurers in which no man is honest and no woman virtuous, had been reflected, before the Sun King drew his last breath, in the satire of Le Sage. With the *Diable boiteux* of 1707, and *Turcaret* of 1709, says a French writer, *quelle rancoeur d'âme honnête* is revealed. When, with the first part of *Gil Blas*, in 1715, Le Sage showed his hero living on his wits and making fools of the rich and powerful, he was not discovering the new world of the regency, he was merely beginning to feel more at home in a world that was already there before Louis XIV had died. Gil Blas joins hands across the century with Figaro. Meanwhile, out of the personal tragedy of the runaway priest, the abbé Prévost, grew the history of *Manon Lescaut*, sounding a deeper note than the eighteenth century proper could commonly reach. There is more in *Manon* of Racine than of Rousseau. The chevalier des Grieux descends from the high lineage of Phèdre, and could pray like the abbé Prévost, but so unlike the eighteenth century, 'Deliver us from love.'

In politics also the regency must not be dismissed as a mere upstart *opéra bouffe* episode in French history. It represented the culmination of a real attempt to remedy the ills which serious observers detected in French society. The *noblesse de l'épée* had never become reconciled to the position of powerlessness to which the cardinals and Louis XIV had reduced it. As early as 1664 a group of peers commissioned the abbé Le Laboureur to write a history of the peerage for the purpose of putting their claims on a sound historical basis. His work circulated in manuscript, though it was not published until 1740. Fénelon, who had been tutor of the young Duke of Burgundy, the grandson of Louis XIV and heir apparent in 1711–12, denounced royal absolutism. 'I call to my support,' he said, 'the memory of past centuries, because it would be blindness to reject the methods that maintained a moderate monarchy during thirteen centuries and to substitute for them others which only facilitate a despotic power, more appropriate to the genius of the Persians, Turks or oriental nations than to our constitution.' These were no isolated sentiments. La Bruyère, in the editions of his *Caractères* published after Louis XIV's invasion of Germany and ravaging of the Palatinate, wrote, 'There is no *patrie* in the despotic state, other things take its place:

interest, glory, the service of the prince.' An Oratorian, Michel Levassor, was, it is suggested, the author of the pamphlets entitled *Les Soupirs de la France Esclave, qui aspire après la liberté*. The ideas of Fénelon, who in *Télémaque* taught implicitly the evil of absolutism, were taken up and developed by the Jacobite exile, the chevalier Ramsay.

There was a moment when it seemed as if those who formed the small, secret, aristocratic opposition under Louis XIV had the future at their feet. In 1711 the Duke of Burgundy became dauphin. Fénelon and the Dukes of Beauvillier and Chevreuse, who shared his views, had indoctrinated the new heir and began to draw up plans to abolish despotic monarchy and restore an idealized aristocracy. A year later the Duke of Burgundy died, but Philip of Orleans, with Saint-Simon to urge him on, was himself influenced by the views of what was called 'the faction of the Duke of Burgundy' and as regent he was to attempt to put them into practice. Symbolically, after the death of Louis XIV, the court abandoned Versailles, though the move to Paris was only the continuation of a trend that had begun while he was still on the throne, when the younger nobles, tired of the abode of boredom and constraint that the great king had created, deserted the cramped and crowded discomfort of Versailles for the elegant *hôtels* they built or bought in Paris. The boy king was sent first to Vincennes, but in what was then only a village there was no lodging for his entourage; in 1716 the court was established at the Tuileries, where Louis the *bien-aimé* grew up, a pretty, spoilt boy, under the admiring eyes of his people. The regent continued to live close by at the Palais Royal.

One of the prime objects of the aristocratic reaction was to reduce the power of the secretaries of state, described by Saint-Simon as the monsters who had devoured the *noblesse*, the all-powerful enemies of the *seigneurs* whom they had reduced to dust beneath their feet. Three secretaries out of four were kept by the regent; but side by side with them he established the so-called Polysynodie, a system of six councils for war, navy, finance, home, foreign affairs, and religion composed each of ten members, half official and half noble. This has been treated by some historians as a mere device of the regent to establish a clientèle for himself, a piece of lip-service to the new ideas which he never intended seriously. He treated personally with the president of each council, it is said, and neglected to bring many matters of state before the council of regency. The fact that Orleans called to the councils his foremost opponents, the bastards, the chief figures of the old court and the former ministers of Louis XIV, makes it difficult to accept this hostile interpretation. No such hypothesis is needed to explain the failure of the Polysynodie. Saint-Simon, himself one of its chief promoters, confessed that the difficulty was the ignorance, frivolity, and lack of application of a *noblesse* that was good for nothing except to get itself killed in war. By 1718 the experiment had failed, the six councils were suppressed and the regency returned to the old king's system of government through secretaries of state.

Aristocratic nostalgia for a past that had gone beyond recall was to be dormant for nearly three-quarters of a century more, and when it reawoke was to provoke a catastrophe that those who were aiming in 1715 to overthrow the system of Louis XIV did not dream of, even though another and ultimately fatal ill, which had manifested itself under Louis XIV, had already reduced the state to a condition of acute crisis. This was the problem of the royal finances. The regent thought of declaring the Crown bankrupt and summoning the States-General, so close does 1715 seem to 1789. The deficit was indeed greater, proportionally, than that which brought about the fall of the absolute monarchy under Louis XVI. The last controller-general of Louis XIV had proposed to meet the financial difficulty by the imposition of taxes which would be paid by *noblesse* and clergy as well as the rest of the nation. The aristocratic reaction was real enough to prevent this solution from being put into effect· The interest of the *rentiers* were not yet strong enough, as it had become by 1789, to prevent the other solution of a partial repudiation of the royal debts. A Chamber of Justice was set up 'to make the financiers disgorge'. Composed of magistrates taken from the parlement, it set about its task with a characteristic heavy-handed indifference to justice, condemned petty financiers to the galleys, provoked suicides, and upset commercial relations to the point at which the merchants were forced to protest. The wealthier financiers escaped, the friends of the regent sold immunity to those who could afford to buy it, and the whole operation produced little gain to the state. Meanwhile the duc de Noailles, the effective head of the *Conseil des Finances*, was able to make limited reforms in financial administration and effect some modest economies.

The regent fully saw the need for more drastic changes and he believed that he had found the man who could bring them about. This was the Scot, John Law, son of an Edinburgh goldsmith and banker, who in the course of an adventurous life had made the acquaintance of Orleans in the gaming dens of Paris, to which Law was reputed to resort with a bag of gold coins in each hand. In the financial capitals of Europe he had learnt that money was only a means of exchange, that real national wealth depended on population and supplies, that these depended on trade and that trade depended on money. The shortage of currency, he truly saw, was one of the chief handicaps to French economy. The issue by a royal bank of paper money, guaranteed on the king's credit, could remedy this deficiency. Credit was the open-sesame to wealth, and therefore power. How, otherwise, had two tiny states like England and the Dutch Republic been able to face and defeat the great French monarchy, to raise and support national debts such as France was crushed by, and to extend their trade through all the seas and into all the continents of the world? The regent, nothing if not intelligent and adventurous, saw the force of Law's arguments. The *Conseil des Finances* was suspicious and the merchants and financiers jealous, but in May 1716 Law obtained authorization from the regent to establish a private bank. Conducted on sound principles, it proved a great success. In August 1717 Law gained a further concession in the

form of the trade monopoly with Louisiana, for the exploitation of which he founded the Company of the West.
To this was soon after granted the monopoly of trade with
the West Indies and Canada. In December 1718 the bank
became a royal bank, and in 1719 the company absorbed
the old and languishing companies of Senegal, the East
Indies, China, and Africa. The financiers, who had not
viewed the growth of this banking and trading colossus with
equanimity, opposed it as well as they could, the chief
centre of financial opposition being the Farmers General –
the financiers who bought from the state for a lump sum the
right of collecting the indirect taxes and made what profit
they could out of them. Law therefore next proceeded to
outbid the Farmers General and gain for his company the
farm of the taxes. Finally, he took over the royal debt, offering its holders shares in the company and asking from the
state only a reduced interest of 3 per cent. In 1720 the bank
and the company were officially united and Law, who had
become naturalized and accepted the Catholic religion, was
appointed to the revived office of Controller-General of
Finances.

Many reforms were sketched out in the short period of
Law's System. Direct and indirect taxes were united under a
single system of collection. Following a proposal which had
been put forward earlier by Louis XIV's great fortress-
builder, Vauban, in his book on the *dîme royale*, a tax to be
paid by all classes in the community was planned; it was
proposed to suppress a host of unnecessary venal offices;
capital was advanced to manufacturers at a moderate rate
of interest; debtors were released from prison; a programme
of public works was started. But all this was only a beginning, largely on paper in more than one sense. To build up
the credit of the company, on the success of which his system
depended, Law had painted a picture of Louisiana as the
new Eldorado, its mountains of gold, rocks of emerald,
mines littered with diamonds, and its inhabitants simple
Hurons ready to exchange all these for the cheapest gew-
gaws or manufactures of Europe. To cope with the trade

that was expected from *le Mississipi*, as the company was known, Lorient was founded in France and New Orleans in America. To provide colonists, in the absence of volunteers the government took criminals, vagabonds, foundlings, prostitutes and shipped them to America by force; and on the desolate shore where Manon Lescaut died in the arms of the chevalier des Grieux in romance, many of her sisters perished in hard fact.

The trade of the company, though not negligible, fell pathetically below expectation and was quite inadequate to support the inflated paper currency of the system; but this was the age of speculation, of the Darien Company and the South Sea Bubble. Noble and base joined in a frantic struggle for shares in *le Mississipi* and pushed their value up to a fantastic figure. Law was besieged by would-be purchasers: one lady, it was alleged, hired men to shout 'Fire!' to get him out of his house, and another invaded his bedroom by way of the chimney. The rue Quincampoix, centre of the stock-jobbing, had to be closed by the police because of the disorder and bloodshed that the crowds of speculators from all classes of society caused, but they only transferred their activities elsewhere. And now the financiers, helpless in the first days of the system, moved into action. Public suspicion was aroused that the shares in the company were not really worth forty times their face value. Great speculators, princes of the blood like Bourbon and Conti, sold out while the mania was still at its height. The shrewder copied them. Law struggled bravely to maintain the stability of the house of cards he had erected. To keep up the value of his shares he decreed that gold and silver should no longer be valid currency, but people had begun to believe that perhaps after all they were safer than paper. In a desperate attempt to restore the system to solvency Law ordered a progressive reduction in the value of the shares, but the official reduction could not keep pace with what soon became a catastrophic fall. The mob of speculators was now fighting to sell instead of buy. October 1720 saw the bankruptcy of the system. Law's paper money ceased to be valid currency and in December he fled to London, where, it is said, a special performance at Drury Lane was held in his honour. The play chosen was *The Alchemist*.

Some had made great fortunes out of the system and thousands had been ruined. 'All those,' wrote Montesquieu, 'who were rich six months ago are now in the depth of poverty, and those who had not even bread to eat are swollen with riches. Never have the two extremes of society met so closely. The foreigner turned the state inside out as a tailor turns a suit of clothes.' All Law's reforms were lost in the ruin of the system, and the prejudice against a state bank was such that France did not again possess one until Bonaparte was Consul. Interest in maritime and colonial enterprises, on a reduced scale, remained. Lorient and New Orleans survived and slowly grew, to provide visible evidence that *le Mississipi* had not been entirely a dream. Industry and public works had been given a stimulus, the peasantry had cleared off some of their debts and the financiers had in many cases increased their fortunes at the cost of the small owners of stock, who were doubtless expendable.

In the economic as in the political structure of France, the attempt under the regency to break away from the régime of Louis XIV and introduce new principles and methods into the running of the state had failed. In foreign policy also a new line had been struck out. Louis XIV in his final years seemed to have learnt the lesson of his defeats and under compulsion to have abandoned the struggle for the hegemony of Europe which had brought him almost to disaster. His last moves have been interpreted as an anticipation of the long eighteenth-century struggle against the natural enemy, England, and a foreshadowing of that Austrian alliance which has been seen by some historians as the masterstroke of French policy, albeit one that miscarried. This is to read too much into what was primarily an attempt to consolidate the one gain that had resulted from twenty-five years of war, the connexion with Spain that was the consequence of the presence of a Bourbon on the Spanish throne. It was difficult for the regent to envisage the Spanish alliance in quite the same light. Philip V was, if it were not for the restrictive clauses in the peace treaties, the rightful heir to the French throne. He was, therefore, the rival and enemy of the regent. The ambitions of Philip V and his domineering wife Elizabeth Farnese and minister Alberoni, which led to the organization of a conspiracy against Orleans by the Spanish ambassador, Cellamare, in 1718, forced the regent to look for external support elsewhere. There is a fashion for calling the diplomacy of the eighteenth century secret and attributing it to the personal interests of the ruler, as though the diplomacy of other periods were not secret and were not also influenced by the interests of rulers. The *secret* of the regent was the English alliance, and he had to aid him in putting it into operation his Foreign Minister, the spare, sparkling, intriguing, ambitious abbé, Dubois. The alliance with Great Britain in 1716, which became the Triple Alliance after the accession of the Dutch in 1717, was the work of Dubois and the British minister, Stanhope. By it George I was promised French support against Jacobite claims, and the regent English support against those of Philip of Spain. After a short war Philip V yielded. In 1721 Dubois obtained recognition by Spain of the right of the regent to the French succession, the betrothal of a Spanish Infanta to Louis XV, and – despite his personal life, which was what might have been expected of a regency abbé – a cardinal's hat for himself. The policy of the English alliance was not to last, but at least it was to endure longer than the Polysynodie or Law's system. Despite the failure of his reforming plans, the personal position of the regent was now stronger than ever. All his enemies had been defeated when, in December 1723, he died. Dubois had preceded him by four months. And what might have seemed the beginning of a new chapter proved to be merely an episode in parentheses.

3. FLEURY AND NATIONAL RECOVERY

THE duc de Bourbon was ugly, blind in one eye, bandy-legged, and stupid, but as the next prince of the blood he succeeded to Philip of Orleans. The best thing about him was his mistress, Mme de Prie, pretty, intelligent, and ambitious, as was the way of mistresses, daughter of a financier and moving in financial circles, as was also often the way of mistresses in the eighteenth century. Bourbon, for all his limitations, was pleased with the possession of power and conscious that only the life of the young Louis XV stood between the throne and the succession of the son of the regent. To guard against this calamity, or such it seemed to a Condé, the only safeguard appeared to be to marry the king off at once, though he was still only fifteen. As the Spanish Infanta to whom he was officially betrothed was only five, France would have had to wait some time before an heir to the throne could be expected from this marriage. The little Infanta was therefore hurriedly packed off back to Spain, to the fury of the Spanish court. To Bourbon, or his advisers, it seemed a stroke of genius to promote Marie Leczinska, daughter of Stanislaus, ex-King of Poland, to the vacant place in the young Louis XV's affections. True, her father was only a dethroned king, living on a French pension in a modest residence in Germany, while Marie was six years older than Louis XV and no beauty, but the poorer her claims the greater would be her gratitude to her benefactor. Moreover she was healthy and seemed capable of guaranteeing the succession. Stanislaus had an eye to the main chance, Marie was delighted with her good fortune and the pretty boy to whom she was so unexpectedly offered, and Louis XV all anxiety to be a devoted husband.

The marriage took place in 1725, but the duc de Bourbon did not profit by it for long. He brought about his fall by an unwise attempt to strengthen his position. He tried to make use of the queen to secure the removal from the king's presence of his old tutor, Fleury, Bishop of Fréjus, whose influence seemed dangerously great. This was a fatal error of judgement, for Louis now manifested that capacity for affection and unwillingness to separate himself from those he was used to which was a dominant feature of his character. In June 1726 the young king sent Bourbon to Chantilly and exiled Mme de Prie, with her husband for company, to their château in the country, where she bored herself to death and died, perhaps by suicide, a year later. Without apparent effort Fleury emerged triumphant at the head, under the king, of the machine of state, and the most prosperous and successful period in the history of eighteenth-century France began.

The government of France had been left by Louis XIV half-way between the medieval personal and the modern administrative régimes. It has still in the eighteenth century to be written of mainly in terms of individuals, but there was a governmental machine through which personal rule had to operate. This was, since the regent's attempt at reform had failed, the machine that had been given its final shape by Louis XIV. With few exceptions – the most important being the parlements and the provincial *états*, of which I shall have to write subsequently – the whole governmental system of France was embodied in the person of the king: he was the state. Divine right was more than a phrase. The king, wrote Bodin at the time of the Religious Wars, is the image of God on earth. When Montesquieu, in his *Lettres persanes*, mocked the memory of Louis XIV, it was clear that the intellectual climate was changing, but the change had not yet touched common opinion, still less affected the assumptions on which the state was based. The court painter Rigaud, who had portrayed Louis XIV in his pride, long after painted Louis XV wearing the same velvet and ermine of majesty, standing in almost the same pose of authority as his great predecessor, so that one almost fails to notice that the subject is a little boy of five years old. Whatever his age or character, the king in person embodied all authority. The law was his and emanated from his simple will. In practice, Fénelon wrote, the king is much more head of the Church than the Pope. The army was a royal army, commanded by the king and fighting under the personal standard of the house of Bourbon. Justice was royal, and whatever the law courts might decide the king could always use his power of *justice retenue* to forestall or override their decision: he could summon any case from the ordinary courts to the Royal Council by *lettre de cachet*. In short, the authority of the king was not that of the titular head of an administrative régime, it was the personal exercise of his individual *bon plaisir*.

Ruling as an individual, the king of France delegated his authority to individuals, and in this way the principle of absolutism passed down through the administrative hierarchy. According to his rank every official was endowed with a fraction of the royal *bon plaisir*. Each, like the king, was in a sense an arbitrary ruler in relation to those subject to his authority, appointed to exercise his discretion, not to act under instruction. This is the meaning of the saying attributed to Louis XV, 'If I were Lieutenant of Police I would ban cabriolets.' Unfortunately he was not Lieutenant of Police, he was merely king, and his only sanction was to dismiss an official who refused to carry out his wishes. Even this power was limited, for most of the royal officials held their offices for payment; their posts were venal and hence assimilated to private property, and could only be taken away from them if compensation equal to their market value were paid. For a royal officer to lose his post was a very rare thing. The result was that the great bureaucratic machine, the product of many centuries culminating in the work of the cardinals and Louis XIV, was to an extraordinary extent in its actual operation independent of the royal will at its lower levels, and at the same time extraordinarily dependent on it at the top.

In theory the king, as well as being supreme judge and lawgiver, head of the armed forces and of the Church, was also the executive in person. He wielded this power through a series of councils. The highest, the *Conseil d'état, Conseil d'en haut*, or *Conseil secret* as it was variously called, dealt with the great questions of government and especially with foreign policy. It was presided over by the king and composed of the Ministers of State, who were nominated and dismissed by the king. A second council, the *Conseil des dépêches*, was concerned with all internal administration and judicial appeals. Affairs brought before it were reported by Masters of Requests, who, as they had to stand, literally did not have seats in the council and were not members of it. There were, in addition, the *Conseil des Finances*; a *Conseil de Commerce* with a fluctuating existence, sometimes separated from and sometimes united to the *Conseil des Finances*; the *Conseil de Conscience*, which dealt with the granting of benefices; and finally, the *Conseil privé* or *Conseil des Partis*, composed of Councillors of State and Masters of Requests, which exercised the private jurisdiction of the king and was described as 'a tribunal established to judge the judges'. It dealt in particular with conflicts of jurisdiction. The *Conseil des Partis* was composed, in 1789, of eighty-two Councillors of State and eighty Masters of Requests, who acted as *rapporteurs*; it was the direct ancestor of the modern *Conseil d'état*. It is sad to have to say, after giving this imposing picture of a conciliar régime, that it was largely a mere façade. The real work of government in the eighteenth century was conducted by other persons and in another way. The heads of the departments of state, who, apart from the Secretary for Foreign Affairs, were not necessarily included in the *Conseil d'en haut* which in principle decided matters of high policy, were the men who wielded the actual executive power and took the important decisions.

The first of the great officers of state was the Chancellor. President by right of all tribunals, sitting in the parlement above the *premier président*, he embodied under the king all justice. As a sign that while majesty passed away justice was eternal and never died, he alone wore no mourning for the death of a king. The chancellorship was a life office, the last of the great medieval offices of the Crown. For this very reason all effective power had been removed from the Chancellor and given to the Keeper of the Seals, who might or might not be the same person. With the power also went the fees. It was said, 'Chancelier sans les sceaux est apothicaire sans sucre', not without justification, for under Louis XV the Seals were worth some 120,000 livres a year.

There were normally four Secretaries of State, for Foreign Affairs, War, the Navy, and the *Maison du Roi*. The last of these had responsibility for questions of internal security and in particular for Paris, so that he was often called the *ministre de Paris*. Fifthly, the Controller-General had charge of royal finances, of agriculture, industry, bridges and high-ways, and in general all matters of internal administration except those in the attribution of the *Maison du Roi*; and as the complexity of domestic government increased, so his importance grew. The four secretaries and the Controller-General, each at the head of large and highly developed *bureaux*, provided the effective government of France, the councils being pushed on one side.

Louis XIV had worked individually with each secretary, decided with them separately the policies of their offices, and himself provided the unity and coordination required if the whole government were to function effectively. If the king could not undertake this task his place could be supplied by a *premier ministre*, such as Richelieu and Mazarin had been. The office was revived in 1722 for Dubois; on his death in 1723 the regent took it for himself and he was succeeded by the duc de Bourbon. Fleury never took the title but he acted as a very powerful *premier ministre* and while he lived, at least until the last few years, when age began to show its effects even on him, France had a government and a policy, though the secretaries were increasingly restive under his control. After the death of Fleury, Louis XV decided, or was persuaded, to step into the shoes of his great-grand-father as the effective head of the government, but he had neither the assiduity nor the strength of character to impose his will effectively on the secretaries. The result was that for the last fifty years of the *ancien régime* France had no *premier ministre*. When one was appointed, in 1787, apart from his personal inadequacy, it was too late to remedy the ills of nearly half a century of weak and divided government. But this is to look ahead. In 1726 Fleury was to take up office with the full authority of the king behind him, though, at the age of seventy-three, it could hardly have been anticipated that he would continue in the same position for another seventeen years.

The modest, smiling abbé, who had become Bishop of Fréjus and was to be cardinal, won the devotion of the young king when he was his tutor and was to retain it to the end of a long life. In the absolute monarchy favour was the first and necessary basis of power, but Fleury was more than a mere royal favourite. In private life a timid, unassertive, friendly though reserved, cautious old ecclesiastic, in office he showed himself to have a will of iron – 'the proudest man in himself and the most implacable that I have ever known', Saint-Simon described him. It was a pride that was put to the service of France. His early poverty had engendered no love of riches in him and his way of life remained simple and unpretentious. While the regent has been condemned for his adventurous policy of innovations, Fleury has been criticized for his conservatism and caution; but they both of them gave France what she needed most, a government.

Fleury brought into the administration hard-working and able ministers. D'Aguesseau, Chancellor for life, was recalled from exile and devoted himself to the continuation of the great work of legal codification begun under Colbert. The former intendant, Orry, Controller-General from 1730 to 1746, provided an orthodox, methodical administration. Maurepas built up the navy, while he also functioned as Secretary for the *Maison du Roi*. D'Angervilliers, Secretary of State for War from 1728 to 1740, was another who had learnt administrative habits as an intendant. From 1727 to 1737 Chauvelin, officially Keeper of the Seals, conducted foreign affairs in collaboration with Fleury, until his efforts to divert French policy on to lines which Fleury did not approve of led to his disgrace and replacement by yet another former intendant, Amelot de Chaillou. France was hardly to know again such a period of stability in governmental personnel.

The third of the great cardinal ministers was not unworthy of the succession to Richelieu and Mazarin. Like his contemporary Walpole, with whom he had more than a little in common, Fleury preferred to let sleeping dogs lie. They both saw the advantage to their countries of a continuation of peace and the opportunity for economic recovery from the wars of Louis XIV, rather than in the adventures that the war party in each country was urging and that some subsequent French historians would have preferred Fleury to have undertaken. The European situation when he came into power was uneasy, but Fleury and Walpole were both anxious to preserve peace and rapidly established a personal understanding. The most powerful financier in France, Pâris-Duverney, in a memoir read to the Council, warned that war would be a disaster for French economy. At the beginning of Fleury's term of office Great Britain, under the energetic pressure of Walpole's colleague, Townshend, seemed to be moving in the direction of war with Spain and Austria. The situation of France in the pattern of European powers, and the personal proclivities of Fleury, cast him for the role of honest broker. By continual activity he kept the imminent conflict within the field of diplomacy, and at the price of being charged, at the time and subsequently, with subservience to British policy, he preserved the peace of Europe. The treaty of Vienna in 1731 closed this episode. None of the fundamental problems of international politics had been solved, no glory had been gained; Fleury had merely preserved peace, which was at the moment the most valuable thing that France could have.

Those who were so anxious to push France into war, preferably with Austria or Great Britain but it did not matter seriously with which, were soon to find a better opportunity. In 1733 Augustus, Elector of Saxony and elective King of Poland, died, leaving as his heir Augustus III of Saxony. The dispossessed Stanislaus of Poland saw in this situation his opportunity; with the backing of a strong French party he proceeded to Warsaw, where a Diet of Polish nobles restored him to the throne. As was usual in Poland, an opposition was immediately formed which chose Augustus III as anti-king. Russia and Austria supported Augustus; and an invading Russian army chased Stanislaus from Warsaw and placed his rival on the Polish throne.

This insult to the father of the French queen and injury to French interests played so completely into the hands of the war party in France that Fleury could do nothing but accept the inevitability of an armed conflict. He let Chauvelin organize a coalition with Spain and Sardinia against Austria; but whereas Chauvelin was also directing his diplomacy against Great Britain, Fleury used his influence with Walpole to secure British neutrality and took care to divert French military action from the Low Countries where it would have aroused British hostility. While Chauvelin was aspiring after war on the grand scale, Fleury was determined that it should be limited in its scope and profitable in its results. He made no serious attempt to reverse the situation in Poland. A French army occupied Lorraine, but though it crossed the Rhine and captured Phillipsburg, where its commander, the Duke of Berwick, was killed, no attempt was made to penetrate farther into Germany. In Italy some territory was conquered in the Milanese by Villars, but he was recalled from an attempt to invade Austria through the Tyrol and died on his way back, the last of the great generals of Louis XIV.

Content with these successes, Fleury began negotiations for peace. At the back of his mind there was the thought that by giving Chauvelin his head and allowing him to push on with an agressive policy there was a danger that the coalition of Austria, Great Britain, and the Dutch Republic, which had proved fatal to Louis XIV's ambitions, might be recreated. The cardinal was determined to pursue a policy which would not alarm Europe. Secret peace negotiations were therefore begun in 1735, and in 1736, after a short two years' war with no great campaign, France emerged with the virtual acquisition of the duchy of Lorraine. Stanislaus was compensated for the loss of Poland by being made king of Lorraine, where he proved a philosophical and benevolent ruler and turned Nancy into one of the most beautiful minor capitals in Europe, while under his French chancellor the little kingdom was administered practically as a French *généralité*. When Stanislaus died in 1766 it was absorbed uneventfully into France. To reconcile the Emperor to this concession, Francis of Lorraine, destined to marry the Emperor's daughter, was given the succession to Tuscany, and France recognized the Pragmatic Sanction guaranteeing the unity of the Habsburg dominions. Fleury had not only secured a peace which was profitable and a settlement which within its limits was likely to be lasting, he had outmanoeuvred his own more reckless colleague and the war party. For his part, Chauvelin had been building up a network of intrigue which, he believed, would intimidate the cardinal. He did not know his man. Rapidly and ruthlessly the ambitious minister was hurled from office into exile. Those who continued to intrigue, or even to correspond with him, paid the price in Fleury's disfavour. Towards Chauvelin the cardinal was henceforth implacable.

Fleury had restored France to the position in Europe which her population and resources justified. In 1739 a French ambassador negotiated a peace between the Holy Roman and the Ottoman Empires which restored Belgrade to the Turks and signified a resurgence of the power of one of France's traditional Eastern allies. At home Fleury's administration was marked by no correspondingly striking achievements. He damped down the fires of conflict over Jansenism and the reviving claims of the parlements, but these, and the connected problem of financial reform, will be best dealt with subsequently, at the point when they effectively take the centre of the stage. The most important feature of Fleury's period of office was undramatic and unmarked. It was the opportunity that a generation of stable government, with no great wars, gave for recovery from the disasters of the reign of Louis XIV and for positive economic advance. For some sections of French society at least this was the golden age of the *ancien régime*.

4. PROSPERITY AND POVERTY

By abstaining from expensive adventures abroad, and providing competent government at home, Fleury established the conditions in which the resources of France could be directed to the task of restoring economic prosperity. Though foreign adventures were subsequently to undermine and finally bring about the collapse of royal finances, until the Revolution they never wholly diverted the country from that pursuit of economic advantage which became a major characteristic of French society in the seventeen-thirties. The effect of increasing economic prosperity was to introduce a solvent into its rigid pattern, but we must be careful not to exaggerate the novelty of this factor. The society of the *ancien régime* was never the simple stratification of classes that has so often been described and denounced. Privileged classes and *tiers état* were already, when the eighteenth century began, little more than juridical categories, a formal legal framework which did not correspond to the actual complexity of social life. Acquired riches, which cut across and conflicted with these categories, had become a great force in French society even in the age of the *roi soleil*.

The reign of Louis XIV offered opportunities of wealth and power to the financiers and contractors who raised the loans and furnished the supplies necessary for his wars, fitted out his ships, provided the capital for overseas trade, and began, with government concessions, the exploitation of the colonies. The financier Crozat had, before Law, the monopoly of trade with Louisiana. Samuel Bernard went bankrupt for 30 million *livres* in 1709 and rebuilt another great fortune on the ruins of the first. The great bankers and financiers inserted themselves intimately into the financial machinery of the state. They fitted out the expeditions to seek overseas supplies, provided the bullion which the

French system, lacking adequate credit facilities, required, and farmed the indirect taxes. The constant and indispensable associates of the Controller-General, they were received as honoured guests by Louis XIV and his ministers at Versailles, were viewed with jealousy by the old aristocracy, and reviled by the populace as infamous *traitants*. They erected great town houses, and châteaux in the country, decorated them with the works of the finest artists of the time, entertained on a princely scale, married their daughters into the aristocracy, and bought nobility for their sons. Law's system, with its royal bank and company, was an attempt to take the control of French finances and commerce out of their hands. Its failure, to which they contributed to the best of their ability, brought them back to the position they had won under Louis XIV. The Pâris brothers controlled the liquidation of the system and the ablest of them, Pâris-Duverney, whose fortune had been built on war-contracts, emerged as one of the powers of eighteenth-century France.

Throughout the century profits came easiest from loans to the king to finance wars and meet deficits, from farming the taxes and from playing the exchanges; commerce interested the financiers less and industry least of all. The highest rank among them was held by the Farmers General, the group of forty financiers who, every six years, united their resources to buy, through a nominal purchaser, the right of collecting the indirect taxes. For all financiers, however, the career was wide open to their particular talent, especially in the first half of the century. The Pâris brothers were sons of an innkeeper; the Farmers General Teissier and La Bouexière began life as valets. More often, however, money bred money. Financiers were apt to find their best jumping-off place in the service of the state, among the army of tax-collectors, receivers, controllers, and treasurers of a host of public services. One small provincial town, say Rennes, with a population of about 20,000, might have nearly twenty of these, all with a foot on the ladder that led to fortune.

There was wealth in eighteenth-century France not only for the financiers. In the eighteenth century, and particularly after 1730, prices began slowly to rise and French economy reacted to the increased stimulation. Another factor was the stabilization of the currency. The relation of the livre and the écu to the gold louis had fluctuated wildly in the past, at the whim of the government. Thus in February 1724 the louis was worth 24 livres and the écu 6; in December 1725 the louis fell to 14 livres and the écu to 3 livres 10 sous. In 1726 they were fixed at 24 livres and 6 livres respectively, at which figures they remained unchanged from this date until the Revolution.

French overseas trade had suffered from Louis XIV's wars. A quarter of a century of peace at sea enabled it to recover to a point at which the competition of French merchants both alarmed and inspired a bellicose spirit in their English rivals. The French colonies were naturally the basis for this commercial expansion. Canada, with some fifteen ships reaching it a year, and Louisiana with only two or three, were of little economic value, while the French stations in India, so long as their trade was monopolized by the *Compagnie des Indes*, were generally in financial difficulties. The jewels of the French crown were the little islands of the West Indies. From the Atlantic ports of France four or five hundred ships a year sailed to take part in the trade in slaves from Africa (its morality as yet barely a subject of discussion) and in wine, food supplies, and other goods from France to the Antilles. From the islands the ships returned laden with sugar, rum, and molasses, and a little coffee, cotton, and indigo. All this trade, by the colonial pact called *l'exclusif*, was confined to French ships. The fisheries off Cape Breton Island and the Grand Banks, saved at the Treaty of Utrecht, drew a fleet of little fishing boats, a fine sight as they put out annually from Saint-Malo to share the dangers of the passage together. They won their profits particularly from the fish they sold to provision the slaves in the Antilles. The Atlantic trade was the most important, but trade with the Levant also experienced a notable revival, stimulated by the success of French diplomacy in the Ottoman Empire.

Colonial trade had increased from some 40 million livres

a year in 1716 to 204 in 1756, when the Seven Years War broke out, for what such statistics are worth. By this time France had some 1,800 ships engaged in overseas commerce, which roughly quadrupled between 1715 and 1789. To assist this trade a *Bureau de commerce* was set up in 1722, and gradually developed a stable and competent administrative personnel, though, especially after 1736, when the *Compagnie des Indes* lost the monopoly of the trade to the Antilles, the expansion was primarily attributable to the enterprise of individual merchants and shipowners.

The great commercial development was reflected in the growth of the ports. Saint-Malo, held back by the limited draught of the ships that its harbour could take, was confined to the fisheries. The free port of Marseille flourished on the trade with the Levant. Dunkirk, also a free port, dealt particularly with the Baltic. Le Havre, breaking into the Atlantic trade, was rapidly increasing in prosperity. The port founded at Lorient by Law slowly increased by the trade of the *Compagnie des Indes*. La Rochelle shared, so far as its harbour permitted, in the Atlantic commerce. Nantes was the town of the wealthy slavers, sending 150 ships a year to the isles. Above all Bordeaux, with the great estuary of the Gironde to shelter its ships, the canal du Midi to link it with Languedoc, and its centuries-old export of wines and brandy to England and Northern Europe, exploited the trade to Africa and the Indies. Its commerce and wealth never ceased from increasing till the time of the Revolutionary Wars. Its maritime trade, on one estimate already worth 40 millions in 1724, by 1789 had increased to 250 millions. The merchants of Bordeaux built for themselves great town houses, commissioned the architect Gabriel to plan a fine open place fronting the Garonne and flanked by the magnificent Hotel des Fermes and the Bourse, and housed their Chamber of Commerce in a princely palace. Arthur Young, when he saw the town in 1787, reluctant as he was to admit that anything could be done better in France than in England, had to confess that Liverpool was nothing to Bordeaux.

The most obvious external evidence of the increasing wealth of the eighteenth century was indeed to be seen in the cities. Building enjoyed an unprecedented expansion. Paris grew, on the right and the left banks, into the fashionable new faubourgs of Saint-Honoré and Saint-Germain. In the provincial cities, each a little Paris to its surroundings and separated by a long and tiresome journey from the national capital, governors, intendants, bishops, the aristocracy of sword and robe, financiers, and men of affairs, erected their town houses, many of which, surviving as the homes of the wealthy, divided up into bourgeois apartments, or sunk into vertical slums, still constitute a notable feature of the older towns of France. 'Who,' it has been asked, 'has not spent some part of his life in these dwellings with their thick walls and large panelled rooms or more intimate salons, the marks of age covered by successive layers of paint, with tall casements opening on the green of garden lawns or on the big paving-stones of a court, and whose attics huddle together under red tile or blue slate?'

Rennes, devastated by fire in 1720, was largely rebuilt in the eighteenth century; in other towns, even without this adventitious advantage, the work of demolition and rebuilding went on apace. Who would have guessed, even before the Revolution, that in 1700 Bordeaux had still been a medieval city? While private individuals built their eternal mansions on earth, elegant, grand, but in their frequent repetition of the same themes ultimately a little boring, town planning and the creation of imposing set-pieces on a larger scale was the work of the royal intendants, who rivalled one another in the task of beautifying the seats of their authority. After Louis XIV the threat of invasion or civil war no longer hung over France, and the ramparts round the cities, which had already often spread beyond them, having become useless, were converted into public spaces and promenades, where formal gardens, enclosed with balustrades, peopled with statues and shaded by trees, were laid out. At Nîmes, in the Jardin de la Fontaine, the genius of the eighteenth century was wedded, with uniquely happy results, to the remains of the Roman temple and baths. The creation of a *place royale* was essential to every town that aspired after dignity and standing – that now called by the name of its own little king, Stanislaus, at Nancy, with its long, low ranges of buildings and the magnificent ironwork of its gates and trellises, the loveliest of all. Paris itself naturally had to have a *place royale*, but since to clear a space in the heart of the capital would have been intolerably costly, the site chosen was in the outskirts, on a patch of waste ground between the gardens of the Tuileries and the wooded Champs Élysées. Begun in 1757, it took twenty years to complete. The plans were those of Louis XV's chief architect, A.-J. Gabriel, who, if he introduced no new motives into architecture, was supreme in his tactful arrangement of the elements he employed, and by his constant striving after simplicity achieved a restrained elegance. The place Louis XV, completed in good time to become the place de la Révolution, and now place de la Concorde, proved an admirably convenient site for the austere and functional operations of the guillotine.

Building was perhaps the greatest outlet for the new wealth of France. In addition, the fructifying influence of commercial wealth spread round the great ports, providing distilleries, sugar refineries, shipbuilding yards at Bordeaux, and cotton manufactures in the neighbourhood of Rouen. On the whole, however, the picture presented by French industries in the eighteenth century is very different from that of commerce. Small-scale enterprise, most often that of a single craftsman and his family, or a master with one or two journeymen, predominated. The masters were organized in corporations which, instead of declining as they had done in England, had been given a new lease of life by the legislation of Colbert. This was the high-water mark of the gilds in France, at least in respect of numbers. Poitiers, which had fourteen gilds in the fourteenth century, had forty-two in the eighteenth. Though in some towns, such as Clermont, the state failed to establish or re-establish them, and in the great ports local hostility kept the system in check, even where the corporation, gild, or *métier juré* did not exist, police control to some extent took their place.

One of the main functions of the corporations was fiscal: they were a means by which, through creating a mass of largely unnecessary offices – either for sale to individuals, whose prime function was to collect fees from the members, or to be bought up by the corporations to prevent them from being purchased by individuals – the state could draw in a little extra revenue. Thus the silk industry of Lyon, which was continually being hindered by the creation, suppression, and re-creation of useless official posts, in 1745 bought up 150 offices of alleged inspectors at a price of 200,000 livres; in 1758 it had to repeat the process at a cost of 133,000 livres. Again, the corporations were obliged to furnish and equip militia men for the army and replace them if they deserted. The silk corporation of Lyon had to provide eighty soldiers in 1742 and another fifty in 1743. The corporative system served also to protect the masters, for the aristocratic character of the gilds was accentuated during the eighteenth century: fees for reception as a master commonly amounted to as much as 2,000 livres and the gilds became largely hereditary. Their aim was in all ways to restrict competition. In 1751 an ordinance was issued prohibiting the circulation of notices in Paris announcing the sale of goods at cheap prices.

To give effect to government control of industry a continual stream of orders poured out, regulating such matters as the quality of raw materials, method of manufacture, and the standard of the finished articles. All these regulations required another horde of officials to enforce them and the imposition of fees to pay for the process of inspection. They prevented, and were intended to prevent, the development of new methods of manufacture. French industry had in fact been put into a strait-jacket by Colbert just at the time when a continual stream of new technical inventions was to call for the greatest flexibility and liberty. Up to the middle of the eighteenth century controls were effectively maintained despite increasing opposition. In the second half of the century the enforcement of the system gradually became laxer, one sign of which was the conclusion of the great struggle over 'toiles peintes' – printed fabrics – by an edict of 1759 which legalized their importation and manufacture. Fashion broke down a ban against which economic theory was powerless.

Industry was held back perhaps even more by shortage of capital than by the regulations of the gilds and state control. Many individual examples of industrial investment could, of course, be given, but such examples should not be allowed to obscure the fact that on the whole comparatively little finance capital flowed in this direction. Large-scale industry, therefore, tended to depend for its capital on the support of the state. The luxury manufactures of the Gobelins and Sèvres were carried on in state factories, as was also the soap manufacture. Other *manufactures royales* were created lavishly and supported by state loans, subsidies, and sometimes monopoly rights. The Jacobite exile, John Holker, who fled from England after being involved in the '45 and set up a textile factory in a suburb of Rouen with the aid of a small team of skilled workers brought over from England, obtained considerable success in his venture. The result was that in 1752 he became a royal manufacturer of velvets and cotton cloths, and in 1755 was appointed Inspector-General of Manufactures.

Here and there, in the eighteenth century, industry developed on a larger scale. At Reims nearly half the textile workers were grouped in factories. There were some iron works and paper factories. Coal-mining, where it was on any scale, required a concentration of labour, for the control of which a code was drawn up by Orry in 1744. By this, no mining was to be undertaken without the permission of the Controller-General; concessions for mines were granted by the king, proprietors of the surface land being paid compensation; and rules for safeguarding workers in mines were laid down, though as was usual with government regulations they were more often broken that observed. Though many mines were still little better than holes in the ground worked by a handful of miners, under royal encouragement a few fairly large mining establishments were developed. The largest, the mines of Anzin, had 4,000 workers in 1789. Especially in the textile trades, new machines were introduced from England or invented in France; but the fate of the improved methods of silk weaving developed out of earlier experiments by Vaucanson in 1747 is not untypical. The hostility of the silk workers at Lyon prevented their adoption until the idea was taken up by Jacquard at the end of the century and put into practice under Napoleon. For spinning, by 1789 there were perhaps 900 jennies in France: at the same time there were 20,000 in England.

An impressive picture of French industrial advance in the eighteenth century could be drawn by giving a collection of individual examples, and this is sometimes done. In fact, industry was mainly dependent on an army of domestic workers following traditional methods. In the less developed areas, such as Brittany, the peasants continued to weave their own cloths. In Flanders, Picardy, Upper Normandy, and elsewhere, the domestic system of industry prevailed and rural craftsmen worked up the material supplied by merchants, who sometimes also provided the tools of the trade and who collected the finished articles for sale. To avoid gild restrictions there was a tendency for industry to move into suburbs or into the countryside and this movement was encouraged by the government in the second half of the century.

The control of merchants and masters over their workers, and the hierarchical structure of industry, was upheld not only by the system of corporations but also by direct royal edicts. By letters patent of 1749 workers were forbidden under a heavy penalty to leave their masters without written permission or to organize the disposal of their own labour. At Lyon the master weavers had fallen into almost total dependence on the silk merchants. Strikes and violent outbreaks, such as that of 1744 in which the silk workers of Lyon practically took control of the town by violence, were not rare, but they were always repressed, that at Lyon by armed force followed by the torture and execution or sentence to the galleys for life of the leaders. Though some of the masters resented the tutorship of the state over industry, they readily used it to maintain control over their workers and to prevent the introduction of new methods. In the control exercised by the corporations, and the system of state regulation, is to be found one reason why industry in eighteenth-century France, unlike overseas trade and in striking contrast to English industry, remained comparatively stagnant.

Undoubtedly another factor which also contributed to the industrial backwardness of France compared with England at the same time, was the system of internal tolls, customs, seigneurial dues, *octrois*, and hindrances of all descriptions on domestic trade. Large parts of France were freer to trade with the foreigner than with the main customs area of the *Cinq grosses fermes* which extended over the old provinces of the monarchy. Throughout the century a series of reforming officials devoted themselves to the preparation of plans for the unification of France into a single customs unit, only to be frustrated, time and again, by the opposition of the vested interests of provinces, cities, Farmers-General. The existence of an army of officials to collect the internal customs, and a counter-army of smugglers trying to avoid them, was the chief positive result of this antiquated system. Once again the source of the weakness of eighteenth-century France must be sought in the failure of Louis XIV or his successors to complete the work he had begun. Colbert had initiated the process of customs unification with the creation of the *Cinq grosses fermes*; provincial rights and privileges of all kinds prevented his successors from completing it.

These considerations may help to explain why the great scientific and technical achievements of French genius, although much encouraged by the state, remained to such an extent in the realm of theory and did not produce more positive results in practice. The most successful achievements were in respect of transport. The roads of France, by gradual deterioration of the paved highways of the Romans through neglect or the pilfering of stones, had probably reached their lowest level in the seventeenth century. In 1736 they were put under the *Contrôle Général*. The great technical Corps of Bridges and Highways, created in 1747, by 1787 consisted of 1 first engineer, 4 inspectors-general, 28 engineers, 60 sub-engineers, 124 inspectors and an army of inferior grades; its annual budget amounted to 7 million livres for technical services and supervisory personnel alone. The actual work of construction was performed by means of the *corvée*, the forced labour of the population within reach of the main roads, organized and extended to all France by Orry in 1738. Funds were provided by the Treasury or by local and special taxes for those works with which the *corvée* obviously could not cope, and by the end of the century a network of main roads had been created. Radiating out from Paris, and for the needs of the century unnecessarily wide and straight, they were determined by the political predominance of the capital and by military considerations rather than by economic requirements. Arthur Young repeatedly comments on the fineness of the French roads and the lack of traffic on them, even in the neighbourhood of great cities. Transverse connexions, linking up the smaller towns and villages and cutting across the great highways, were still inadequate or non-existent. However, to travel from Paris to Lyon by coach, which had taken ten days in the seventeenth century, on the eve of the Revolution only took five. Because of the expense of land transport, goods and even passengers were still conveyed as far as possible by water. Any picture of the Seine at Paris in the eighteenth century will show it lined with long rows of boats discharging supplies from the great hinterland which its tributaries tapped to provision the population.

To draw up a balance sheet of the changes in French economy in the eighteenth century is almost an impossible task, for the picture must seem a contradictory one. Some broad general impressions alone can be given. Overseas trade was developing rapidly and methods of transport were improving. More efficient industrial methods were being adopted only slowly and on a very restricted scale. Meanwhile population was increasing rapidly. The causes of this growth of population remain mysterious. One can only notice the absence of great famines, though there was frequently scarcity, and that no foreign invasions or civil wars ravaged the soil of France. The plague which swept Marseille in 1720 was the last of its kind, though an epidemic is estimated to have carried off 80,000 in Brittany in 1741. Emigration was on a small scale. New crops, such as maize and potatoes, were slowly coming into use in some areas. But the expansion of population, beginning, or at least first becoming marked, in the eighteenth century, is too widespread a phenomenon to be explicable by any local or restricted causes. The actual figures are speculative. France had long been the most populated state in Europe. Its numbers were not surpassed, even by those of Russia, until after 1789. Under Louis XIV its population had probably been stationary or perhaps even declining. In 1715 it may have been no more than 16 or 17 million; by the middle of the century one may guess at a figure approaching 22, and by the time of the Revolution it had probably reached 26 million.

Commercial prosperity and the growth of the state machinery inflated the size of the towns. Paris, in the middle of the century, had a population of half a million and was steadily increasing, Lyon had perhaps 160,000, Marseille and Bordeaux were approaching 100,000. On the other hand, provincial capitals like Rennes, Dijon, or Grenoble were towns of little more than 20,000. All told, by the end of the *ancien régime* the urban population of France can hardly have exceeded two and a half million at most, which left a rural population of perhaps some 22 to 24 million. It is difficult to avoid the conclusion that France must have been suffering from intense and increasing rural over-population. This is the other side of the medal, to be set against the wealth of the mercantile, financial, and official classes, and of the professional men who to a considerable extent lived on them and shared in their prosperity.

Only agrarian and industrial revolutions could have

saved the swelling population of France from severe distress as its numbers pressed increasingly on the means of subsistence, and I have already given reasons why industrial production was rising only slowly. New agricultural methods made practically no headway against the conservatism of the French peasantry, while the limit of profitably cultivable land had possibly already been reached. At any rate, the limiting factor in this respect was not so much land, as fertilizers, and these were in short supply because livestock was deficient. The shortage of cattle, horses, and sheep in France was partly attributable to the need for each area to be self-sufficient in arable crops, and this in turn was due in part to lack of transport and in part to government policy. The result of the inadequate supply of fertilizing material, as Lavoisier pointed out, was that taking new land – and usually poorer land – into cultivation did little to increase production, for it merely meant that the same quantity of manure was spread over a larger area.

In some parts of France the surplus rural population turned to poorly paid domestic industry, one result of which was to depress wages in the towns. A large floating population worked when it could for the more prosperous farmers, especially at harvest time, and drifted into the towns to provide casual labour at other seasons. The number of vagabonds and beggars, forming themselves sometimes into bands which terrorized large areas of the country-side, increased to the point at which they became a social menace. The charitable foundations of the Church had largely disappeared or their resources had been diverted to add to the revenues of more influential if less needy sections of society, though the state gradually began to intervene for the relief of distress in the course of the century. Taine's comparison of the situation of the rural population to that of a man walking through a pond with the water up to his chin – a slight fall in the economic level and he goes under – is not misleading. Only the well-to-do *laboureur*, or the *fermier* who could rent a fair-sized farm, could really live on the product of his land. The majority had to eke out a living by working on the lands of others, engaging in domestic industry, migrating seasonally into the towns, scraping a bare living off the commons and waste, or else starve. That in such conditions the population continued to increase is a mystery which it is for the demographer to explain.

France in the eighteenth century was thus literally a land of prosperity and poverty: but the poverty was concentrated in the inarticulate rural masses, and bad as their conditions were, given the general absence – until 1789 – of rural uprisings or great famines such as had marked the reign of Louis XIV, and the continued increase of population, one is left with the feeling that perhaps, in spite of all, they were better off than they had been in the previous century.

5. DISORDER AT HOME

WHETHER anything that any eighteenth-century government could have done would have remedied the poverty of the rural masses in France is more than doubtful. But if we cannot assign the blame for this poverty, we can attribute some credit for the prosperity of other sections of the community to the government of Fleury. However, even he could not last for ever. The disgrace of Chauvelin in 1737 was a warning to those who opposed the cardinal, but though Louis XV, who clung to old friends and disliked new faces, refused to be parted from his great minister, the cardinal's age was not to be ignored. Factions were growing up at Versailles and among the interested public in Paris, each with its own candidate for the succession. The fallen minister, Chauvelin, had his adherents. The cause of the Cardinal de Tencin, leader of the Ultramontane anti-Jansenists, was energetically promoted by his intriguing sister, Mme de Tencin, in her salon. A military faction gathered round the comte de Belle-Isle. The marshal de Noailles drew support from the ramifications of his numerous and influential clan at Versailles. The king's mistress, the duchesse de Châteauroux, and her cousin the duc de Richelieu, hoped by means of the king's favour to secure a monopoly of patronage. Finally, the secretaries of state, strengthened by their long tenure of office, in spite of their rivalries joined in an effort to save themselves from subordination to a new *premier ministre*. The king himself, aged twenty-eight in 1738, might even have been regarded as a candidate for the succession. Returning, after much hesitation, to the traditions of his house, he had taken a *maîtresse en titre*, a post occupied in turn by the three Nesle sisters, Mailly, Vintimille, and Châteauroux, the last of whom, not without an eye to her own advantage and that of her friends, encouraged him to take a more active role in the government of his country.

When at last Fleury died, in January 1743, the struggle over the succession reached its climax. Chauvelin, still in exile, had prepared for the long-awaited day by entrusting to an adherent at Versailles a memorandum setting forth his claims to the vacant position and enumerating in no measured language all the faults of the cardinal, which he took it upon himself to correct. Presented with indecent haste to the king immediately after Fleury's death, this memorandum ruined for ever Chauvelin's prospects of returning to office. The duc de Noailles, less ambitious or more subtle, offered Louis for his guidance the instructions which Louis XIV had drawn up for Philip of Anjou when he became king of Spain. 'Do not let yourself be led,' Louis XIV had written, 'be master yourself. Never have a favourite or first minister. Listen to and consult your council, but decide yourself. God, who has made you king, will give you all the necessary wisdom so long as your intentions are good.' Did this echo from the past give the hesitating Louis XV resolution? In any case he announced that he would in future have no first minister but would himself govern.

What this meant in reality was that the faction of the secretaries of state had won. The business of government would henceforth be done, as it had been under Louis XIV, separately with each secretary, the king himself providing the necessary coordination. Unfortunately this was just what Louis XV was incapable of doing. Intelligent, well-intentioned, conscious of what a king of France and the successor to the *roi soleil* should be, he was self-distrustful in the extreme, *un grand timide* in whom, said the duc de Croÿ, modesty was pushed to the extreme of a vice. He was incapable of deciding on a policy and supporting it steadily and consistently. Under Fleury, wrote the abbé de Bernis, who was to know the government of France from the inside at a later and less happy stage, 'the king's council had more authority and kept its secrets better, the great corporations of the state were more submissive, the ministers more respected and France more worthy of respect.' Against this we may set the description of the council given by the Cardinal de Tencin after Fleury's death. 'It must be admitted,' he writes, 'that the king's council is a council *pour rire*. Only a very small fraction of the business of the state is discussed in it; and after the rapid reading of a memorandum our opinion is asked on the spot, without any time for undisturbed reflection and summing up. Moreover, the lack of interest the king appears to show and the profound silence he maintains is shattering.' D'Argenson, admittedly writing with the bitterness of an ambitious man who had failed in his ambitions, was nevertheless justified when he described the royal council as 'a republic not of citizens assembled to take counsel concerning the well-being of the state, but of heads of factions, each thinking only of his own concerns, one of finance, another of the navy, another of the army, and each achieving his own ends according to his greater or less facility in the art of persuasion.'

Louis XV is hardly to be blamed for not being a Louis XIV. It was his misfortune to have to occupy a representative position for which, either by nature or from the constant and premature publicity which he endured as a child-king, he had acquired a horror. He carried on with aloof dignity the life of a king, surrounded by crowds of courtiers he hardly knew, moving daily through the fixed routine of court ceremonies, stared at from morning to night, the principal boy in a perpetual pantomime; but to concern himself continually with public affairs, to be the statesman who pulled the strings, as well as the puppet who was controlled by them, was beyond his capacity. The intrigues of the court, the appointment or dismissal of officials, his personal and secret system of diplomacy, these could arouse his interest, but public affairs involved so much boring work that they bored him. He had better things to turn his attention to: he sought distraction in hunting and in women, two occupations which if they were always the same were always different, and which filled up the emptiness of his life.

There was never a pause in the holocaust of animals slaughtered, almost daily, for Louis XV was an indefatigable hunter; but the death of the last of the Nesle sisters in 1744 left a gap in the other of his two chief pursuits. It was to be filled by Jeanne-Antoinette Poisson, daughter of a steward to the Pâris brothers, the bankers who after the collapse of Law's system were for a time the most powerful figures in French finances. A financial scandal which made a temporary absence from France desirable for M. Poisson enabled his wife to form a profitable connexion with a wealthy Farmer General, who in due course married off her daughter to his nephew, Le Normant d'Étioles. The world of high finance in which Jeanne-Antoinette had been brought up was also a world of culture and of what was beginning to be called enlightenment. Young Mme d'Étioles, with her financial connexions, intelligence, skill in drawing-room accomplishments, wit, beauty, and a kind of charm which even her enemies had to acknowledge, soon attracted to her house men like Crébillon, the fashionable society novelist, Fontenelle, now getting on for a hundred and a legendary but still lively figure in the world of letters, Montesquieu, not yet the author of *De l'esprit des lois*, but with a reputation for wit based on the *Lettres persanes*, Voltaire, who found her amiable and sincere.

All this was good, but not quite good enough for an ambitious little beauty. There was a higher world than those of finance or letters to conquer. To become accepted in aristocratic society was difficult, the private life of the court was easier to enter if you had something to bring to it, as Madame d'Étioles had, and knew the right person, as she did. A distant relation was body-servant to the Dauphin and so in touch with the king, who was on easy terms with his servants. How the first meeting between Louis XV and the new candidate for the vacant place in his affections was arranged is not known, but by September 1745 she was installed at Versailles as recognized mistress, endowed with an estate in the country and the title of Marquise de Pompadour. She was to be the king's mistress for five years and his close friend for twenty.

The name of the Pompadour is associated with a world of *objets d'art* – she herself the loveliest if the most ephemeral of them all – in a period when the cult of the lesser arts reached perhaps its height. Paris, in the middle of the century, had five hundred goldsmiths, and a host of skilled craftsmen and shopkeepers were occupied in the production and sale of works of art of all kinds. Mme de Pompadour was one of the most assiduous of their patrons. In one shop, in the rue Saint-Honoré, the account books of which for the ten years 1748–58 have survived, her name appears on an average once a week. When she died it took two notaries, working for a whole year, to draw up the catalogue of her possessions. She is particularly associated with the china manufactory at Sèvres, for it was founded at her instigation to compete with Meissen. Under royal patronage, Gobelins, Aubusson, and Beauvais continued to produce their famous tapestries. Luxury, in ample measure, was tempered by a sense of restraint, an acceptance of limitations, which is evident also in the music that flowed gracefully through such elegant salons. With composers like Rameau and Couperin the music of the century is noble, sober, and classical in operas, or gay but sedate in *bergeries*, *contre-danses*, and the accompaniments of *fêtes galantes*. There is little incongruity in adding that this was also the age of the perfection of French cuisine and of the invention of the great wines and cheeses.

To the artistic achievements of the *style Louis XV* the intelligent encouragement of the Pompadour and her brother

Marigny, who became *Intendant des Bâtiments*, contributed much. Exotic influences, particularly in the form of chinoiserie, contributed to the decorative arts of the period, but France escaped the exaggerated styles that prevailed elsewhere in Europe. Perhaps the works of Meissonier represent the only true examples of rococo to be found. Elegance was at its height: one could not ask for more from writing-desks and mirror frames, salt-cellars, fruit bowls, china statuettes. One becomes conscious of the limitations of the period when one approaches the greater arts. Carlo Vanloo, spoilt child of court and capital, produced innumerable undistinguishable society portraits. Nattier painted royal princesses, noble ladies, and wealthy bourgeoises, all with the same gracious smile and vacant countenance, whether they are represented as Diana, Venus, or any other pagan deity or mythological figure. Only Boucher – favourite of Mme de Pompadour – emerges from the crowd of fashionable painters, his pictures, with masterly technique, perpetuating the thoughtless charms of the lascivious little beauties to whose representation in all attitudes he devoted so much of his talent.

In literature it was an age of wit rather than wisdom, of optimism rather than a sense of tragic destiny. Voltaire, it is true, could not persuade himself, at least after the Seven Years War and the earthquake of Lisbon, that all was for the best in the best of possible worlds. The new spirit of pre-romanticism was to come in soon with Rousseau, but that strange Genevan genius did not belong to the France of mid-century. For the imaginative literature of the age of Louis XV we must look to lesser figures. 'O to read eternal new romances of Marivaux and Crébillon,' exclaimed Thomas Gray. Are the libertine novels of Crébillon still read? Marivaux began to produce his comedies in 1720. The title of the best known of them, *Le Jeu de l'amour et du hasard*, would do for all. Love is no longer the tyrannical goddess of the classical age, but a mischievous Cupid who gets his arrows mixed up in a world of lesser nobles and well-to-do bourgeois, whose too witty valets can pose as gentlemen and whose too pretty chambermaids be mistaken for their mistresses. In these comedies we are in a world not of sentiment but of sensibility. With Marivaux's long novel, the *Vie de Marianne*, there is added an astringent dose of realism in glimpses of the people, remote in their lives and thoughts from the elevated sphere in which the Pompadour glittered and had her being. She has been unduly identified with an age which she only represented in its transient beauty. For the political disasters of the period she has unfairly been held responsible, because she has come to symbolize a generation in which, under a weak king, the irresponsible intrigues of a frivolous court determined the constant changes of ministers and policies.

The fundamental weaknesses of the *ancien régime* go deeper than this, however. The commonest charge against the court, and in particular against the Pompadour, was extravagance, which, it was believed, ruined French finances and so brought about the Revolution. That a lot of money went on palaces, parks, works of art, and even more on places and pensions for courtiers and their hangers-on, is undeniable; but in relation to the whole cost of the government of France the expenditure of the court, excessive as it may have been, does not play a decisive role. The expense of even a small war was greater than that of the biggest palace. This does not mean that the court can be absolved of responsibility for the distress into which royal finances fell, but the root of the trouble lay rather in the system of collection of the taxes than in expenditure. Once again we are forced to seek the source of the evil in the reign of Louis XIV. The great king had endowed France with a modern system of government while retaining a semi-medieval system of financing it. It is sometimes said that the preservation of fiscal privileges was the price paid for the extinction of the political power of the privileged classes, but this is probably to underestimate what royal authority could have done under Louis XIV. The result of his and Colbert's failure to reform the royal finances was that his successors were left not only with a state which at

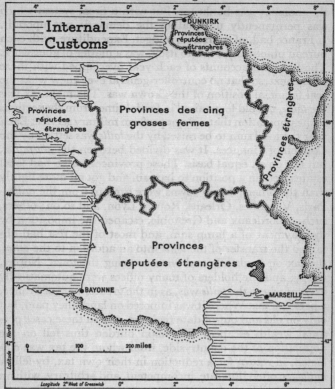

The major divisions of France for internal customs were:
1. Provinces des cinq grosses fermes
2. Provinces réputées étrangères
3. Provinces étrangères

The *cinq grosses fermes* were made into a customs union by Colbert in 1664. The *provinces réputées étrangères* were those excluded from the tariff union of 1664. They retained a congeries of criss-crossing internal customs barriers as well as those on their frontiers. The *provinces étrangères* were those subsequently annexed, which traded freely across the frontiers of France but were separated by customs barriers from the rest of the country. There were three free ports – Dunkirk, Marseille, and Bayonne – but of these only Dunkirk was totally free from external customs of any kind and cut off by a strict customs barrier from the rest of France.

57

the moment was bankrupt, but with a fiscal system which was permanently unequal to the demands put upon it.

France had, of course, no budget. Expenditure, with each bureau practically a law to itself, was a matter of guesswork. The financial accounts of each year overlapped with those of the next, so that no controller-general ever knew what the real financial position of the Crown was. The main tax was the *taille*, the old levy raised in feudal times from the sections of the population that did not perform military service. Each year the total sum to be raised by the *taille* was settled by the Council of Finances. It was divided between the *généralités*, but not on an equal basis. Those provinces which had local estates were in a position to bargain and got off more lightly than the others. Many towns were exempt from the *taille* — Paris, Versailles, Orleans, Rouen, Lyon, and so on; others, such as Bordeaux and Grenoble, escaped the imposition by the payment of a lump sum, and most of the rest had obtained the transfer of the *taille* into an addition to the *octroi*, the tax on foodstuffs and wine entering the town. Nobles, clergy, and the holders of many offices were automatically exempt where the *taille* was, as in the greater part of France, a personal tax. Where it was imposed on land, they paid, but only on old and out-of-date registers, and in these cases personal wealth escaped. The main burden thus fell on the population of the countryside, from whom the tax was collected, in return for a reduction in their own tax, by fellow *taillables*, often illiterate, incompetent, and arbitrary, with an army of bailiffs and sergeants to enforce payment. The *capitation*, established in 1695 and intended to supplement the *taille* by a tax on wealth admitting of no exceptions, had been whittled down until it was a mere addition to the *taille*. The *dixième*, established in 1710 with a similar object, met with a similar fate.

These direct taxes were supplemented by a vast and complex system of indirect taxes. The *gabelle*, the hated salt tax, which between 1715 and 1789 was raised from 23 to 50 million livres, was imposed with such diversity in different parts of France that the price of salt varied from half a sou to

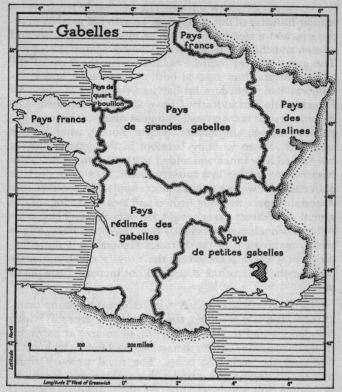

1. pays de grandes gabelles
2. pays de petites gabelles
3. pays des salines
4. pays de quart bouillon
5. pays rédimés des gabelles
6. pays francs

These were the main divisions, but within each of these areas there were many sub-divisions and local variations. The price of salt ranged from 60 livres 7 sous a minot (72 litres) to 1l. 10s. Average prices in each area, though these conceal a wide range of differences, were – 1. 57l.; 2. 33l.; 3. 24l.; 4. 13l.; 5. 9l.; 6. 3l. 15s.

twelve or thirteen sous a livre. The inevitable result was a regular industry of salt smuggling, an army of *gabelous* to repress it, and a steady procession of men to the galleys and women and children to prison for offences against the *gabelle*. The great bulk of indirect taxation took the form of the *traites*, customs dues exacted both at the frontier and at innumerable internal customs barriers, the effect of which on French trade and industry I have already mentioned, and the *aides*, excise taxes on such things as drinks, tobacco, iron, precious metals, and leather. Arthur Young, when he saw men and women working barefoot in the country, might have asked how much was added by the *marque de cuir* to the price of shoe-leather in a country where, because of the lack of livestock, it was already in short supply. To describe in a reasonable space the complexities and local variations of this system of indirect taxes would be impossible. They were collected, much more efficiently than the direct taxes, by the great organization of the Farmers General, but the efficiency, which was reflected in the rapidly mounting price paid for the lease of the taxes, did not increase their popularity.

The *Contrôle Général* added to its resources by stamp taxes, lotteries, the sale of offices, the *don gratuit* or free gift which the clergy voted to the Crown, not, of course, at an excessively burdensome rate to themselves, and finally by loans to tide over the recurrent crises. The royal treasury could manage to stagger along under this cumbersome system in peacetime, but war inevitably brought a financial crisis. If one is looking for a single reason why France, with its population and resources, should have been defeated by far smaller powers such as Great Britain and Prussia in the eighteenth century, it is to be found in its inability to mobilize the wealth of the country for war. Fleury, by avoiding large-scale war, and Orry, by economical administration, had managed to carry on without grave financial difficulties, though his attempts at economy and his uncourtierlike personality made Orry one of the most hated men in France. It was perhaps not a mere coincidence that the

Pâris brothers, to whom his austere financial methods were by no means congenial, succeeded in bringing about his fall in December 1745, just after their *protégée*, Madame de Pompadour, had risen to favour.

However, if Louis sacrificed Orry to personal enmities and the scheming of the financiers, it was not without giving him a worthy successor. To know how or why anyone was ever chosen for any office, it would be necessary to have a daily, or indeed hourly, bulletin of the intrigues and gossip of the court, but the king was not unconscious of merit when the report of it, or personal impression, could penetrate to him through the network of scandal and back-biting that constituted Versailles. Machault d'Arnouville, the new Controller-General, brought from the intendancy of Valenciennes, was a cold, taciturn, rigid, honest administrator, with a broader horizon than his predecessor had possessed. Called to office with the task of raising the necessary finance for the War of the Austrian Succession, by expedients of all kinds he succeeded in the immediate task. The restoration of peace gave him the opportunity to begin on fundamental reform. In 1749 he introduced the *vingtième*, a tax of one-twentieth on all incomes without exception, for the collection of which he began to organize and train a new administrative personnel.

The struggle over the *vingtième* may be taken as an object lesson in the difficulties of financial reform under the *ancien régime*. The noblesse, naturally, refused to pay, and what sanction could a simple collector of taxes employ against a noble? The parlements and the Provincial Estates had to be compelled to register the edict. The clergy, to whom the idea that they should pay a tax other than their 'free gift' savoured of heresy, took the lead in opposition. They were supported by the *dévot* party at court, with the backing of the queen, the dauphin, and the king's daughters, by the Jesuits, and by the comte d'Argenson, Secretary of State for War and a personal enemy of Machault. The bitterness of the clergy at the prospect of being subjected to compulsory taxation can be appreciated when it is realized that, according to one calculation, on an annual revenue of some 120 million they paid in voluntary taxation some 2 or 3 million. The Pompadour, who had as little love for the clergy as they had for her, put all her influence behind Machault; but the king was susceptible to religious arguments and to pressure from his daughters. The clergy launched a great campaign of prayer to be spared this new affliction, which touched them where they felt it most, and the bishops threatened to abandon their churches. Meanwhile the nobles and *parlementaires* held their fire, more than content to see the battle fought for them by such a powerful ally. Machault could not overcome this opposition. In December 1751 he had to admit defeat. The raising of the *vingtième* on the property of the clergy was suspended and after this the attempt to reform the fiscal system was abandoned.

A weak and divided government was not only incapable of bringing about financial reform, it could not, when the great corporations of the state – the Church and the parlements – were involved, even maintain its own authority and suppress disorder. Curiously, considering that this was the eighteenth century, the prime cause of domestic disturbance was at least nominally religious. There had been in succession three religious struggles in France. The first and bitterest, against the Huguenots, had been effectively ended by Richelieu but reopened by the persecution of Louis XIV. Huguenot despair flared out in the terrible revolt of the Camisards, the last echoes of which reverberate through the eighteenth century. An edict of 1724 forbade heretical religious assemblies, under penalty of sentence to perpetual galleys for men and life imprisonment for women. For Protestant preachers the punishment was death. As late as March 1751 a Protestant religious meeting in the Cevennes was dispersed by the bullets of royal troops. In March 1752 a Protestant preacher was hanged at Montpellier. In 1749 the parlement of Bordeaux ordered forty-six persons to separate for concubinage, that is, for being married by Protestant rites, and declared their children illegitimate and incapable of inheriting their property. In 1752 there was a small Huguenot jacquerie and a new wave of emigration. However, though the case of Calas was yet to come, the persecuting spirit was spending itself and toleration appeared in practice before it was admitted in theory. Even in the first half of the century the treatment of the Protestants depended on the attitude of the local authorities in each *généralité* and varied greatly from time to time; and after 1751 the Church was increasingly on the defensive against a more dangerous enemy.

The second struggle, between Versailles and Rome over the Gallican liberties, had ended in a compromise by 1715. The third, over Jansenism, had apparently ended in 1709 when, under pressure from Louis XIV, the Pope decreed the extinction of Port-Royal, now inhabited, for Jansenism had been rapidly declining in its appeal, only by twenty-two aged nuns. They were dispersed, the property of the convent confiscated, the buildings razed to the ground, and even the bodies in the cemetery dug up to be put in some unknown grave or scattered to the winds. The Jesuits could feel that they had decisively avenged the *Lettres provinciales* of Pascal, but to consolidate their influence over the Church in France it was necessary also to eliminate its deep-rooted Gallicanism. The position of the Archbishop of Paris, Noailles, was the obvious objective to attack, and an opening was provided by the fact that a work published by Quesnel in 1671, which had been recommended by Noailles, was Jansenist in its tendency. Papal condemnation was secured for 101 propositions in Quesnel's book by the famous Bull Unigenitus.

Noailles yielded, but whereas the former controversy had largely been a matter for theologians, this one concerned a popular and widely read work, written in French and not in Latin, and involved the question of the Gallican Liberties. For the first time since the Fronde the parlements, so submissive to Louis XIV, refused to register a royal edict, that enforcing acceptance of the Bull. Regarding themselves as the guardians of the rights of the Gallican Church, they took the lead in a struggle that was to continue for fifty years.

Though the struggle was still labelled with the name of Jansenism, the so-called Jansenism of the parlements was really a combination of Gallicanism with an attempt to revive their own political power. It enabled them to disguise as an assertion of the independence of the secular power their own claim to authority in matters of ecclesiastical discipline. In the words of the parlement of Paris, they held that 'The temporal power is independent of all other powers, to it alone belongs the task of coercing the subjects of the king, and the ministers of the Church are accountable to the parlement, under the authority of the monarch, for the exercise of their jurisdictions.' Public opinion, finding little outlet for its religiosity in the official Church, joined in the new Jansenist controversy, especially in the thirties, when at the tomb of a Jansenist deacon, Pâris, miracles very inconveniently started to occur. The crowds who gathered to watch the antics into which religious emotion threw the *convulsionnaires* over the tomb became such a menace to public order that, miracles or no miracles, the cemetery was closed by the police.

There followed a struggle over *billets de confession*. The Archbishop of Paris who followed Noailles was Christophe de Beaumont, virtuous, pious, stupid, and a violent partisan of the Jesuits and the Bull Unigenitus. He excommunicated and deprived of the last sacraments those who had not a ticket to show that they had confessed to a priest who accepted the Bull. The parlements retaliated by arresting priests who refused the sacraments to suspected Jansenists. The struggle was now one inside the Church as well as with the parlements, and it was intensified by a new tendency which was developing among the lower clergy. The upper clergy in the eighteenth century were almost exclusively noble, for the Church might well have been described as a system of out-door relief for the aristocracy. A Prince de Rohan, Bishop in partibus of Campe at the age of twenty-six, could become in succession to his uncle, Bishop of Strasbourg, Grand Almoner of France, Provisor of the Sorbonne, Abbot of the wealthiest abbey in France, and Cardinal. The

Cardinal de Polignac, Archbishop of Auch for fifteen years, never once set foot in his diocese. The revenues of many religious houses went to *abbés commendataires*, exercising no religious functions. A large part of the tithes and other revenues of the parish priests was alienated to such nominal *abbés* or to wealthy upper clergy, save for a meagre *portion congrue* which had to be left for them to live on. The lower clergy therefore provided fruitful soil for the ideas first put forward early in the seventeenth century by Edmond Richer, who had claimed that the government of the Church belonged of right to the whole community of pastors; and the so-called Jansenism of the eighteenth century, which for the parlements was a kind of Gallicanism, for the lower clergy became a kind of Richerism.

To trace the long running fight which went on between the parlements and the Church would be an exhausting and fruitless task. The king, influenced by the *dévot* party, usually took the side of the bishops, public opinion that of the parlements; and while in financial matters the parlements were able to prevent reform, in ecclesiastical matters they succeeded in perpetuating discord. The Crown found in them its bitterest and most dangerous enemy. It may well be asked how it was that under an absolute monarchy mere law courts could acquire such power.

France had twelve parlements and three sovereign courts, which filled similar functions. The parlement of Paris, its jurisdiction extending over one-third of the country and by far the greatest of these hereditary and venal law courts, dated from the thirteenth century. The other courts, set up when fresh provinces were taken under royal administration, had played an important part in the extension of royal authority. The members of the parlements and of the other courts which shared their powers numbered in the eighteenth century a little over 2,000 in all. Originally recruited from middle-class lawyers, by the eighteenth century membership of the parlements was determined by birth and money, and since the offices were venal they were properties of which their possessors could not arbitrarily be dispossessed.

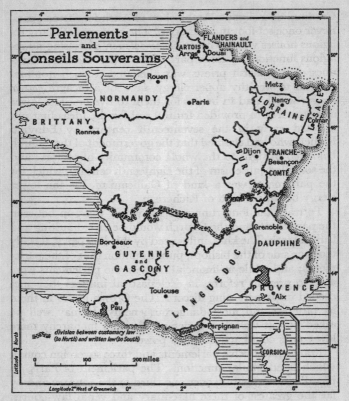

Parlements
and
Conseils Souverains

There were, in 1789, 13 parlements and 4 conseils souverains with similar powers. The vast area from which cases had to be brought to Paris will be noted, and also the small extent of the jurisdiction of some of the lesser courts. If the boundaries of the jurisdictions of the Chambres des Comptes and the Cours des Aides were added, it would be seen that these often failed to coincide with one another or with those of the parlements. In addition to the traditional division of France between the areas of customary and written law, there were a host of varying local laws and feudal customs.

Primarily law courts, the parlements also had extensive police powers over such matters as religion, trade and industry, morals and censorship. Most important of all were their political claims. Registration by the parlements was the normal method of promulgating royal decrees. They could protest against these by *remontrances*, which, intended for the king's eye alone, in the eighteenth century were often published by the parlements for the purpose of stirring up public opinion. If the parlement refused to register a decree, the king could enforce registration by the formal procedure of *lit de justice*. Finally, in the event of continued resistance he could exile individual magistrates or the whole court to some other part of France. The parlements, for their part, could reply by suspending their sessions, thus holding up the course of justice, causing great inconvenience. and arousing public opinion in their favour.

Under Louis XIV the parlements knew too well the determination of the great king and feared him too much to provoke his wrath. Louis XIV, it has been said, did not have to crush the parlements; he showed that he did not fear them and that was enough. Under the weaker governments that followed they became the centre of opposition to the royal will. As the last relic of the medieval constitution left at the centre of government, the parlement of Paris, though no more in fact than a small, selfish, proud, and venal oligarchy, regarded itself, and was regarded by public opinion, as the guardian of the constitutional liberties of France. From the revival of its claims under the regency to the moment when it brought the monarchy crashing down in a general destruction of the *ancien régime*, which it shared, it conducted a running war with the Crown. The defence of so-called Jansenism and opposition to financial reform provided the main themes of the agitation. The provincial parlements, in the second half of the century, encouraged by the example of that of Paris, started local wars against the *intendants*. Thus, while standing in the way of all reforms, the parlements spread a spirit of opposition and revolutionary ideas throughout the country. They undermined respect for the Church and the monarchy, prevented the reform of royal finances and finally, as will be seen, opened the door to revolution. But this is to look far ahead, and meanwhile the weakness and instability of French government after Fleury was to have more immediately harmful consequences in the field of foreign affairs.

6. DEFEAT ABROAD

THE disappearance of governmental cohesion in the declining years of Fleury, which led to failure in religious and financial policies, had even more disastrous consequences in the field of foreign policy. The most powerful of the factions which were struggling for the succession to the cardinal in his last years, when he was increasingly unable to hold his own against them, was that which surrounded the ambitious and brilliant comte de Belle-Isle. Grandson of that Fouquet whom Louis XIV had flung from the highest office to perpetual prison in 1661, he had gradually worked his way back into favour. Belle-Isle was a good soldier and distinguished himself in the last battles of Louis XIV. He made a fortune out of Law's system. Charm, ability, tireless energy, ambition, and a mastery of intrigue enabled him to build up a party for himself at court. His chance came when the death of the Emperor Charles VI, leaving a young girl, Maria Theresa, as his successor, threw middle Europe into the melting-pot.

Belle-Isle's aim, or one of his many aims, was to be Marshal of France and Duke, and war was the only short-cut to the achievement of this ambition. The young nobles at court, lacking occupation and the opportunity for glory and promotion under the peaceful régime of Fleury, wanted nothing better than war, and Belle-Isle was able to put himself at the head of a powerful faction. The entourage of Louis XV and Mme de Châteauroux encouraged the king to break away from the inglorious caution of his aged minister. The cardinal, though more opposed to foreign adventures than ever, was no longer in a position to treat Belle-Isle as he had treated Chauvelin, and had unwillingly to accept the fact that the ambitious noble was a power at Versailles and let him have his head.

After the death of Charles VI the politics of Europe were centred on the election of a new Holy Roman Emperor. Belle-Isle's grand plan was to secure the choice of a French client, the Elector of Bavaria. To put this plan into operation he was given the key position of ambassador to the electoral diet at Frankfurt. There, in feverish communication with the French envoys to all the German courts, with his supporters at Versailles, and with the ambassadors to other courts, he practically made himself the effective Foreign Minister of France. But while Belle-Isle intrigued, Frederick II acted. The Prussian invasion of Silesia in December 1740 precipitated war. Belle-Isle saw the possibility of using Frederick to further his own ends, which was a more excusable mistake at the beginning of the king of Prussia's career than subsequently. He promoted the conclusion of a Franco-Prussian alliance in June 1741, and obtained the command of an army to fight in Germany. Fleury, weakened by age and troubled in mind and body, could not stem the enthusiasm for war. A reconciliation with the Pâris brothers, formerly his enemies, assured Belle-Isle that the necessary supplies would be forthcoming. In August 1741 the French army crossed the Rhine and, in alliance with the Bavarians under the Elector, invaded Austrian territory and captured Prague; another French army occupied Westphalia and menaced Hanover; and in January 1742 the Elector of Bavaria was chosen as Holy Roman Emperor. Belle-Isle's policy seemed to have been crowned with rapid and complete success.

It was a precarious triumph, based upon a combination of circumstances which might not prove lasting – the faithfulness of Frederick II to the French alliance, the continued passivity of Great Britain under Walpole, the disintegration of the Habsburg Empire, and not least the effective maintenance of control of the French military and diplomatic

effort by Belle-Isle himself. The year 1742 was to see all
these conditions vanish. Maria Theresa came to terms with
the Magyars, reconstituted the Habsburg army, and carried
the war into Bavaria. Worse followed. Walpole resigned
office, British foreign policy passed into the hands of a
minister who favoured intervention against France on the
Continent, and by British mediation Frederick II was
bought out of the war at the price of Silesia. The secretaries
of state at Versailles, jealous of the predominance of Belle-
Isle, intrigued against him, and with the backing of the
secretaries and the queen, Broglie was appointed to command the French army in Bohemia. This change in command was not without its influence on Frederick's desertion,
for the King of Prussia admired Belle-Isle and had no faith
in de Broglie. Finally, Belle-Isle himself, under the strain of
his intense military and diplomatic activities, fell ill, despite
which he succeeded, by a brilliant retreat, in extricating the
French army from the impossible position into which de
Broglie, despite his ability, allowed it to fall at Prague.

But Belle-Isle's halcyon days were over. So recently in all
appearance the destined successor of Fleury, the failure of
his plans robbed him of all influence. 'If the Marshal of
Belle-Isle was not a great man,' wrote a contemporary, 'he
was certainly an extraordinary one, but he was soon forgotten.' When Fleury died, in January 1743, there was no
question of Belle-Isle as his successor. I have already referred to the victory of the secretaries of state. Maurepas,
d'Argenson, Orry, and Amelot, four able professional administrators, were to hold the government in a sort of commission, with the king himself to direct and coordinate
their policy. The defects of Louis' character – his uncertainty and self-distrust, his domination by personal motives
and interests, lack of assiduity, sudden reversals of opinion –
were for the next twenty years to be those of the government of France.

The war – no longer of the Austrian Succession, for
Maria Theresa had settled that – dragged on for another
five years. Any purpose it had possessed for France at the

beginning had been lost by 1742. Lacking any rational objective the campaigns became a series of diversions – an attack on Sardinia, a projected invasion of England in support of the Young Pretender, a major invasion of the United Provinces. The victories of the most successful of the French generals, Maurice de Saxe, in the last of these campaigns, were ended when he had to be called back to repel an Austrian invasion of Lorraine, where Louis XV, inspired by Mme de Châteauroux – for the Pompadour had not yet come on the scene – to prove himself in the combats of Mars as well as of Venus, had put himself at the head of a French army, only to experience a set-back. Then, at Metz, in August 1744, he fell critically ill. This led to an episode which he did not quickly forget or forgive. The *dévot* party, seizing their opportunity, determined that he should not die in the arms of his mistress, who was driven away, pursued along her route by the hisses of the population and stoned in her carriage. Louis himself, believing like everyone else that he was dying, was bullied into making a public confession of his sins and asking pardon for the scandalous example he had set his people. The neglected queen and the heir apparent, surrounded by the clergy and the *dévot* party, prepared to inaugurate a new reign. They were thirty years too soon. Louis recovered from his illness with astonishing rapidity, *Te Deums* were sung all over France in a great wave of popular enthusiasm and Mme de Châteauroux returned to the royal arms, though briefly, for she died soon after.

The war continued with better fortune, for Frederick II, alarmed at the Austrian successes, re-entered the fighting. Meanwhile the direction of the foreign policy of France had fallen into new hands, those of the marquis d'Argenson, a man full of ingenious plans for the re-establishment of that French hegemony in Europe which Louis XIV had for a time exercised and which continued to haunt the imagination of French Foreign Ministers. But even if the plans of d'Argenson had been more practicable, the opposition of the other ministers and of the factions at court would have prevented them from being put into practice consistently. In May 1745 Maurice de Saxe won the battle of Fontenoy, last glorious victory of the *ancien régime*, and French troops occupied Flanders. D'Argenson, weaving a complicated and flimsy web of diplomatic intrigue, failed to take advantage of the belated military success. Once again, in December 1745, Frederick of Prussia, most treacherous of allies, withdrew from the war, having consolidated his hold on Silesia. D'Argenson, exposed to violent criticism at Versailles, continued with his tortuous and unavailing schemes, which were collapsing round him even before he had properly started to put them into effect; but he was now no more than nominal Foreign Minister and Louis XV was taking advice from a variety of diverse and opposed sources. At last, in January 1747, the king dismissed him.

The chief influence over the conduct of diplomacy and the war now fell into the hands of Maurice de Saxe, a bastard of the king of Poland, who had entered the military service of France and who alone had gained in reputation from this unhappy war. With Maurice a definite, limited, and attainable objective for French policy at last emerged: by means of a renewed attack on the United Provinces to force Great Britain to accept peace. Victory at Laufeldt and the capture of Berg-op-Zoom brought this end within sight. Deprived of British support, Maria Theresa had to reconcile herself to what she thought would be the temporary loss of Silesia, while under the patronage of Maurice a 'Saxon' party at the French court secretly prepared a *rapprochement* between France and Austria. Both Great Britain and Austria were now ready for peace, which after the usual prolonged and intricate negotiations was signed at Aix-la-Chapelle in 1748. Despite the ambitious diplomacy of Belle-Isle and d'Argenson, and the military successes of Maurice de Saxe, France had gained nothing; and this was not strange, for short of European hegemony, which the balance of European forces did not render a practicable end, there was no specific objective to be gained.

True, outside Europe a real conflict of interests between

Great Britain and France was developing; but in respect of the struggle for colonies and trade the war settled nothing, and the peace, with a mutual restoration of conquests, represented only as an armistice. Moreover, while English concern with the overseas struggle was primary, to France, traditionally aiming at dominance in Europe, it appeared only as a secondary issue, a mere side-show. Therefore, after Aix-la-Chapelle, Louis XV and his ministers, faced with the task of paying for the war and hampered by the opposition of the parlements, forgot the unfinished conflict overseas. Unfortunately for them, whereas their European wars were avoidable and unnecessary, the colonial struggle with England was in the nature of things.

In the New World French missionaries and explorers from the settlements in Canada had been working inland, and by way of the great rivers tracing a route south to Louisiana. A continent was waiting to be opened up, but the royal government was little interested in a colony which cost far more than it brought in. Nor were the French people more interested. Canada attracted few immigrants and its population grew only slowly. The French Canadians slowly increased in numbers from 24,500 in 1710 to 65,000 in 1760. Quebec had 7,000 inhabitants and Montreal 4,000. At the same time the whole of Louisiana, far to the south, was inhabited by 5,000 Europeans. To set against this the English colonies along the seaboard had a population of over one and a half million. On the other side of the world, in the East Indies, France had a network of trading stations, and here the *Compagnie des Indes* competed with the East India Company not without success, which was increased when, in 1751, Dupleix was appointed Governor-General.

It is easy to comprehend why neither government nor public opinion in France should have cared about Canada or Louisiana, or even the East Indies, when a comparison is made with the resources and profits of the French West Indian islands. Martinique, in the middle of the century, had 17,000 whites and 57,000 slaves, Guadeloupe 9,000 and

33,000, St Domingo, 'the pearl of the Antilles', 20,000 whites and 160,000 slaves. The West Indies accounted for 20 per cent of the total external trade of France in the first half of the eighteenth century. Here was something worth fighting for, but the colonial struggle could not be confined to the West Indies. It continued throughout the world during the years of nominal peace after 1748. French and English colonists clashed in America in the neighbourhood of the Great Lakes. In India, Dupleix entered into the rivalries of the Indian princes and established a protectorate over the Carnatic and a large sphere of influence in the Deccan. The English copied his methods, and in the guise of struggles between local princes a regular war was waged betwen Dupleix and the representatives of the East India Company from 1750 to 1753. In 1754 the Anglo-French conflict in Canada and India was intensified. The British government decided, although the two countries were nominally at peace, to settle the Canadian struggle by cutting off supplies and reinforcements from France. In June 1755 a French convoy was attacked by Admiral Boscawen off Newfoundland; two French ships were captured, though the rest escaped. On land, military expeditions dispatched under Braddock against the outlying French forts were repulsed with heavy loss.

The French government, in the face of these attacks, could not do less than recall its envoys at London and Hanover. War had still not been declared, but the British navy was ordered to seize all French ships wherever they might be. Over 300 French merchant ships were captured in a few weeks, by what can hardly be described as other than an act of piracy. Versailles sent an ultimatum to London, and by January 1756 the two countries were openly at war. France had done nothing to provoke this war. Neither court nor country was interested in the icy wastes of Canada, while the *Compagnie des Indes*, only concerned with trading profits, disavowed Dupleix, who was replaced in 1754 by a governor instructed to liquidate his policy. The trade of the West Indies was another matter. France could hardly sit by passively while French merchant ships were being seized or driven off the seas in time of peace by the British. This war with Great Britain, therefore, could not be avoided. There was, however, another war, starting concurrently, on which a very different verdict must be passed.

Maria Theresa was determined that Silesia should not be permanently lost. To recover it she required an ally on the Continent and that ally could only be France. The brilliant young Austrian diplomat, Kaunitz, sent to Versailles to lay the foundations of an Austro-French alliance, found the French court wedded to pacific ideas. At the same time the British government was negotiating with Austria to secure an alliance which would protect Hanover. Though neither the Austrian nor the British government wished to break their traditional alliance, no agreement for this purpose on mutually acceptable terms could be reached; and since Britain could not rely on Austria to protect Hanover, in January 1756 she concluded the Convention of Westminster with Prussia.

Kaunitz now turned again to France. The difficulty for Austrian policy was that while her prime aim was the recovery of Silesia from Prussia, France was completely unconcerned in this quarrel. It was, therefore, necessary to work on French dynastic ambitions by offering to support a French candidate for the throne of Poland, and even by venturing the suggestion that a son-in-law of Louis XV might be established as ruler of a large part of the Austrian Netherlands. The French royal council was still for the most part committed to the Prussian alliance, and Frederick, by his patronage of enlightened writers, had won for himself propagandists in France who were influential even if they were not conscious of the use that was being made of them. But the influence of writers on foreign policy was limited, and in the state of French government nobody could tell from the ministers nominally in authority what its policy would actually be.

Austrian intrigues might not have succeeded if French foreign policy had not already been confused and confounded. Diplomacy by factions was the natural corollary of government by factions. The '*secret*' of the regent had been followed by those of Chauvelin, of Belle-Isle, and of the Saxon group. Most important of all, though least suspected at the time, was *le secret du roi*. It was hardly reasonable to suppose that the king would have his own secret diplomacy working in rivalry with and often in opposition to his official agents, yet this was the situation that developed. A habit of private consultation between the king and the prince de Conti on foreign affairs, begun in 1743, developed into a candidature by the latter for the Polish throne, in support of which a system of secret correspondence with French agents to various European courts was built up. In 1752 the comte de Broglie, as ambassador to Poland, became the central figure in this network and he continued as the effective head of it, under the king, after Conti withdrew. The *premier commis* at the ministry of Foreign Affairs, Tercier, was also in the *secret*. Diplomats at foreign courts who were in the organization sent their private reports, as well as copies of the dispatches they had received from the Secretary of State, to the king by way of Tercier and de Broglie. When Tercier was dismissed by Choiseul, in 1759, the last link between the official diplomacy and the king's *secret* was broken, but the latter survived until the king's death fifteen years later. It may well seem extraordinary that Louis should have been willing to toil away, in the privacy of his cabinet, reading the correspondence, personally answering the reports of de Broglie and through him controlling a network of agents in pursuit of one policy, while all the time his Secretaries of State for Foreign Affairs were following contrary policies.

The king's *secret*, aimed at maintaining the alliance with Turkey, Poland, Prussia, and Sweden, separating Austria from Russia, and excluding Russian influence from Poland, was closer to traditional French policy and, it might be argued, more in keeping with French interests than the policy that was officially to be adopted in 1756. Even this, however, was not the work of the Foreign Minister, Rouillé, who was a mediocrity. The secretaries of state were committed to the Prussian alliance, and Kaunitz, who knew of Louis XV's taste for secret diplomacy, therefore determined on an indirect approach. The catalyst to bring about the desired reaction in French foreign policy was found in the person of Mme de Pompadour. The titular mistress had ceased, at some time in 1751–2, to exercise her official functions, in which, as she and the king had both come to realize, she could not share the satisfaction that Louis obtained. For the next twenty years, until the time of Mme du Barry, the king took his pleasure with an apparently unending series of passing beauties, whose names are largely unrecorded. Their obscure origins aroused the indignation of the court, which felt that the king was ready to confer on mere facile charms an honour that should have been reserved for birth and breeding. Serious hopes were only aroused when it was thought that one of them might usurp the position of the *maîtresse en titre*. For this was not the end for Mme de Pompadour: in a sense it was only the beginning. She ceased to be the mistress to become the closest friend and *confidante* of the king. Her direct political power has been grossly exaggerated. Her influence, as might have been expected, was in the field of personal relations rather than policies; but in a state whose politics were determined by the factions of a court, personal relations were apt to be the decisive factor. So the Austrians thought when they astutely chose her as the intermediary in their decisive diplomatic manoeuvre.

Direct negotiations were engaged between the king and the Austrian ambassador. The council and the ministers were largely excluded from the discussions, the details of which were entrusted to an amiable little friend of Mme de Pompadour, the abbé de Bernis. The revelation of the Westminster agreement between Prussia and Great Britain, which seemed to demonstrate for a third time how treacherous an ally Frederick II was, clinched the issue. In May 1756 France and Austria signed the Treaty of Versailles. Thus was concluded the Austrian alliance, which was to

dominate French policy up to 1789. The famous Reversal
of Alliances was completed. It represented the abandonment of France's old and decaying allies, Sweden, Poland,
Turkey, and the German states, in favour of new links with
Vienna and St Petersburg. Yet, throughout the long and
involved diplomatic manoeuvres, which had extended from
1750 to 1756, no positive aim emerged on the French side.
At best the treaty with Austria might have been regarded,
though mistakenly, as guaranteeing France against war in
Europe while she waged the naval and colonial war with
Great Britain. But it should not have required great per-
spicacity to see that Maria Theresa's object was to secure
French support in a war for the recovery of Silesia. Apparently this was not realized at the French court. Frederick II
appreciated his danger soon enough, all the more because
there were alarming indications also on the Russian side,
and rather than allow time for the coalition against him to
take the offensive, in August 1756 he fell on Saxony and
occupied it and Louis XV, who had gradually been led on
by Austrian diplomacy, found himself committed to a full-
scale war in Europe.

The war into which France had been dragged at least began promisingly. Minorca was captured and the British
fleet under the unfortunate Admiral Byng repulsed. The
French navy, which had been strengthened during the long
term of office of Maurepas as Secretary for the Marine,
more than held its own on the seas. It was reasonable to
suppose that the coalition of France, Austria, Russia, Sweden, Saxony, and other German states would rapidly overcome the resistance of Prussia. What had not been allowed
for was the incompetent generalship of the allied armies, the
military ability of Frederick, and the coming into office of
Pitt in Great Britain. Moreover, for France to join in a
system of alliances which enabled Austria to group the German states, with the exception of Prussia and Hanover,
both at war with France, under her banner was a flagrant
repudiation of the classic policy of France towards the
Empire, which, adumbrated by Henry IV and put into

execution by Richelieu and Mazarin, had triumphed in the Treaty of Westphalia.

The French, however, began the continental war with success by invading Hanover. Defeated at Hastenbeck, the Duke of Cumberland signed the Convention of Closter-seven by which he undertook to disband his army. But once again domestic factions prevented France from taking advantage of military victory. The victorious French general, d'Estrées, had made the mistake of quarrelling with Pâris-Duverney, who was in control of supplies, and the powerful financier used his influence with the Pompadour to secure a change in the command. It was, however, her chief rival at court, the duc de Richelieu, professional charmer and favourite of Louis XV, who replaced d'Estrées and proceeded rapidly to fritter away the fruits of victory. In charge of the largest French army, he let it loose on Hanover to pillage the, country and fall into a state of complete indiscipline. He disregarded all appeals to join forces with the other French army under the prince de Soubise, which was now closing with Frederick II. The rivalry of court factions thus even determined military policy, for there was no love lost between Louis XV's closest companions, Richelieu and the Pompadour, and Soubise was an old friend of Mme de Pompadour. In November 1757 Frederick took advantage of Richelieu's inaction and routed the French and German troops under Soubise at Rossbach. In December, by the victory of Leuthen over the Austrians, he kept his hold on Silesia. In the early months of 1758, the Convention of Closter-seven having been repudiated, an Anglo-Hanoverian army under Ferdinand of Brunswick drove the French out of Hanover and Westphalia. Richelieu had already been recalled to Versailles, to resume there conquests more appropriate to his talents, but he had done all the damage he could do. A subsequent attempt by French armies to invade Germany was only to lead to the defeat of Minden in 1759.

Overseas, Senegal and Goree fell to the English. Clive's victories in India put Bengal into his hands and enabled him to supplant French influence in the south. In Canada, the

strong points of Louisburg, Fort Duquesne, and Fort Frontenac were lost. Wolfe defeated Montcalm at Quebec and
the whole colony passed into the hands of the English. In the
West Indies, Guadeloupe, Martinique, Grenada, Saint-
Vincent, Santa-Lucia were captured by British naval expeditions. At Lagos and Quiberon, the Toulon and the Brest
fleets were routed. France itself was exposed to hampering if
unsuccessful British raids.

The abbé de Bernis who, according to the memoirs he
wrote later, had unwillingly been responsible for launching
French policy on this sea of disaster, was already anxious by
1758 to find some haven of peace. He found one, but for
himself not for France. He was made a cardinal and sent off
to the country. Who was to replace him? The king's council
was almost denuded of ability, most of its members aged,
and only Belle-Isle rising above mediocrity. The king had
even personal grounds for concern. In 1757 a dagger attack
had been made on him by the half-mad Damiens, who had
taken the anti-royal propaganda of the parlements at its face
value. Though Louis was not seriously injured he was
alarmed and perhaps even more shocked. Damiens was subjected to the correct legal *question*, and finally tortured to
death in a great public ceremony. The opportunity might
have been taken to deal with the parlements on a charge of
complicity with him. Instead, the two competent, though
rival, secretaries of state who were most hated by them were
dismissed from office. Thus it was that another d'Argenson,
at the Ministry of War since 1743, and Machault, former
Controller-General and now Minister for the Marine, fell.
Their successors were nonentities. Some means of strengthening the government was urgently required. A protégé of
Mme de Pompadour, the comte de Stainville, was therefore
called from the embassy at Vienna and made duc de
Choiseul and Secretary of State for Foreign Affairs in
December 1758.

It was too late to restore the balance of the war: the following year saw the culmination of French defeats. Choiseul
had no hope but to extricate France with as little loss as

possible. He improved the position by the conclusion, in 1761, of the *pacte de famille* between the Bourbon rulers of France, Spain, the Two Sicilies, and Parma, and in 1762 Spain entered the war on the side of France. With inexhaustible energy Choiseul took over the Secretaryships of War and the Marine, sharing the control of Foreign Affairs with his cousin, Choiseul-Praslin. He was able to conclude peace with Great Britain by the Treaty of Paris in 1763, at a heavy price, but not quite so heavy as the year of disasters, 1759, had seemed to foreshadow. Canada, Senegal, and the West Indian islands of Grenada, St Vincent, Dominica, and Tobago were lost; French possessions in India were confined to a few trading stations; Louisiana was ceded to Spain in compensation for the loss of Florida. As a result of the Seven Years War the first colonial empire of France had been lost and nothing had been gained. The Peace of Paris was the price paid for government by weak and wavering ministerial groups and court factions.

II

THE AGE OF REFORM

———

I. THE REVOLUTION IN IDEAS

WHILE eighteenth-century France remained politically the France of Louis XIV without the Grand Monarch, socially the nation was changing rapidly and the conflict of social realities with the juristic and formal pattern of society was becoming increasingly acute. Moreover, in ideas this was already a century of revolution, though of a revolution whose roots lay deep in the past. Even while Reformation and Counter-Reformation were tearing France to pieces in the Religious Wars, Rabelais and Montaigne had initiated a more sceptical attitude to religion, which was continued by the libertine writers of the next century. In the seventeenth century Pascal challenged the moral basis of orthodox thought and Descartes provided an intellectual alternative to it. While Louis XIV was on the throne there had been little possibility of the open expression of unorthodox ideas, but under the more liberal English and Dutch régimes new ideas were developing rapidly. Newton provided a mathematical system which reduced the physical world to order and demonstrated the reign of law. Locke evolved a theory of human psychology which, through the principle of association, showed how complex ideas could be built up out of the simple data of sensory experience without assuming the existence of any innate ideas. His theory of morals marks the emergence of utilitarianism; in politics he justified the English Revolution of 1688 and parliamentary government, and in religion deism.

The infection of new ideas could not be wholly excluded from France during the reign of Louis XIV, even if those who were tempted by dangerous thoughts kept silent or fled abroad. Among the latter the greatest name is that of Pierre Bayle. Because his writings were scattered, unsystematic, often anonymous, his influence is difficult to estimate and may appear less than that of Locke; but in Bayle's writings are to be found all the leading themes of the advanced thinkers of the next century. Locke's ideas had to be translated into the terms of an alien tradition when they crossed the Channel, but in Bayle's writings, though he himself perhaps remained more fundamentally religious, and even Calvinistic, at heart than has been commonly recognized, the climate of opinion was already that which was to become dominant with Voltaire and the Encyclopedists. He fell under the ban of the French state as a Calvinist, even worse, as one who had temporarily accepted Catholicism and then relapsed. The year of the comet, 1680, produced an outburst of superstition, which Bayle, now a refugee teaching at Rotterdam, criticized in his *Pensées diverses sur la comète,* explaining the manifestation on the basis of observed facts as a purely physical phenomenon. He followed this up with a study of the history of the Religious Wars, which set off Catholic and Calvinist accounts against one another and tested both by rational historical criticism.

Bayle was a sceptic, but his scepticism differed from that of Montaigne or La Motte de Vayer, because while he questioned everything he did not end up by disbelieving everything. He accepted what was soundly based on scientific and historical evidence, rationally criticized. The theoretical arguments of Cartesianism and the metaphysics of Leibnitz were not for him. To theories he opposed the facts of observation and experience. He was essentially concerned with practical questions. Above all he was a moralist who believed that there was a 'natural idea of equity' in man which was independent of religious revelation. Conscience, he agreed, is the supreme rule of human life, but its judgement on human actions must be in accordance with their results. It was his rejection of the criterion of religious dogma which separated Bayle from his fellow exile, the Huguenot pastor, Jurieu. Bayle's object was to spread the spirit of rational criticism, that of Jurieu to inspire a Calvinist revolt against the Catholic monarchy of Louis XIV. Jurieu's aim was liberty for the true religion, and when he argued for the theory of the sovereignty of the people, it was only the people chosen by God whom he meant. Bayle equally maintained the sovereignty of the political state, but he meant the whole community, held together not by religion but by its common secular interests. No system of government was an absolute good: they all depended on circumstances and should be judged by their results. The whole of this philosophy of life was poured pell-mell into Bayle's *Dictionnaire historique et critique* of 1697, and although he died, at the age of fifty-nine, in 1706, he set the tone and provided the ideas which were to dominate the following century.

Bayle, though he stood above all other critics, did not stand alone. The death of Louis XIV released a dammed-up flood of criticism. Montesquieu's *Lettres persanes*, published when the regency had relaxed the censorship, mocked at the idols, religious and political, of the previous reign. The abbé de Saint-Pierre applied his utilitarian inventiveness, with a range worthy of Bentham himself, to everything from perpetual peace to a patent portable arm-chair. The Jacobite Ramsay followed in the steps of Fénelon with a plea for toleration. Such men, and their kindred spirits, met at the Club de l'Entresol, to which Bolingbroke in exile joined himself, until it was suppressed by Fleury in 1731.

Censorship, of course, was still partially effective in the early years of Louis XV's reign. In 1717 an act of sacrilege was punished by the burning of the culprit, and a charge of speaking with impiety of religion by a sentence to the galleys for life. In 1739 all the printing establishments in forty-three towns were suppressed. Unorthodox ideas, particularly in the field of religion, had to find expression largely in manuscript form. This limited their influence, though the number that have survived of some of these manuscripts is surprising. One investigator found copies of as many as 102 different manuscript treatises expressing unorthodox religious ideas which had been in clandestine circulation in the first half of the eighteenth century. The comte de Boulainvillier, author of the *Vie de Mahomet*, was the centre of one group of heretical thinkers amongst whom such manuscripts circulated; it met at the houses of the marquis d'Argenson and the duc de Noailles, or at the Académie des Inscriptions, until the death of Boulainvillier in 1722. The works of English deists and free-thinkers were translated and circulated in manuscript by such men, but being translations it was also less risky to print these.

By 1730 French writers had passed beyond the moderate deism of most of their English predecessors, though the most notorious of the clandestine writings, the *Testament* of the curé Meslier, was begun as early as 1722–3. Voltaire declared that he knew of over one hundred copies of this extraordinary work, ruthlessly materialist in its views, which treated man as a 'human machine' and not a very successful machine at that. One chapter in Meslier's treatise was entitled, 'The world is not ruled by an intelligent being'. Theology, it declared, made of its God 'a monster of unreason, injustice, malice, and atrocity'. Even Voltaire, when he published, much later, extracts from this work, dared not print its violent political and social criticism. In respect of this, indeed, it stands alone, for the general attack was directed almost exclusively against the Church and religious teaching. Published works were much more moderate in tone and are represented by Voltaire's *Lettres philosophiques* of 1734, in which the author popularized Newtonian mathematics, still generally rejected in France in favour of the mathematical theories of Descartes.

Clandestine writings declined after 1740, as the censorship became more lax. The middle of the century marked the turning-point, with the publication of a number of major works expressing the new ideas. *Les Mœurs* of Toussaint, in 1748, expounded a secular morality. La Mettrie's *L'homme machine*, in the same year, proclaimed crudely that pleasure is man's only end. Diderot, in a series of philosophical writings of which the most important is the *Lettres sur les aveugles* of 1749, speculated on the relativity of knowledge and morals. Montesquieu's *De l'Esprit des lois*, in 1748, proclaimed the rule of law and inaugurated the comparative study of institutions. Buffon published the first volume of his *Histoire naturelle* in 1749. Condillac, building on Locke, in his *Traité des sensations* of 1754 gave systematic form to a psychological theory which derived all human ideas from experience. By now there was a considerable body of advanced thinkers in France imbued with new and revolutionary ideas on religion, science, history, society, and anxious to spread the enlightenment of which they believed themselves to be the possessors. Diderot conceived the idea of a great Encyclopedia which should be at the same time a compendium of all knowledge and a work of propaganda for the new ideas. Its first volume appeared in 1751.

Orthodox thought was on the defensive, and those who should have been defending it were more concerned with the struggle against the so-called Jansenism of the parlements. The censorship of books was still vigorously carried on by the latter, but with more show than effect. Regularly books were condemned to be burnt by the executioner, and as regularly the publishers produced piles of unwanted remainders to be ceremonially destroyed, and continued to circulate and sell the condemned works as freely as before. Writings which might fall under the ban were published in Switzerland, Holland, and England, or at least alleged to be so on their title-pages, and issued without an author's name, attributed to a dead writer, or described as translations.

Fuel was provided for the fire that was now raging against the Catholic Church by episodes of religious persecution which were all the more shocking for being sporadic. Memories of the Camisard revolt, stirred up in a period of economic difficulties and fear of foreign invasion, produced a local panic in Toulouse, of which the bourgeois Huguenot family of Calas, charged with the murder of a son who had been converted to Catholicism, were the victims. The parlement of Toulouse had Calas broken on the wheel and all the property of his family confiscated. The conduct of the trial was so flagrantly unjudicial and incompetent that Voltaire, moved by a combination of genuine indignation at the cruel and irrational verdict of the parlement, pity for the fate of the Calas family, and desire to exploit the judicial murder in the interests of his campaign against the Church, was able to make great play with it and in the end secure the quashing of the verdict by the king's council in Paris. Another case which secured much publicity was that of the young chevalier de La Barre, aged nineteen, who had indulged in some adolescent obscenities which were held to be sacrilege. The *procureur du roi* attempted to save him by means of a *lettre de cachet*, but the local parlement was not willing to let a possible victim evade its clutches in this way. Despite the intercession of the Bishop of Amiens in La Barre's favour, the parlement knew its duty. The rights of religion, which Church and Crown had shown themselves regrettably reluctant to enforce in this case, were vindicated by the law. La Barre was sentenced to have his tongue cut out and to be burnt with a copy of Voltaire's *Dictionnaire philosophique* round his neck. The executioner, more pitiful, only made the semblance of cutting out the tongue and the young man was decapitated before his body was thrown on the fire.

In spite of the excesses of the parlements it was clear that the persecuting spirit was dying down in the Church, itself influenced by the new ideas. This did not temper the force of the cold blast of scepticism and mockery that Voltaire and the *philosophes* were directing against Catholicism. The period from 1748 to 1770 may be said to mark the victory of the new anti-religious ideology. To dismiss this simply as a new kind of unorthodox orthodoxy, as Carl Becker does, is unfair. The thought of the eighteenth century was essentially practical. The so-called *philosophes* had no time for metaphysics or dogma, but they were intensely concerned with ethics. They were essentially empirical in their outlook. They judged the Church and all other social institutions by their practical results. Utilitarianism dominated the century and it taught the gospel that pain was evil and pleasure good. Limited this doctrine may have been, but in its simple way it appealed to the ordinary educated man of the age of reason.

In the long run the anti-clerical campaign of Voltaire and the literary men was to leave the greater mark on the national mind, but at the time the internecine warfare of the defenders of religion, the parlements and Jesuits, was the more dangerous to both Church and Crown. By the middle of the century the parlements had succeeded in reinstating themselves as a power in the land. Their victory over Machault was followed by an offensive against subsequent controllers-general, which was copied by the provincial parlements, waging guerilla warfare against the intendants. In 1763 the parlement of Paris consolidated its political victory, in alliance with Choiseul, by securing the appointment as Controller-General of a *parlementaire*. The royal administration, in the hour of defeat, capitulated to the parlements and abandoned its attempts at financial reform.

The success of the parlements in frustrating financial reform was followed by the triumphal conclusion of their campaign against the Jesuits. The Jansenist controversy, even in its limited eighteenth-century form, was by now dying of inanition: what was left was the *richérisme* of the lower clergy. But the vendetta of the gallican *parlementaires* against the Jesuits was inexhaustible, and the current of opinion, even if the parlements repudiated and did their best to persecute their unwanted, infidel allies in the literary world, was running against the Society of Jesus.

In this situation the Jesuits were unfortunate enough to have given hostages to fortune. Père Lavalette, Superior of the Mission to the Leeward Isles, had built up at Martinique a great commercial enterprise, which the Seven Years War reduced to bankruptcy. His creditors obtained judgement at Marseille against the Society, which with great folly appealed to the parlement of Paris. The parlement leapt at its opportunity, condemned the Society to pay all the debts of Lavalette, and then proceeded to set up a commission to examine the Jesuit Statutes. On receipt of the report of this

Commission, in 1762, the parlement decreed the abolition of the Society of Jesus, as a political body which, on the pretext of combating heresy, had established an alien authority in France and repudiated the sovereignty of the throne. Jesuit doctrines were declared 'perverse, destructive of all principles of religion and even honesty, injurious to Christian morals, pernicious to civil society, seditious, a challenge to the rights of the nation and royal authority, to the safety of the sacred person of the king and to the obedience of subjects, proper to arouse the greatest disturbances in states and to create and support the profoundest corruption in the heart of man.' Louis XV, whose rights were thus vindicated by those who were conducting the bitterest campaign against his government, did what he could to protect the Jesuits and stand between them and the wrath of the parlements; but, emerging discredited from a disastrous war, his government dared not face another domestic conflict. The Society was abolished by royal edict, its property confiscated, and its members dispersed. The *philosophes* may have been spreading irreligious ideas among the educated public: it was the parlements which delivered the greatest blow before 1789 to the Church. One result of the destruction of the Society of Jesus was the cessation of their teaching functions. Oratorians and other Orders attempted, as far as possible, to fill the gap that was left in the schools. Many teachers who were either laymen or else in very minor orders had to be introduced – Fouché and Billaud-Varenne both taught in the great schools of the Oratory at Juilly. The effect of their teaching on the minds of the coming revolutionary generation can at present only be guessed.

Though exceptions may be found, it is not unfair to say that religion in eighteenth-century France had become largely an external thing, repeating – except when it unconsciously adopted the language and ideas of its opponents – the formulas of the seventeenth century emptied of their feeling; just as religious architecture continued to copy the models of the previous century, exaggerating the theatrical character which even then had given to churches and abbeys something of the feeling of pieces of stage scenery. By the last years of the *ancien régime* the campaign for the secularization of thought appeared to have triumphed, at least in the educated mind. The more positive aspects of the revolution in ideas remain to be mentioned, for this was not merely a negative and destructive movement; but these are so closely bound up with practical developments that they are best discussed along with them as a formative element in the age of reform with which the *ancien régime* was to close.

2. REVIVAL OF AUTHORITY

THE Seven Years War left France, potentially still the greatest power in Europe, defeated and humiliated. However, the greatest loss, that of Canada, was of a territory of future and as yet unsuspected potentialities rather than of an immediately valuable one; and its loss was soon to be avenged by the difficulties which the removal of the French threat produced for the British government in its American colonies. Peace, moreover, provided an opportunity for renewing French strength. Choiseul, if he was not a great minister, was an able and energetic one and took advantage of it. Government by the secretaries of state and their bureaux was now so firmly established that he could not become an all-powerful *premier ministre*, as Fleury had been without the title, still less a Richelieu or a Mazarin, even if he had been built on that scale. But by accumulating in his own hands and those of his cousin, Choiseul-Praslin, the major offices of Foreign Affairs, Marine, and War, as well as many minor posts, Choiseul was able to provide something more like a united government than France had known since the hey-day of Fleury. That for all his talent and inexhaustible energy Choiseul was not a great minister, was shown at the outset. To ensure himself a peaceful life on the home front he concluded a tacit alliance with the parlements, allowing them to suppress the Jesuits and giving up any prospect of financial reform. This was to abandon from the start the one thing that was essential. Choiseul had willed the end, which was the re-establishment of French power in the world and a war of revenge against England; he did not will the necessary means, which was the restoration of royal authority inside France and the reform of royal finances, without which all other reforms would be in vain.

The bases of Choiseul's foreign policy were the Austrian alliance, which he had inherited, and the Family Compact with Spain, which was his own special creation. Since the Seven Years War had demonstrated how vital naval power was in any war with Great Britain, he vigorously set himself to rebuild the French navy. The fisheries were encouraged, to provide men to man the fleet; an *ordonnance* of 1765 reformed naval administration, giving increased authority to the officers responsible for the navigation of the ships; naval arsenals were multiplied. In 1763 France had some 30 to 40 ships of the line, mostly in bad condition: by 1771 there were 64 well-equipped ships and 50 frigates.

Military changes were introduced at the same time. Choiseul reformed the system by which the captains personally recruited and paid their companies, receiving in return a lump sum: it was naturally to their interest to swell the size of their regiments with dummy entries and to economize on supplies and equipment. Similarly, the colonel was the proprietor of his regiment. Choiseul bought out and retired, despite much noble indignation, many officers, and put recruitment and equipment into the hands of officials of the Ministry of War. He established a school for young nobles preparing to enter the *École militaire*. He converted factories for arms and munitions into royal establishments. The artillery, which had been an independent, self-governing corporation, became a *Corps royal* of six regiments, and the process of equipping it with the new mobile artillery invented by Gribeauval was begun.

The army and the navy, Choiseul and his able technical advisers could deal with directly. The colonies, after the Peace of Paris a mere relic of the former French empire, presented greater difficulties; reform in this field meant going against the national tradition and accepting, at least to some extent, the new ideas of free trade put forward by the Physiocrats. This was done all the same. The trading monopoly of the *Compagnie des Indes* was broken and imports from the East Indies multiplied two and a half times between the date of the breaking of the monopoly in 1769 and 1776. Efforts at colonization in Madagascar and French Guiana proved expensive failures, but the attenuation of the system of restriction in the French West Indies was reflected in the growth of their population and trade. French strength in the Mediterranean was increased when, in 1768, Choiseul purchased for two million livres from the Republic of Genoa its rebellious possession of Corsica. The opposition of the Corsicans under Paoli, which, although on such a small scale, may perhaps be regarded as opening the history of modern struggles for national independence, was crushed, and Corsica became a French *généralité*. In 1766, on the death of Stanislaus Leczinski, Lorraine was quietly incorporated into France.

Soldier, diplomat, and administrator, ugly and fascinating, calculating and fiery, full of expedients but given to long-range plans, gay and friendly, a frivolous courtier and an incredibly hard-working minister, Choiseul seemed to have everything that was needed to gain high office and make good use of it. Mme de Pompadour was devoted to him. France had had no luck for the twenty years while she was helping Louis XV to keep the boredom of a court and throne at bay: perhaps fortune would change with the brilliant new minister. If it was to do so, the Pompadour was not to know it. She died in 1764 at the age of forty, generally regretted, says the British Ambassador, but not by the people of France. From the balcony of the palace, on a wild, stormy day, Louis XV, wiping the tears from his eyes, watched the funeral cortège leave Versailles. Unequal, despite herself, to his passion, their friendship was unmarred till death separated them. Her political influence has been greatly exaggerated.

The death of the Pompadour had no effect on the position or power of Choiseul. Indirectly at least his fall was to come about, as that of so many other ministers, through the parlements. Choiseul having given way to the parlement of Paris all along the line, it was difficult for it to pick a quarrel with the government. But now the provincial parlements had been aroused to the assertion of their claims, and the struggle against the royal administration was shifting to the provinces. Brittany had been, in 1689, the last of the provinces to receive a permanent royal intendant; it possessed in its provincial estates an organ for the expression of the opinion of a tumultuous horde of petty, poverty-stricken provincial nobles; and its parlement, at Rennes, felt certain of their support in any quarrel it undertook with the king's representatives. The *casus belli* was the construction during the Seven Years War, for purposes of military defence, of a system of roads in the province. These roads could only be made by means of the royal *corvée*, but the estates of Brittany claimed that to do so was to invade their provincial rights. The parlement supported the estates and opened a struggle with the intendant, who in this case was collaborating with the military commandant, d'Aiguillon. The representatives of the king carried the war into the enemy camp by depriving the leader of the parlement, the *procureur général* La Chalotais, of the right of *survivance*, that is, of the right of passing his office at death to his son, who as it happened, though this, of course, was no reason for his exclusion from office, was notoriously weak-minded. La Chalotais knew no bounds in the violence of his attacks on d'Aiguillon, who proceeded to have him arrested. The other parlements of France now joined that of Rennes in a chorus of denunciation, and in the assertion of their powers came close to denying the sovereignty of the king. Louis XV repudiated their claims in the *lit de justice* of 1766, in language such as the parlements had not heard for many years. In the face of the tempest, however, d'Aiguillon resigned, though this did not prevent the parlement of Paris from summoning him for trial. Such flagrant defiance of the royal will and open persecution of the king's agents brought even Louis XV to the point of action.

Choiseul's complacency, indeed his secret support for the parlements, now threatened his own position. He seemed at the height of his power when, in 1770, he cemented the alliance with Austria and apparently ensured his future influence by negotiating the marriage of Maria Theresa's daughter, Marie-Antoinette, with the dauphin. This was not to be, from his point of view, as successful a move as he had hoped. Louis XV admired the youthful charm of the new dauphine, but personal difficulties arose when Marie-Antoinette found that the duty of being polite to a royal mistress was too much for a Habsburg princess. She was not entirely to be blamed for this. The new favourite, Mme du Barry, had risen from the poverty of a shop-girl to the rank of royal mistress with the aid of one talent and the most ravishing beauty that the court had seen. Good-natured, easy-going, with charm and charity she won many hearts, including the king's, and became *maîtresse en titre*, an office unoccupied since Mme de Pompadour had died. The du Barry had no political interests and Choiseul's bitter hostility to her, unless it is accounted for by the story that he had aspired to place his sister in the vacant office of titular mistress, is difficult to explain. Though it did not bring about his fall directly, this quarrel can hardly have strengthened his position with Louis XV.

Despite Choiseul's dominance over foreign affairs and the armed services, his position in the government had not remained unchallenged, for an ambitious and able lawyer, Maupeou, known as an upholder of the king's interests against the parlements, had been given the seals. This was a sign that Louis was not willingly following Choiseul in his subservience to the parlements. Maupeou brought into the ministry the abbé Terray as Controller-General. A curious pair they formed, little, dark, bilious Maupeou, whom his enemies called the Seville orange, and tall, stooping, sombre Terray; alike in their capacity for hard work, ability, ruthlessness, and contempt for popularity.

They had not long to wait before power fell into their hands. Choiseul himself provided the occasion for his downfall. A dispute had broken out between Spain and Great Britain over the Falkland Islands. Choiseul urged the Spaniards not to yield, with promises of support based on the Family Compact. When the question was raised in the royal council, in December 1770, Terray exposed the bankrupt state of royal finances, the result of years of subservience to the will of the parlements. The Choiseuls replied by attributing it, very unreasonably, to Terray's own administration and a furious debate took place in the king's presence. But Louis had learnt his lesson: he had been pushed into disastrous wars by bellicose ministers in the past. At this moment, war with England over the irrelevant Spanish claims to the Falkland Islands, when the restoration of French strength after the Seven Years War was still incomplete, when royal finances were at their lowest ebb and the parlements were engaged in open hostilities with the king's administration, would have been the height of folly. For once the king asserted himself. Choiseul and his cousin were stripped of all their offices and exiled to their country estates. Parlements, *noblesse*, public opinion were with the fallen ministers, whose fate was attributed to the intrigues of the new mistress. In fact the king had saved the country from yet another foreign adventure, which it was in no condition to undertake; and the reforming movement that Choiseul had initiated in the fields that interested him was now to be extended to the domestic field where it was even more needed.

After six months of struggle and intrigue for the succession to Choiseul, d'Aiguillon was brought in as Secretary of State for Foreign Affairs, which was equivalent to throwing down a gage of battle against the parlements. Terray had persuaded Maupeou and the king of what was true enough, that without drastic measures the Treasury could not overcome its difficulties. Such measures could only be carried through by overriding the opposition of the parlements. Maupeou was prepared to undertake this task, and at last

Louis XV had been brought to see that either his government or the parlements must rule France.

In a desperate situation Terray began with desperate remedies: repudiation of part of the debt, suspension of payments of interest, and forced loans. These measures dealt with the immediate problem: to put royal finances permanently on a sound basis a general reform was required, which could only be achieved at the price of a bitter struggle with the parlements. Instead of waiting to be attacked, Maupeou took the offensive. By calculated provocations he enticed the parlement of Paris into open rejection of the king's authority. Then, in January 1771, by *lettres de cachet*, he exiled the magistrates, not, as was customary, to some pleasant country town such as Blois, but to varying and distant destinations, the more violent to remote villages of barren Auvergne in the heart of winter. This act of atrocity, as it was considered, aroused a public outcry, but Maupeou went his way undeterred. He abolished the venal offices of the *parlementaires* without compensation, divided the vast area over which the parlement of Paris had jurisdiction into six parts, and set up new courts, nominated by the king, in which justice was to be free.

It was a veritable *coup d'état*. Provincial estates, Princes of the Blood, nobles, the whole world of dependants of the parlements, and the bourgeoisie of Paris, long accustomed to regard the parlements as the defenders of their interests, joined in a furious outcry. Many even of the literary men, who had themselves suffered from the censorship of the parlements, were carried away by the wave of emotion, though Voltaire, with greater understanding of what was at issue, threw himself into the struggle on the side of Maupeou. In spite of it all the new courts were set up and after initial difficulties began to function. The *parlementaires* weakened and accepted concessions which allowed them to return home. Maupeou, having won his initial triumph, proposed to follow it up by a fundamental reform of the whole judicial system of France, reducing the mass of unnecessary jurisdictions, codifying and unifying the laws, reforming the antiquated and barbarous procedure, and creating out of the existing *Conseil des Partis* a new Court of Appeal and an administrative *Conseil d'État*. He was not to have the time to put these plans into operation, but it was his secretary, Lebrun, who, as third consul, was to see them brought into effect in the Consulate of Bonaparte.

With the opposition of the parlements eliminated, Terray was able to proceed with some of the financial reforms which they had so long blocked. Machault's edict of 1749, establishing the assessment and collection of the *vingtième* on a sounder basis, was put into operation. The *pays d'états* remained in a privileged position, but the inequity of the distribution of the taxes was at least reduced. The *capitation* of Paris, the collection of which had fallen into great disorder, was reformed by a new assessment and its product nearly doubled. The new lease of the indirect taxes to the Farmers General, in 1774, brought in an extra 20 millions.

The weak link in the triumvirate was d'Aiguillon, jealous, petty, and unscrupulous, who in spite of his incompetence at the Ministry of Foreign Affairs was able to keep in office with the aid of court intrigues and even to add to his existing ministry that of War. What may have helped him to keep his job was that he, as well as the du Barry, who was less stupid than was commonly supposed, knew all about the *secret du roi*. Even Choiseul had only suspected its existence. The king's *secret* had become rather disorientated in these last years. The imposition of Stanislaus Poniatowski as king on Poland in 1764 by Catherine had robbed it of the last relics of its original *raison d'être*. However, de Broglie had provided a new objective in the form of a plan for a war of revenge on Great Britain, and recruited as the representative of the *secret* in London the able young secretary to the French embassy, the chevalier d'Éon. A French agent was sent to report on the defences of the English coast, and a scheme was drawn up by which France, in alliance with Spain and the Northern powers, should be able, when the time came, to throw an invading army across the Channel. These plans were destined to repose in the dossiers of the

ancien régime, save for an abortive attempt at invasion during
the American War, till Napoleon pulled them out; but they
provided the occasion for a farcical last episode in the history
of the *secret*. D'Éon quarrelled with his ambassador, who
was supported by Versailles. He then threatened to reveal
the schemes of the *secret* to the British government. Louis, in
panic, had an attempt made to kidnap d'Éon, who evaded
it and brought a successful lawsuit in the English courts
against the ambassador, who had to abandon his post. In
1766 d'Éon agreed to return the documents conveying
Louis' instructions, in exchange for a pension of 12,000
livres a year; but he retained other papers with the revelation of which he periodically threatened the French government. However, it was about this time that the chevalier
adopted female attire and declared that he was a lady, after
which he was taken rather less seriously.

Meanwhile, at Vienna the new French ambassador, the
Cardinal de Rohan, discovered that the Austrians had in-
tercepted and deciphered the correspondence of the *secret*,
a fact which, through his relation the prince de Soubise, he
passed on to the king. The enmity which he experienced
from Maria Theresa is doubtless more reasonably explained
by the cardinal's inconvenient discovery than by his alleged
exploits among her maids of honour. Inherited by Marie-
Antoinette, this enmity was at the root of the unhappy and
influential diamond necklace affair.

The correspondence of Louis XV in the final years gives
one the impression that he himself was beginning to lose the
thread of his own secret diplomacy. Although de Broglie
more than once begged to be allowed to abandon it, the
king was too much a creature of habit to give it up, though
it was by now practically meaningless. The *secret* ended only
with his death when, on the orders of Louis XVI, the papers
were deposited with the new Foreign Minister, Vergennes –
himself, ironically, a member of the *secret*; so that in him
official and secret diplomacy may be said to have come together at last.

Possibly, in these years also, Louis XV may have been

paying more attention to home than to foreign affairs, and in this connexion d'Aiguillon counted for a good deal less than his colleagues. His irresponsibility was finally demonstrated when he began to negotiate with his old enemies of the parlements against them. But he was a light man and could hardly have swung the balance down against Maupeou and Terray, who had so dramatically and successfully restored royal authority after a generation of weakness. Given a few more years for the country to appreciate the benefits of the new system, and there could hardly have been any question of a restoration of the parlements. Freed from their incubus, the reforms which were already in the minds of many, and in the dossiers and *mémoires* of the administration, could be brought out and applied. The tragedy was that the few years that were needed were not given. In 1774 Louis XV was taken ill with smallpox and in fourteen days he was dead. The reforming wave was to continue and to gain in strength, but the forces of resistance that Louis XV had been brought to face and defy only in the last years of his reign were to prove even stronger under his weaker successor, and the contradictions which had been inherent in the social and political system of France since the time of Louis XIV were within fifteen years to bring the monarchy down in ruins.

3. PRELUDE TO REFORM

THE former dauphin, with whom the *dévot* party might have come to power, had died in 1765. The successor was therefore Louis XV's grandson. Louis XVI, king at twenty years and full of good intentions, was determined to break with the ways of the corrupt old court and in particular with the tyrannical triumvirate, the *protégés* of Mme du Barry as he had been taught to see them. All too conscious of his own youth and inexperience, he looked around for an adviser, and was given one by his aunt Mme Adélaide, in the person of the elderly courtier, Maurepas. A capable and successful minister a quarter of a century earlier, at the age of seventy-three Maurepas found himself called from the wings, where he had long exercised his wit at the expense of the players, back to the centre of the stage, delighted at the freak of fortune which brought him so unexpectedly to the height of influence. If Louis XVI thought he had found his Fleury he was sadly mistaken. Maurepas' only aim was to enjoy his new elevation as long as he could and not to overburden his aged frame with work or his flippant mind with serious thoughts.

The dismissal of Maupeou – last of the great ministers of the Bourbon dynasty – was a foregone conclusion. This was not enough. The *parlementaires*, conscious of their role as the defenders of the constitutional liberties of France, and their supporters who had labelled themselves the 'Patriot' party, rapidly recovered from the disarray and hopelessness into which they had fallen after four years of firm handling by Maupeou. They organized demonstrations in Paris, exploited the legend that Louis XV had speculated in grain to profit from the distress of his people – the so-called *pacte de famine* – and brought out the mob to invade the courts where the *parlement Maupeou* sat. It was a tactic that was to be repeated in 1788 and it succeeded in conveying the impression of a great public movement, to which the government yielded by restoring the old parlements. All the achievement of Maupeou was undone. True, the restoration was on conditions, but no one who knew the history of the parlements in the eighteenth century should have expected them to abide by these. In the provinces, as in Paris, the triumph of the combined *noblesse* of the robe and the sword was celebrated as a victory for the people over a despotic monarchy.

But even in this Indian summer of reaction the spirit of reform could not be suppressed. Nothing could be more mistaken than the idea that the eighteenth century was an age of abstract thought. It was, on the contrary, in all the countries where the Enlightenment was a force, and particularly in France and England, one of intense interest in practical reform. To appreciate why this was so we

must look a little more closely at some aspects of its intellectual history; for this was the age when science descended,
in a sense, from the study to the market-place. Naturally,
something was lost in the process, but the strength of the
new ways of thought that science brought with it was evident
even when they were turned to old uses. The theme of the
abbé Pluche's *Spectacle de la nature* (1732), which went
through at least eighteen editions in France, was to prove
the existence of God by the evidence of the divine plan in
nature. 'Some animals,' wrote Pluche, 'are pre-ordained by
Providence to live with, and be serviceable to mankind;
others to reside in woods and deserts, . . . to prove a scourge
to all such of the human species as grow profligate and abandoned wretches.' Or again, 'The same hand which made the
fishes of the sea, prepared from the beginning the water of
which they had need.' Popular science of this sort admittedly
demonstrated no more than a growth of interest. The barriers against acceptance of new scientific ideas on a higher
intellectual level were strong. Even Fontenelle, for all his
modernity, clung to Descartes and the *tourbillons* and rejected the Newtonian system. The Jesuits, who, until
their expulsion, dominated French education, only accepted
Cartesianism about 1730, when it was losing its intellectual
validity. Maupertuis, on the other hand, defended Newton's
explanation of the movement of comets as early as his *Discours sur la figure des astres* of 1723. Voltaire wrote effective
propaganda for Newtonian science, and by 1747 the triumph
of the new ideas could be described in the marquis d'Argens'
La philosophie du bon sens as 'la fureur de l'attraction'.

We must not exaggerate the scientific achievements of
eighteenth-century France. The distinguished mathemati-
cian d'Alembert, the careful observer of insects Réaumur,
among many others, catch our attention; but until we come
to Lavoisier it was a period of diffusion, popularization, accumulation, rather than of fundamental discovery. The important new fact was the spread of the empirical attitude.
Voltaire, in his *Lettres philosophiques*, and d'Alembert in the
Discours préliminaire to the *Encyclopédie*, saw behind Newton

the founder of experimental science in Bacon. Abstract, *a priori* thought was almost universally condemned. 'What could be more ridiculous,' wrote Condillac in his *Traité des systèmes* (1749), 'than that men awakening from a profound sleep, and finding themselves in the middle of a labyrinth, should lay down general principles for discovering the way out? Yet such is the conduct of the philosopher.' Observe, experiment, collect: this was the method of the eighteenth century and these were activities in which many could join. Salons could be laboratories and literary journals spread scientific news, until even Voltaire thought that the craze for science was going too far. 'I loved physics,' he wrote in 1741, 'so long as it did not try to take precedence over poetry; now that it is crushing all the arts, I no longer wish to regard it as anything but a tyrant.'

Empirical science, linked with the sensational psychology and the materialist doctrine, was destined profoundly to influence man's attitude to himself and his institutions. The result was to make environment and education all-powerful over man; the chain of custom, the bondage to the past, was broken at its strongest link. Progress became possible and therefore conceivable. 'We arrive, so to speak,' wrote the abbé de Saint-Pierre early in the century, 'at the beginning of the age of gold.' And at the end Condorcet could envisage the human race, 'emancipated from its shackles, released from the power of fate and from that of the enemies of its progress, advancing with a firm and sure step along the path of truth, virtue, and happiness.'

The idea of progress provides ample scope for mocking at the shallow optimism of the age of *lumières* from our own peak of disillusion, but it was not unqualified. 'What is optimism?' asked Cacambo. 'Alas,' said Candide, 'it is the mania for pretending that all is well when all is ill.' Voltaire was no stranger to pessimism:

> *L'homme, étranger à soi, de l'homme est ignoré.*
> *Que sais-je ? Où suis-je ? Où vais-je ? et d'où suis-je tiré ?*
> *Atomes tourmentés sur cet amas de boue,*
> *Que la mort engloutit, et dont le sort se joue.*

But his conclusion was not despair, but 'Il faut cultiver notre jardin.' The whole attitude of mind of the eighteenth century led up to one thing: practical reform. By the time when Louis XVI mounted the throne the pressure for reform was such that no government could ignore it. Maurepas, cynical old courtier as he was, recognized the need to make a gesture in this direction. While he was casting round for a reforming controller-general to give tone to the government, the name of the intendant of the Limousin, Turgot, was suggested to him. Maurepas obtained, indeed, rather more of a reformer than he had bargained for: in Turgot a disciple of the Physiocrats came into office.

The Physiocratic school of thought did so much to influence ideas in the second half of the eighteenth century that a brief indication of its major tenets must be given. Quesnay, the founder of the Physiocratic school, was the royal physician. His belief that the land was the only source of wealth had not a great deal to recommend it from the theoretical point of view. Its practical conclusions were more important and, indeed, are the real explanation of the success of the doctrine; for it followed that the land should therefore pay the taxes, and this meant all the land, which was not to the liking of the great proprietors, whether noble, clergy, or bourgeois, but would have been very convenient for the royal controllers-general. The other major conclusion was that any restrictions on the circulation of wealth, and particularly on trade in the products of the soil, was injurious to national wealth. It followed that all national customs barriers by which their movement was restricted should be swept away. If it were asked who was to accomplish these and other reforms, the answer was the king, for in so far as the first school of Physiocrats possessed any political doctrine it was roughly that of enlightened despotism. The most notorious among them was the eccentric marquis de Mirabeau, the 'friend of man' who loved humanity and hated his own family. Loosely connected with the Physiocrats was Gournay, an inspector of manufactures and *intendant de commerce*, who had a higher conception of the importance of trade and industry and extended the idea of the abolition of restrictions into these fields. He was also less convinced of the potential virtues of the good despot and carried the belief in the advantages of liberty from the economic into the political field.

Turgot was the friend and follower of Gournay. As intendant in the backward *généralité* of Limoges he had attempted to put reforming ideas into practice, to find himself, as his biographer, Dr Douglas Dakin, puts it, 'committed to a perpetual drudgery in administrative bad habits, to a wearisome tidying of endless lumber. He had to collect direct taxation under a system which was archaic, bizarre, wasteful of effort; he had to rectify justice which so frequently miscarried; he must promote the arts of agriculture among an ignorant, surly, and beggarly peasantry; he was called to encourage industry and commerce to satisfy a government whose economic wisdom was merely the time-worn prejudice of a medieval town.' His achievements in the Limousin, in these circumstances, if they were on a small scale, were remarkable. Characteristically, of course, it was not his work as intendant but the fact that he had a friend who was also the friend of Maurepas that secured Turgot's appointment to the office of Controller-General.

Whereas Maupeou and Terray had begun by crushing the chief obstacle in the path of reform, Turgot began with the reforms themselves, though on a modest scale. The charge that he tried to force a mass of undigested theories into law *en bloc* is patently untrue. His great mistake, for which perhaps absence from the intrigues of court and council and a certain innocence of the ways of Versailles was responsible, was his concurrence in the recall of the parlements. If he believed that they were likely to pay any attention to the restrictions imposed on them, he was exhibiting a naïve optimism. However, the restored parlements remained chastened for a year or so, and during this period Turgot initiated what enlightened opinion expected to be a great reforming ministry. In finance he was able to do no more than take a few minor and hesitating steps. By small economies here and there, despite the opposition of the court, he checked for a time the ever-swelling expense of places and pensions. He introduced reforms into the collection of the *taille* and the relations of the state with the Farmers General; but if the government was temporarily free from the customary financial difficulties, this is to be attributed to the ruthless policy of Terray rather than the mild reforms of Turgot.

In another matter Turgot reversed the policy of Terray. The price of grain had reached its highest point, before the crisis of 1787–9, in 1770. Terray reacted, as he did to everything, violently, by abolishing the limited freedom of trade in corn which had been introduced during the good harvests of the sixties and reviving the traditional policy of state intervention. The parlements and their supporters, though naturally they had no more belief in the liberty of trade than in any other kind of liberty except their own, seized the opportunity to portray Terray as a sinister monopolist, and Louis XV, by means of the mythical *pacte de famine*, as a speculator reaping colossal profits from the deliberate starvation of his people. Popular disturbances broke out but they were soon suppressed. Doubtless the extent to which any government policy could affect the supply and, therefore, the price of corn, was largely imaginary; but in fact there was a steady and substantial decline in corn prices from 1770 to 1774.

The outcry against Terray's policy, factitious as it may have been, predisposed Louis XVI to accept Turgot's proposal for its abandonment. The new scheme was no doctrinaire one: freedom to export grain was still withheld and special precautions to secure the provisioning of Paris were retained. Unfortunately the harvest of 1774 was a poor one. Scarcity ensued and bread riots and a little *guerre des farines* followed, especially in the countryside round Paris, which was apt to be denuded of foodstuffs because of the demands of the capital. Responsibility for the riots has been attributed to various of Turgot's enemies, but though there is no reason to suppose that they regretted this set-back to his policy, the evidence in favour of the spontaneity of the disturbances is strong. In any case they were suppressed, and the rise in the price of grain, though sharp, was not of long duration.

Other and minor measures of Turgot's reforming administration must be left with a simple mention – the energetic steps he took to deal with a severe outbreak of cattle plague; the replacement of the inefficient old company which had held the monopoly of the manufacture of saltpetre by a *régie*, at the head of which he put the greatest living scientist, Lavoisier, who made the French manufactures of gunpowder the best in Europe and to whose work the later successes of the revolutionary armies were not a little due; the transfer of postal services from a private monopoly into a public service in the department of the Controller-General. More far-reaching plans for the development of education, a measure of local self-government, state provision for the poor, and the reorganization of the army, were also projected.

Both the reforms achieved and those proposed aroused, as all reforms inevitably did, the antagonism of powerful vested interests. Turgot's enemies were soon gathering on all sides. The financiers saw profitable monopolies being taken out of their hands; the Choiseulists, still a strong party at court, their early hopes that Turgot would play their game having been disappointed, turned against him; the *dévot* party and the clergy, well aware of the dangerous intellectual company that Turgot kept and of his commitment to ideas of toleration, had been opposed to him from the beginning – he had tried, unsuccessfully, to secure a modification of the Coronation Oath by which the king pledged himself to extirpate heretics, and subsequently spoke strongly in the council in favour of measures of toleration for Protestants; the parlements, the natural enemies of any reforming minister, were gradually recovering their confidence and only awaited a favourable moment to unmask their guns. The other ministers turned against Turgot, except for Malesherbes, who had succeeded the corrupt and senile La Vrillière, for fifty years in charge of the Maison du Roi, but who lacked the strength of character, though he had the good intentions, necessary for one who would clean out those Augean stables; Saint-Germain, at the Ministry of War, was himself a reformer but resented Turgot's attempts to revive the influence of the *Contrôle général* over the finances of the other ministries; Vergennes, at the Ministry of Foreign Affairs, took little part in domestic disputes; Miromesnil, Keeper of the Seals, a legal mediocrity, sided increasingly openly with the parlements against Turgot; Maurepas, that fine if somewhat faded flower of the old court, could only conceive of government in terms of intrigue. None of Turgot's colleagues, therefore, could be relied on to support him against his enemies.

Despite the gathering clouds and his own ill-health, the Controller-General went ahead with his programme. He submitted his Six Edicts to the king in January 1776. Four of these extended his earlier edicts on free trade in corn to Paris and abolished a host of unnecessary offices which were little more than an excuse for extra impositions on the food trade. The two other edicts were of major importance: the first abolished the *jurandes*, the restrictive gilds which controlled and limited admission to many industries; the other edict suppressed the *corvée* and proposed to raise the funds necessary for the upkeep of roads by a general tax payable by all proprietors of land.

Six Edicts

Now the parlement of Paris felt that the time had come to strike: the edicts on *jurandes* and *corvées* were an attack on privilege, and in view of the general intellectual atmosphere any such attack might open a dangerous breach in the wall of privilege which the *parlementaires* were manning with all the greater determination because of their temporary defeat by Maupeou. Despite the opposition of the parlements, and even of his own colleagues, Turgot persuaded the king to register the edicts by *lit de justice*; but Maurepas, who only wanted a quiet life and was now anxious to be rid of his tiresome colleague, succeeded in turning the king against him. In May 1776 Louis dismissed Turgot. As far as was possible, all the work of his ministry was rapidly undone. Even if he had succeeded in his reforms one can hardly suppose that he could have held back the coming aristocratic revolt or saved the *ancien régime*; but it might have died less discreditably had there been more chances of survival for a minister like Turgot.

Any attempt at large-scale reform was clearly doomed to frustration, but the spirit of the age was not to be denied. Through chinks and crannies in the rotted structure of the old régime reform irresistibly continued to find its way. Two of Turgot's fellow ministers were in their own fields responsible for important reforms. Saint-Germain, an old professional soldier who had served the Emperor and the Elector of Bavaria, had fought under Maurice de Saxe and been Minister of War in Denmark, set about reforming the army on Prussian lines. The household troops, expensive, undisciplined and largely useless, were reduced in numbers, though as their officers, mostly of the higher *noblesse*, had to be bought out at an extravagant price, no more than a beginning could be made in this respect and even so it aroused the indignation of the court. The militia, a ragged military proletariat of conscripts chosen by lot from the poorest of the population, was useless military material, apart from one company of Royal Grenadiers. Saint-Germain ceased to mobilize them, except for the Grenadiers, and in their stead increased the recruitment of regular troops. He suppressed the *École militaire* of Paris, which was monopolized by the sons of the higher nobles and wealthy bourgeois, and founded instead twelve provincial military schools, with 600 scholarships for the sons of poor nobles. Among the new officer material thus drawn in there was soon to be a boy called Bonaparte. The administrative system of the Ministry of War was reorganized and a beginning was made in the reduction of venality which prepared the way for its abolition by the Constituent Assembly. Perhaps the most important change of all was the continuation by Gribeauval of the reform of the artillery, commenced under Choiseul but subsequently dropped, thanks to which France entered the Revolutionary War with the most modern artillery in Europe.

All these reforms, as well as improvements in the material conditions of the soldiery, were ignored or opposed by public opinion, which was revolted by the more vigorous discipline that Saint-Germain imposed, and particularly by his rather unhappy introduction of the punishment of beating with the flat of the sword in place of other and not necessarily less severe penalties. Officers and soldiers alike, unused to discipline, showed their resentment. Maurepas was not the man to stand by an unpopular colleague and Saint-Germain went the way of Turgot and Malesherbes. The *noblesse* continued its struggle against what was now a reforming Ministry of War, and in 1781 secured the issue of a decree requiring the possession of four degrees of nobility for promotion to any rank above that of captain. Of course, no law, under the *ancien régime*, tells us much unless we also know if and how it was put into practice. The result of the reforms of Choiseul and Saint-Germain was that when the noble officers fled in the early years of the Revolution the nucleus of an efficient army remained, which was able to absorb the masses of revolutionary volunteers and conscripts and with them prove itself on the field of battle superior to every other army in Europe.

The winds of reform were by now blowing from every quarter. At the Ministry of Marine, Sartine, yet one more member of the great ministry which inaugurated Louis XVI's reign, built up the navy to a point at which it could challenge British naval supremacy in the War of American Independence, though at a frightful cost to the royal finances. Turgot's memoir to Louis XVI in favour of toleration had achieved no positive results in face of the opposition of the Assembly of Clergy; but on the eve of the Revolution, in 1787, an Edict of Toleration granted the Protestants civil rights, including those of entry into various hitherto prohibited trades and professions, and recognized the legitimacy of Protestant marriages registered with the local authorities, a much resented infringement of the rights of the Church which prepared the way for the secularization of marriage under the Revolution. In 1784 the personal tax which Jews had to pay was abolished. The Church itself was not immune from reform. A *Commission des réguliers*, established in 1766, forbade the taking of religious vows before twenty-one for men and eighteen for women, and in four years suppressed more than fifteen hundred moribund or practically deserted religious houses. The *portion congrue* which had to be allocated to the parish clergy was raised from 300 livres for *curés* and 150 livres for *vicaires* to 500 and 200 respectively in 1768, and to 700 and 350 in 1786. State pawnshops, *monts de piété*, of which there had been only six, were greatly increased in number.

Mainmorte, that last relic of serfdom in France, which was as harmful to agriculture as it was to the unfortunate populations that still lived under it, was suppressed by Necker on the royal domain by an edict of 1779. In 1780 the same minister proposed an improvement in the state of the prisons, though whether much was achieved in this respect is doubtful. The *question préparatoire*, torture inflicted on accused persons for the purpose of obtaining a confession, was abolished in 1780, and the abolition of the *question préalable*, the routine torture of convicted criminals before execution to obtain from them the names of their accomplices, followed in 1788, despite the opposition of the parlements to such interference with the good old ways of doing justice. In 1784, even under a minister with such a reputation as a reactionary as Marie-Antoinette's favourite, Breteuil, there was a general inspection of the cases of all prisoners held under *lettre de cachet*; many were liberated, the use of the letters was henceforth confined to serious offences and the duration of the imprisonment was to be no longer than two or three years. The decision was taken to pull down the Bastille, which now never had more than a mere handful of involuntary guests.

The mud, dirt, and congestion of the streets of Paris were notorious, but the idea that the government had a responsibility for the cleanliness and health of the cities was spreading. A regulation of 1783 laid down thirty feet as the minimum width for roads in future and established a ratio between the width and the height of building permitted along them. Water carriers still thronged the public fountains, but in 1777 a company was formed to supply water from the Seine to houses by means of two pumping engines. Necker, who replaced Turgot in effective control of finances, though as a Protestant he was excluded from the titular office, introduced a number of minor reforms. His successor, Calonne, has no great reputation as a reformer, but he organized a bureau of statistics under Dupont de Nemours, increased grants for road and canal building and harbour improvements, and, as will be seen, produced in the end an extensive plan of financial reform. Vergennes, in 1786, negotiated the free-trade treaty with Great Britain. The initiative for the negotiations came from France and was greeted with profound suspicion by the younger Pitt, who suspected the French even when they appeared to bring gifts. The treaty did, in fact, represent a genuine desire on the part of Vergennes to secure an international *détente*: that this would be a little difficult to reconcile with the intense struggle that French and British agents were at the same time waging for the alliance of the Dutch Republic apparently did not occur to him. The treaty was at least an indication of the extent to which ideas of free trade had penetrated the bureaux.

Behind such reforms we can detect in the background the influence of a growing body of officials and professional men, far from revolutionary in sentiment but becoming increasingly impatient with the barriers that parlements, *noblesse*, and clergy put in the way of every step in the direction of a more efficient state. Such men were only the most influential section of an educated public which had become convinced of the need for drastic changes and which viewed the more barbarous and irrational habits of the *ancien régime* with increasing revulsion. If the reforms would also take political power and social status out of the hands of an effete nobility and bestow them on the competent lesser officials and professional men who already performed most of the actual business of the state, that did not diminish their attraction. At the same time, it would be a mistake to

interpret the reforming trend that was now manifesting itself
in so many different directions as the simple expression of
material interests. It was the flowering of a great humanitarian spirit that had been centuries in the growing.
Barbarities and stupidities that were sanctified by the use of
ages and embodied in the most cherished traditions of great
institutions seemed to be on the point of disappearing like
the phantoms of night at dawn.

But much as had been and was being achieved by piece-
meal reform, far more remained to be done before the institutions of France could catch up with educated opinion, and
meanwhile the forces that looked to the past and aspired to
go backward rather than forward were also gathering
strength. The dawn of reform was to open the day of revolution, and the revolution, though it was to bring to fruition
some of the high hopes of the eighteenth century, was to
be fatal to more. The tragedy of the French Revolution lay
not in the reaping of a crop of dragon's teeth, but in the
frustration of so many noble and apparently practicable
aspirations. It was, in the words of Albert Schweitzer, a fall
of snow on blossoming trees.

4. THE EVE OF REVOLUTION

IF we ask why reform had to give place to revolution, the
explanation, as for the weakness of France under Louis XV,
must primarily be given in terms of the personality of the
ruler. The condition on which Louis XIV had bequeathed
greatness to the French monarchy was that the monarch
should be equal to the task imposed on him. It was reasonable, in an age that believed in divine right, to suppose that
any personal deficiencies in the actual physical heirs of
Saint Louis would be made good by the spiritual nature of
their office. Unhappily this spiritual influence had not been
conspicuous in the case of Louis XV, and if he had been unequal to his responsibilities Louis XVI was to be even more
so. What was to be expected of a rather dull and phlegmatic

young man of twenty? Kindly, conscientious, unambitious, devout, he had no vices save a propensity for over-eating. The funeral cortège of Louis XV had been accompanied – or so the story ran – with shouts of 'Voilà le plaisir des dames!': no such cry would ever accompany Louis XVI, alive or dead. Apart from eating, hunting was his chief pleasure and he was a better locksmith – for in true Rousseauist fashion he had learnt a manual craft – than king. He gives the impression of being one of the most uninterested and uninteresting spectators of his own reign. His fate is evidence that good people do not necessarily end happily, especially when they are kings in an age of revolution; but his queen did not end the more happily for being a little less good.

Marie-Antoinette Josephe Jeanne de Lorraine was the daughter of Francis I and Maria Theresa. At the age of fifteen she took the journey from Vienna to Versailles, a living pledge to the Franco-Austrian alliance. On an island in the Rhine near Strasbourg she quitted the Holy Roman Empire, was symbolically and also literally stripped of her Habsburg apparel, passed over to new French ladies-in-waiting to be robed as a French princess, and stepped on the soil of France the dauphine. As she travelled through the country the enthusiasm and tenderness of the French populace, despite its rags and poverty, moved her to tears, but the little Habsburg princess was not to find Versailles a bed of roses. The party opposed to the Austrian alliance was still very strong and had no love for her. The minister who had made the marriage, Choiseul, had just fallen from power, and though the Austrian court, which had found him too independent, had no regrets at this, Marie-Antoinette always favoured the Choiseulists at Versailles. The old roué who was king of France would have been kind enough to her in his way, but the proud little daughter of Maria Theresa was not prepared to demean herself to the point of recognizing the existence of Mme du Barry; the dauphin, for lack of a minor operation, was no husband to her for the first seven years of their marriage; the king's aunts, *dévot* and dull, regulated the monotonous routine of her life; and Marie-Antoinette was made of too lively a metal to endure all this with patience. The French abbé who had tutored her at the Austrian court reported that she was more intelligent than was generally supposed. 'Unfortunately,' he added, 'up to the age of twelve she has not been trained to concentrate in any way. She is rather lazy, extremely frivolous and hard to teach.'

She came to a court whose chief occupation was pleasure, in an age when frivolity had claimed it for its own. Women's attire was becoming more fantasticated, with the queen as the leader of the fashion. The king, said Mme de Campan, disapproved of the excessive luxury in dress but did nothing to check it. The height of elaboration was reached, literally, in the monstrous head-dresses that erected such a heavy burden over such light heads. When the queen passed along the gallery at Versailles, says Soulavie, you could see nothing but a forest of feathers, rising high above the heads and nodding to and fro. Mme de Campan and Soulavie, unreliable on most matters, are perhaps trustworthy on such trifles. Internal decoration, too, was influenced by the same spirit. The nymphs of the opera wanted a less chaste background than the restrained style patronized by Louis XV and Mme de Pompadour and represented by the Petit Trianon, built early in the sixties. Arabesques and polychromatic ornamentation now spread lavishly.

All this was on the surface, at the beginning of the new reign; but a very different current was emerging from below. Luxury was becoming boring. Marie-Antoinette herself revolted against the tiresome etiquette of the French court. This was the age of Rousseau and pre-romanticism. The classicism of the seventeenth century had dried up and faded under Louis XV. Sensibility reigned, but still with a survival of the restraint of the previous century, until, in the second half of the eighteenth century human nature took its revenge on the artificiality of fashionable life in floods of lachrymose sentimentality. The *comédie larmoyante*, so much admired and exemplified by Diderot, released natural emotions and portrayed domestic virtues on the stage. 'Back to nature' was to mean more than this when Jean-Jacques Rousseau became its prophet. To identify it with primitivism is a vulgar error. It was a reaction against formality, luxury, elaborate clothes, and etiquette, against the suppression of simple human sentiments and ignorance of innocent pleasures that was the hall-mark of Versailles and the world of fashion. An elegant simplicity was now *à la mode*. The queen could discard her elaborate dresses and hair-styles and have herself painted for the Salon of 1783, her hair unpowdered and unbewigged, in a simple muslin blouse. It was an age of reverie, sentiment and melancholy, of country fêtes and pastoral pleasures.

Nattier abandoned his mythological portraits to paint his sitters in modern clothing. Chardin devoted his genius to the illumination of humble persons and quiet domestic manners. More popular, and in keeping with the new climate of emotion, were the melting beauties of Vigée Le Brun and the insidious little innocents of Greuze, a finer painter than is commonly recognized. The sorely tried virtue of Rousseau's new Héloïse, close cousin of Pamela, replaced the tougher metal of Marianne and the starkness of Manon. Pictures, Diderot preached in the series of *Salons* which may almost be regarded as founding art criticism, are only good if they teach moral lessons. Under d'Angiviller as Directeur des Bâtiments 'indecent' works were eliminated from the Salon. Fragonard only achieved official recognition by painting, against his nature, the kind of picture that had now the *cachet* of official approval; after which he returned to the more frivolous masterpieces that reflected his own taste and the spirit of the previous generation. Gluck developed the expression of human emotions in opera.

Beaumarchais brings us to the point at which literature acquires a direct social and political significance. The dramatist was in his own person the symbol of a new age. Pierre-Augustin Caron was the son of a master watchmaker of Paris. His invention of a new escapement, and talent in playing the flute and the harp, opened the doors of the court

to him. His charm won for him the office, the fortune, and
the widow of a wealthy official, and he became Caron de
Beaumarchais. Financial speculations, a *lettre de cachet*, and a
famous law-suit, in which he found himself opposed to the
parlement Maupeou and took revenge in vitriolic pamphlets,
followed. More speculations made him, as a supplier of arms
to the American colonies, one of the instigators of French
intervention in the American War. He was destined to make
and to lose two or three fortunes in his life, to be criticized
for dangerous writings under the monarchy and imprisoned
as a counter-revolutionary during the Revolution, when he
barely escaped the September massacres, to be an agent of
Louis XVI and a member of the first commune of Paris.
But he survives as the author of *Le Barbier de Séville* and *Le
Mariage de Figaro*; and to find in Figaro the spirit of the Revolution is to see in the first breezes of autumn, shaking the
petals off the roses one by one, the gales of winter. Figaro,
like his creator, belongs to an age when intelligence allied
to not too much scruple set out to conquer the world and
found only acquired riches and rank in its way. The aim was
not to destroy the citadel of vested interest but to occupy it,
not to end the *douceurs de la vie* but to enjoy them, in which
Beaumarchais was perhaps truer to his generation and class
than the serious, puritanical prophets and politicians of
revolutionary France. Like practically everyone else he was
no revolutionary before 1789 and Figaro ends with a song.

> *Or, messieurs, la co-omédie,*
> *Que l'on juge en cè-et instant;*
> *Sauf erreur, nous peint la vie*
> *Du bon peuple qui l'entend.*
> *Qu'on l'opprime, il pes te, il crie;*
> *Il s'agite en cent fa-açons:*
> *Tout fini-it par des chansons.* (bis)

In this atmosphere Marie-Antoinette withdrew from the
stuffy ceremonial of Versailles. With a small group of friends
she increasingly spent her time in the freer atmosphere
of the little Trianon, that small country-house planned
by Louis XV for the Pompadour but never inhabited by

her. There, a *jardin anglais*, traversed by a meandering
stream, with rustic bridges and an imitation waterfall
and leading to a toy hamlet set round the banks of a diminu-
tive lake, provided the setting in which the queen and her
friends could dress themselves as stage shepherds and shepherdesses and share the simple pleasures of rural life.
Etiquette was thrown to the winds. Marie-Antoinette, fallen
from a donkey she had been riding calls out, 'Hurry up: ask
Madame de Noailles [the chief arbiter of court etiquette]
what a Queen of France should do when she falls off a
donkey.' 'In an age of pleasure and frivolity,' wrote the duc
de Lévis, 'intoxicated with supreme power, the queen had
no fancy for submitting herself to constraint, and she found
court ceremonies tedious. . . . She thought it absurd to
suppose that the loyalty of the common people could depend
upon the number of hours which the royal family spent in a
circle of bored and boring courtiers. . . . Except for a few
favourites, chosen for some whim or because of a successful
intrigue, everyone was excluded from the royal presence.'
The Princesse de Lamballe, whose devotion to the queen
outlasted her loss of favour and who returned to her in the
Paris of the Revolution, to be butchered in the September
massacres and have her head paraded round the streets on
a pike, the Polignacs, greedy and irresponsible, whose
favour cost the state half a million livres a year, the handsome young Swede, Count Fersen, who won Marie-Antoinette's heart – these were not the great names of the French
court. Maria Theresa, to whom it was all secretly reported
by the Austrian ambassador, Mercy, warned her daughter
that she did not realize what she was doing. 'I know well
enough,' she wrote, 'how tedious and futile is a representative position; but believe me, you will have to put up with
both tediousness and futility, for otherwise you will suffer
from much more serious inconveniences than these petty
burdens – you more than most rulers, since you have to rule
over so touchy a nation.'
The France that Louis XVI and Marie-Antoinette never
saw and that never saw them – for apart from one journey

by the king to the new harbour works at Cherbourg they
never travelled beyond the group of royal châteaux in the
neighbourhood of Paris – was to take its revenge upon them;
but the attack was to be launched by the hostile factions at
court, which Marie-Antoinette had done so little to con-
ciliate, their enmity intensified by her favour for the
Choiseulists. A flood of almost inconceivably scurrilous
pamphlets, instigated by her enemies at court, poured out.
They attributed to her as lovers practically every eligible
male at Versailles, except Fersen: if her children could be
bastardized, the king's brother, Provence, might succeed to
the throne, and he was not necessarily innocent of complicity in the campaign against the queen. Her reputation was
almost ruined when the affair of the diamond necklace
came, in 1785, to complete the process.

Napoleon dated the French Revolution from the affair of
the necklace. It burst on the public sensationally enough.
In August 1785 the Cardinal de Rohan, duke and peer,
member of the great Rohan-Soubise clan, one of the three
princely houses of France, Bishop of Strasbourg, Provisor
of the Sorbonne, Grand Almoner of France, was arrested at
Versailles and charged with using the queen's name to pro-
cure a fantastically expensive necklace of diamonds from the
court jewellers without paying for it. He demanded to be
tried by the parlement of Paris. The Minister for the Maison
du Roi, Breteuil, who was responsible for the arrest and
subsequent prosecution, and, having helped the young
Fersen when he first came to court, was also a particular
favourite of the queen, exhibited astonishing folly in his
conduct of the affair, and above all in allowing the case to
be tried before a court composed of the bitterest enemies of
the monarchy. It can only be supposed that his personal
feud with Rohan, dating from the time when the cardinal
had supplanted him as Ambassador at Vienna, robbed him
of his judgement. The Cardinal de Rohan, moreover, as an
enemy of the Austrian alliance, had acquired the ill-will of
Maria Theresa, who passed her prejudice against him on to
her daughter. He himself wanted nothing more than to have

his existence recognized at court and to receive the queen's favour. When the Comtesse de la Motte, pauperized descendant of a bastard of Henry II, offered herself as an alleged contact with Marie-Antoinette, Rohan was easily taken in. He must have been very gullible: among those he patronized was Cagliostro, Italian adventurer and professional mystifier, who cured his asthma and made him a gold ring out of base metal.

The age of reason was already giving place not only to sentiment but also to superstition. Illuminés and Rosicrucians were spreading from southern Germany into more rational countries, Lavater was founding the new science of physiognomy and Mesmer enthralling society with the mysteries of hypnotism. Mme de la Motte worked her wonders in a more practical way. With the aid of forged letters she persuaded the Cardinal de Rohan that if he would pledge his credit to acquire the diamond necklace for the queen, he would be restored to royal favour. A momentary interview at night, in the gardens of Versailles, with a Paris prostitute dressed up to resemble the queen, completed the cardinal's infatuation. This may have been the fatal episode from the queen's point of view also, for she was anxious that above all there should be no mention of meetings on the terrace. Breteuil, as has been said, was a close friend of Fersen. If anyone knew of the affection between him and the queen it was Breteuil, and a plausible guess may be made that both the minister and Marie-Antoinette suspected Rohan of having ferreted out the queen's secret. This may account for the panic-stricken arrests which followed the revelation by the court jewellers of the transactions relating to the necklace, and the lack of a sense of proportion shown in the handling of the whole affair.

The trial dragged the queen's name through the mire with those of the scum of society. A diamond thief and adventuress, some shady pseudo-gentlemen, an alchemist, a prostitute, a cardinal, and a queen: such were the *dramatis personae*. The chief deviser of the affair, Jeanne de la Motte, was sentenced to be flogged, branded, and put in the Salpêtrière for life – in fact she escaped after nine months; the cardinal, though found innocent, was banished from the court. The queen was supposed by the public to have sold her favours to him for a necklace of diamonds and then to have jibbed at paying the price. The part that all this played in discrediting her in general opinion and so preparing the ground for the fall of the monarchy is not to be underestimated.

While the weakness of the king and the indiscretions of the queen thus undermined the prestige of the monarchy, public opinion, influenced by the agitation of the parlements, was learning to talk republican language even before it had thought republican thoughts. In more than one way opinion in France was revolutionary before anyone had dreamed of a revolution. An opportunity for the expression in action of such sentiments had been provided when the American colonies revolted against Great Britain. Ideological sympathies joined with traditional Anglophobia to throw French opinion overwhelmingly on the side of the rebels. The Foreign Minister, Vergennes, connived at the sending of arms and supplies to them. French volunteers, including the young marquis de La Fayette, greedy for glory, crossed the Atlantic to fight in the cause of liberty. After the capture, in 1778, of the British army under Burgoyne at Saratoga, Vergennes was able to intervene more openly. The American envoy, Benjamin Franklin, with his unpowdered hair, round hat, brown clothes, and homespun wit, became the idol of Paris society. Vergennes negotiated a treaty of alliance between France and the revolutionary colonies, in which the French king engaged himself, in the event of France entering into the war on the side of the colonies, to claim no conquests in North America or the Bermudas.

As was customary, fighting between France and Great Britain broke out through British aggression on the seas before war was declared. Spain was brought into the struggle on the side of France with the promise of Gibraltar,

Minorca, Florida, and British Honduras. The Armed Neutrality proclaimed by Catherine of Russia was joined by most of the other powers of Europe. In 1780 the Dutch Republic entered the war on the side of France and the American colonies. The hour for the revenge of France on the proud island empire which had humiliated her in 1763 had struck.

The last plans of the *secret du roi* now seemed about to be realized. An army of 40,000 was assembled on the Channel coast for the invasion of England, which was to be made possible by a union of the French and Spanish fleets. As twenty-five years later, when Napoleon was waiting in his camp at Boulogne, the union of the fleets was not effected and the plan came to nothing. However, a body of 6,000 good troops under Rochambeau was conveyed to America to join La Fayette's volunteers, while the bailli de Suffren with a French squadron harassed the British in the East Indian seas. In 1781 a Franco-American army shut up the English general Cornwallis in Yorktown, while the French admiral de Grasse, who had defeated an English fleet under Hood, held the seas outside. Beleaguered by land, and cut off from reinforcements and supplies by sea, Cornwallis capitulated and the colonies were lost.

This was the high-water mark of French success in the war. Soon after, Great Britain recovered naval superiority with Rodney's victory over de Grasse at the battle of Saintes in the West Indies. Gibraltar, besieged by French and Spanish since 1779, was relieved in 1782, though Minorca was recaptured for Spain. It was clear that France could not hope to gain anything by a continuance of the war. A new ministry in Great Britain was prepared to recognize the independence of the colonies. Both French and American governments were now suspicious that the other would seek to conclude a separate peace at the expense of its ally, and after the customary complicated manoeuvres peace was finally signed at Versailles in 1783. France regained the small islands of Saint-Pierre and Miquelon off the St Lawrence, Santa Lucia and Tobago in the West Indies, and

Senegal and Goree in Africa. It was generally believed that the loss of the American colonies tolled the funeral knell of British greatness, and this was some consolation to France for the meagre results of a war which had entailed so much effort. No one as yet supposed that the price to be paid for American independence was a French revolution.

There were two reasons why this was to be so, the one theoretical and the other material. The second half of the eighteenth century was the period in which democratic ideology rose to influence in western countries. In the American colonies, Great Britain, Geneva, the Austrian Netherlands, Liège, and the Dutch Republic, ideas of democratic government were developing. Except in so far as similar ideas entered, however inappropriately, into the propaganda of the parlements, France had largely been immune from this new current of ideas, for to suppose that the *philosophes* were democrats is an illusion. Alliance with the Americans not merely exposed French society to democratic and republican ideas, but made them fashionable and respectable. Many of the young French nobles who left their wives or mistresses to fight for American independence returned with a new mistress, liberty. ' I was far from being the only one,' wrote the young comte de Ségur, 'whose heart palpitated at the sound of the growing awakening of liberty, seeking to shake off the yoke of arbitrary power.'

The influence of the new ideas on French foreign policy was to be demonstrated even in Europe. Louis XVI was to find himself once again the ally of republicans before he became their victim. The Dutch had been led into the American War by their own republicans, the Patriot party. Though the results of the war had been disastrous for the United Provinces, the Patriots continued to control the government and to conduct a violent campaign against the Stadtholder, the Prince of Orange. Since the house of Orange was traditionally connected with England, the Patriots naturally looked to France for support. The association with the Anti-Stadtholderian movement in the United Provinces, which was to bring France to the verge of war with Great Britain and Prussia in 1787, was not primarily the work of Vergennes, now in his last years and suffering from ill-health, but rather of the chief secretary at the French Foreign Ministry, Rayneval, and the various agents sent by France into the United Provinces. Vergennes died before he could be involved in another war in alliance with republicans, as he had been led into the American War; and though the ministers for the Army and the Marine were prepared to take the plunge, there was one fact which prohibited a new adventure: by 1787, as a result of the American War, the royal treasury was practically bankrupt. The Dutch Patriots had to be left to their fate. But the impending bankruptcy was the second factor, which, though it prohibited another foreign adventure in support of republicanism, was to prepare the way for the coming of revolution in France.

5. THE REVOLT OF THE PRIVILEGED CLASSES

THE financial crisis was the second major consequence of the American War for France. From 1776 to 1781 the Genevan banker, Necker, who having made a fortune for himself by shrewd speculation had come to be regarded as a financial genius, was in charge of French finances. Short, stocky, heavy in appearance and pompous in manner, with an air of self-important benevolence, he seemed to have none of the qualities for success at Versailles. The real architect of his political career was the ambitious Mme Necker, the Suzanne Cuchod of Gibbon's early love, who with the aid of her husband's fortune and her own literary pretensions founded a philosophical *salon* in Paris. Necker himself played his part by writing an *Éloge de Colbert* and a volume attacking freedom of trade in corn. He thus made himself the spokesman of the opposition to Turgot, and when that minister fell, a clever intrigue brought Necker to the notice of Maurepas. A friend of the *philosophes*, but sharing none of the dangerous new ideas of Turgot, enjoying a reputation as a deep thinker and at the same time as a practical man of business with the trust of the financiers and bankers, Necker seemed just the minister needed to restore confidence in royal finances. As he was a foreigner and a Protestant, he was only appointed assistant to the Controller-General, and subsequently Director-General, but he was the effective minister.

In a sense the confidence placed in Necker was justified. He introduced a few minor administrative reforms and made ineffective attempts to limit the extravagance of the queen and her friends. His great expertise, and the one thing he could do really well, was to borrow money. During the American War Necker's reputation, as a minister who could finance a war without new taxation, mounted to the skies. The sum of 530 million livres, which he acknowledged as the extent of his borrowings, was probably a considerable understatement, and the interest on his loans was between 8 and 10 per cent. The total interest on the royal debt, which had been a modest 93 million in 1774 after the operations of Terray, had risen to over 300 million by 1789, and the responsibility was largely Necker's.

With the aid of skilful and intense propaganda he continued to swim on the crest of a wave of popularity, though in the later stages of the war his position in the government was weakening. To strengthen his hand Necker produced his master-stroke of propaganda, by publishing, against all precedent, his *Compte-rendu* to the king of the finances of the nation. Preceded by a preamble, in Necker's usual inflated style, which played up to current prejudices and revealed the expansive soul of its author, the *Compte-rendu* exhibited a happy financial situation, attributable to the wise management of Necker himself, by whose skill, in spite of war expenditure, the royal accounts had been balanced with a slight surplus on the credit side. For the *ancien régime*, in time of war, this was a miracle. It was also completely untrue, though the nation as a whole, and possibly even Necker himself, were taken in by his specious arguments and misleading figures. His enemies delivered a counter-blow by circulating copies of a secret memoir which Necker had presented to the king in 1778, in which he had written of the parlements with considerable contempt. Their ensuing hostility made it impossible for him to continue to raise new loans and without these he was lost. Moreover, Maurepas was becoming jealous of the too popular minister.

At this point either Necker's vanity led him to put forward impossible claims, or, knowing that he was at the end of his financial tether, he deliberately set out to provoke his own dismissal. He proclaimed the need for reform and demanded in particular that the expenditure of the Ministries of War and Marine should be brought under the *Contrôle général*. This was undoubtedly a much-needed reform, since the financial autonomy of the ministries was an important contributory cause of the permanent deficit. Necker also demanded a seat in the *Conseil d'en haut* which took the final decisions on foreign policy. Maurepas was now able to go to the king with the threat that all the other ministers would resign if Necker's claims were granted, and the king and Marie-Antoinette, who both still shared the popular faith in Necker, reluctantly yielded. In five years the Genevan wonder-worker had undone all the work of Terray and imposed on the royal finances a great new burden of debt at excessive rates of interest. What was worse, by his *Compte-rendu* he had cut the ground from under the feet of any future controller-general, for he had demonstrated, to all appearance, that royal finances, even in war-time, balanced and that there was therefore no need for economies or increased taxation. Finally, by linking his resignation with the rejection of proposals for reform he had established his position as a great reformer sacrificed to court intrigues. The Necker propaganda machine was not dismantled and in retirement he remained a power in the land.

The next two controllers-general were only fleeting figures. The first tried to increase the taxes and to introduce economies. Naturally he fell before the combined wrath of the parlements and the court. The second came into conflict with the Farmers General and was eliminated in less than a year by a revolt of the financiers. It is tempting to say that with the financiers a new power had appeared in the land, but the memory of the financiers of Louis XIV and of the Pâris brothers should be a corrective to this error. What is true is that the seventeen-eighties witnessed one of those periods of speculative mania such as the regency had seen at the beginning of the century. Necker's policy of borrowing had at least made the fortune of a crowd of bankers, some French, a few Dutch or English, and many fellow-Genevans. Rival groups of financiers founded banks and companies, such as those for supplying Paris with water or, appropriately linked with these, for insurance against fire. The Company of the Indies took on a new speculative life. The power of the press was discovered by those who were playing the market, and the writers they employed to spread false reports to raise or lower the value of shares included more than a few of the later revolutionary journalists, who thus served an apprenticeship to their trade. The king's ministers were brought into the unseemly scramble for profits as allies of this company or that, and what had begun as a struggle between two groups of financiers easily turned into one between two ministries. To safeguard or increase their profits the financiers began to play at politics as well as playing the market, the Swiss and Dutch bankers being in many cases already exiles from their native lands because of their democratic opinions. The American War and the subsequent outburst of speculation made the fortune of the financiers; Necker was their patron saint; his policy of borrowing supplied their life-blood. It was natural, taking all these factors into consideration, that they should have aligned themselves with the new democratic tendencies in France.

The fortunes that individuals were amassing did not help to remedy the increasing financial distress of the state. To cope with this, in 1783 a new and brilliant controller-general was pushed into office by the favour of the king's younger brother, Artois, and the Polignacs. Calonne, formerly intendant of Lille, had undoubted qualities:

incessantly active, fertile in expedients, possessed of personal charm, eloquence, and unlimited self-confidence, he was to fail in all he undertook with a regularity and a cleverness which would have brought success to half a dozen ordinary men who possessed also a modicum of judgement. However, the new controller-general began by restoring confidence in the stability of royal finances, which had been lacking since the fall of Necker. He reassured the financial world by recognizing the sacredness of the royal debts and paying the interest on them promptly. He rewarded his supporters at court with large gifts and pensions from the funds of the *Contrôle général*. He inaugurated an energetic programme of public works, including the great naval harbour at Cherbourg, destined not to be completed until the middle of the nineteenth century. With confidence thus restored, Calonne was able to resume the policy of borrowing, until by August 1786 he also had exhausted the market and could borrow no more.

Calonne was too intelligent to fail to see the need for a fundamental reform of royal finances, and too self-confident to fear to put it into effect when there was no other choice. He therefore now completely changed his tactics and presented the king with a plan for a general land tax, to which there would be no exceptions, and for the creation of Provincial Assemblies to supervise its collection. Since there was no prospect of persuading the parlements to accept such a proposal, an Assembly of Notables was summoned to deal with them in February 1787. Calonne's belief that he could persuade an assembly of the privileged classes to accept his plans for taxing them is characteristic of that lack of political sense which he invariably exhibited. His chances were not increased by the fact that Necker and his friends had been conducting a virulent campaign against him. Nothing was wrong with the royal finances, they maintained, save the man who was mismanaging them; put Necker back into office and all difficulties would vanish. Inside the ministry, Calonne had a bitter enemy in the queen's favourite, Breteuil, who had managed to secure the support of the successor to Vergennes as Foreign Minister, the mediocre Montmorin. The struggle between Breteuil and Calonne was not decreased in virulence by the fact that they were involved with rival groups of speculators, who were using the ministers to promote their financial interests. Despite support from Artois, the Assembly of Notables rejected Calonne's plans. Exposed to the attacks of the privileged classes on one side and of the partisans of Necker on the other, he was dismissed, disgraced, exiled, and damned as a rogue whose malversations had brought the country to the verge of bankruptcy.

Under pressure from the queen, Louis now appointed to succeed Calonne the Archbishop of Toulouse, Loménie de Brienne; and to increase his authority made him head of the Council of Finances with a controller-general under him. Soon after, the title of *principal ministre* was revived for Brienne. The Ministers for War and the Marine at once resigned, the former, Ségur, declaring that he was accustomed to do his business direct with the king and not be subject to the authority of any other minister. Once again, after more than forty years, France had a chief minister with the full confidence of the queen, if not of the king. Were the prosperous days of Fleury to be renewed?

As Archbishop of Toulouse, Brienne had presided successfully over the Estates of Languedoc and acquired a reputation as an able administrator. He was an advanced thinker, for a bishop almost too advanced. A distant relation of Mme du Deffand, he had attended her salon and been elected to the Academy with the support of the party of the *philosophes*. He had inspired the movement for the reform of the regular orders, was generous with permits for the use of meat in Lent, forbade burials in churches on sanitary grounds, established free courses for midwives and bestowed a great library on the city of Toulouse. Evidently he was an enlightened man. He took his religious duties lightly, in spite of which he made great efforts while he was minister to obtain elevation to the rank of cardinal. A friend described him to Mme du Deffand as good-natured, indulgent, gay, easy-going, *insouciant*. He hardly strikes one as possessed of the character needed to push through a great reform, and nothing short of this could now meet the situation. Nor did his team of ministers inspire confidence. At the *Contrôle général* under him was an old lawyer, honest but without any financial expertise to supplement Brienne's own deficiencies in this respect. Brienne's incompetent brother was placed in the Ministry of War. At the Ministry of the Marine a former ambassador, La Luzerne, and at Foreign Affairs Montmorin, were already turning their eyes towards Necker, still the popular hero. Breteuil, unwilling to submit to Brienne's predominance, followed Ségur and Castries in resigning and was replaced at the Ministry of the Maison du Roi by a mediocrity. Only the Keeper of the Seals, Lamoignon, had intelligence and firmness of character.

The new principal minister, having played his part among the Notables in opposing his predecessor's plans and bringing about his fall, in office could think of nothing better than to adopt Calonne's proposals practically *en bloc*. Naturally the Notables resumed their opposition, and since obviously nothing more was to be expected from them they were dissolved in May 1787. Brienne now reverted to the normal procedure, of which Calonne had seen the hopelessness, of presenting his edicts for registration by the parlements.

The sovereign courts, as they were called, were by now far more than the constitutional nuisance they had been earlier in the century, and their claims were far-reaching. Earlier they had based their powers on historic rights; as the representatives of the ancient *curia regis* they had claimed to be the guardians of the fundamental law of the kingdom. About the middle of the century they borrowed the idea of 'corps intermédiaires' from Montesquieu and conceived of themselves as the intermediary power between the people and the king. The provincial parlements, from 1755 onwards, asserted their solidarity with the parlement of Paris and kept pace with it in the extravagance of their claims. In the Grand Remonstrances of 1753, which drew the conclusion to the defeat of Machault's financial reforms, the parlement of Paris spoke of 'a kind of contract' between the king and the nation, of which it claimed to be the guardian. As the century progresses the influence of the contractual school of thought, deriving from Locke, becomes increasingly evident in the literature of the parlements. An anthology of democratic doctrine could be collected from their later Remonstrances. 'It is the essence of a law to be accepted. The right of acceptance is the right of the nation', declared the parlement of Rouen in 1760. Fundamental laws are 'the expression of the general will', it said in 1771. The words 'subjects' and 'people' were being replaced by 'nation' in the language of the parlements. The law, declared the parlement of Toulouse in 1763, depends on 'the free consent of the nation'. By 1788 the parlement of Rennes was proclaiming, 'that man is born free, that originally men are equal, these are truths that have no need of proof', and that 'One of the first conditions of society is that particular wills should always yield to the general will'. At the same time, though the parlements claimed to represent the nation, they also called for the revival of the old provincial estates. 'Give us back,' pleaded the parlement of Rouen in 1759, 'our precious liberty; give us back our estates.' As early as 1763 the *Cour des Aides* at Paris, through the pen of its president, Malesherbes, had called for a meeting of the States-General.

The Remonstrances and pamphlets in which such ideas were expressed, along with attacks, often in violent and emotional language, on the king's ministers, had wide circulation. Of the Grand Remonstrances of 1753 more than 20,000 copies were sold within a few weeks. One of the constitutional monarchists asked later, 'Who accustomed the people to illegal assemblies and to resistance?' and answered, 'The parlements'. In 1787 their popularity was such that they seemed to be in a position to dictate their will to the king. When Brienne presented his proposals for new taxation they rejected them with contumely and demanded the calling of the States-General. After the edicts had been registered in *lit de justice*, the parlements declared the registration null and void. Amid mounting popular excitement they were exiled to Troyes in August 1787. Brienne, still attempting conciliation, sent agents after them to try to win over individuals by bribes and promises, and even offered the dismissal of Lamoignon, who was known to favour stronger measures. On the promise of the withdrawal of the edicts, the parlement returned to Paris in November and consented to register further royal loans on condition that the States-General was summoned. But the Ministry and even the more moderate members of the parlement were becoming alarmed at the popular clamour that the agitation had aroused, and it was agreed that the States-General should only meet after several years' delay. However, the proposed loan proved too large and the delay too long for the parlements, and the agreement was almost at once broken.

From its return in November 1787, to May 1788, the parlement harassed the Ministry with protests and remonstrances, and the provincial parlements joined in the hunt. The weakness of government at the centre was reflected in the *généralités* by the intendants who, apart from the fact that, being nobles themselves as well as royal officials, their loyalties were divided, dared not take strong measures, which were only too likely to be disavowed at Versailles, against the local parlements. To add to the financial distress of the Crown, the collection of taxes was beginning to break down. Even the loyalty of the Army, under its noble officers, was in doubt. The Keeper of the Seals, Lamoignon, the only man with any strength of character in the ministry, now forced Brienne's hand. At last a minister of Louis XVI had been brought to realize that there was only one way out of the impasse, and that the way of Maupeou. Two of the wildest of the *parlementaires* were arrested, and on 8 May 1788 the parlements were suspended, forty-seven new courts being created to take their place. A plenary court, nominated by the king, was entrusted with the duty of registering royal edicts. At the same time a number of legal reforms which the parlements had hitherto blocked were passed into law. The parlements had now the choice between submission and open resistance. Conscious of the strong forces that supported them, they chose the latter. What were these forces?

In the first place, they had the backing of the Church. The Assembly of the Clergy, invited to vote a *don gratuit*, drew up Remonstrances in its turn, protested against the suspension of the parlements, and insisted on the immunity of clerical property from taxation. Then the dukes and peers of France associated themselves, by a collective letter, with the protests of the parlements. The duc d'Orléans, representative of the next line in succession to the throne after the Bourbons, had put himself forward as a spokesman for the parlements in November 1787 and been exiled to a château in the country for his pains, but an agitation was continued in Paris by a little mercenary Orleanist faction which saw the possibility of greatness descending, even on such scabrous shoulders, if the difficulties of Louis XVI became insuperable.

The *noblesse*, in former times the enemies of the magistrature, now made common cause with it in defence of their financial privileges, which they needed all the more because of the debts which their gaming, their extravagant mode of life, and the passion for building had piled on them. Indebtedness had almost acquired a prestige value: he who owes two millions, it was said, is obviously twice as great a noble as he who only owes one. They too had learnt to nourish aspirations for provincial self-government. Following on largely abortive attempts by Necker and Calonne, in 1787 Loménie de Brienne had established a system of Provincial Assemblies; but these were intended to facilitate royal administration, not to put authority into the hands of the *noblesse*, who were demanding not these limited assemblies but full-blown provincial estates. The *parlementaires* were long practised in the art of stirring up popular disturbances through the lesser world of *avocats*, clerks, and ushers who depended on them for their livelihood. Seconded by the *noblesse*, they organized riots in the provincial capitals, at

Bordeaux, Dijon, Pau, Toulouse; in two provinces, Brittany and Dauphiné, the disturbances went beyond mere rioting. At Rennes the intendant and the commandant were attacked in the streets and besieged in the latter's town house. The poverty-stricken nobles with whom Brittany swarmed organized seditious assemblies and prepared for battle against the royal troops. At Grenoble the parlement remonstrated against the royal edicts. Exiled by royal order, it refused to obey, and, supported by the *noblesse* of Dauphiné and the people of Grenoble, organized a revolt which sacked the house of the commandant and took control of the city by force. Representatives of the *noblesse* and of the towns illegally convoked the Estates of Dauphiné, for the first time since 1628.

Before this nation-wide revolution of the privileged classes the king capitulated; for it was a confession of defeat when, on 8 August, the States-General were summoned to meet on 1 May 1789. The situation was desperate and Brienne patently unequal to it. He resigned, to be followed shortly by Lamoignon, and on 25 August the king called Necker back to office. The exposure of the falsity of the *Compte-rendu*, and the intrigues of Necker and his partisans against subsequent ministers, had destroyed the king's trust in the Genevan banker; but the nation looked to him as a saviour. He was, indeed, indispensable. The treasury was empty and payments had been suspended, while the privileged classes were in open revolt. Necker's reappointment solved, if only momentarily, both difficulties. His earlier record reassured the privileged classes – for had he not proved that it was possible to meet the needs of the state without fresh taxation – and the confidence that the financial classes had in him enabled the government to raise a loan. He knew his power and insisted on the rank of Director-General of Finances and Minister of State: the other ministers were nonentities. 'At last,' commented Mirabeau, 'M. Necker is king of France'. If he was, he knew as little what to do with his power as the real king. He had no policy but to wait for the States-General somehow miraculously to cure the ills of the nation.

Meanwhile, the order for the recall of the parlements was issued and a second Assembly of Notables was summoned to give advice on the manner of convocation of the States-General. For long enough the privileged classes had sown the wind: they were now about to reap the whirlwind.

On 23 September 1788 the parlement made its triumphal re-entry into Paris, amid the plaudits of the crowd, the ringing of bells, and firing of cannon. On 25 September it registered the declaration convoking the States-General, with the instruction that they should be composed in the manner observed the last time they had met. This was in 1614, but legal memories were long. It was a fatal move. There was an outburst of indignation. The falsity of the propaganda of the parlements was at last revealed. By 'the nation' they had all along meant themselves, but there was another nation, outside the ranks of the privileged classes, which would not be content with a National Assembly in which its representatives were restricted to one-third of the membership, and were always in a minority of one to two when the three orders voted. The Third Estate, suddenly and dramatically, appeared on the scene. The eighteenth century had seen a great increase in its numbers and wealth. The royal bureaucracy, with its host of minor juridico-administrative officers, the professional civil servants of the great ministries, the crowds of lawyers, the doctors, surgeons, chemists, engineers, lower army officers, artists, writers, bankers, merchants and their clerks – all these formed a social nexus which provided the men who did most of the work of government as well as of the professions, but who were kept out of the higher offices by lack of *noblesse* or of sufficient wealth to purchase it, and humiliated socially by the thought that they belonged to a lower caste. For a generation they had supported the demands of the parlements for the recognition of the rights of the people, because they took the people to be themselves. Towards the manual workers of the towns and the tillers of the soil in the countryside, of course, their attitude was very much that of the privileged orders towards themselves: the masses did not exist for them except as supporters of their natural leaders of the educated middle classes.

The declaration of the parlement of Paris on 25 September produced a rapid intensification of the debate which was being conducted in a vigorous pamphlet literature, and a change in its tone. It has been calculated that for the next six weeks new pamphlets appeared at the rate of twenty-five a week, and the main target was the privileged orders. Memorials and petitions poured out demanding double representation for the Third Estate and voting by head instead of by order. Though sudden changes are admitted in practical affairs, there is a tendency to regard movements in ideas as only taking place slowly, by the process of a gradual evolution. This is not necessarily so. In a period of intense political excitement the development of new political attitudes may be catastrophic in its suddenness. Such a period was that from 1788 to 1794. The few weeks after 25 September 1788 witnessed the most revolutionary change of all. The Third Estate, which had been faithfully seconding the struggle of the privileged classes against royal despotism, suddenly discovered that its supposed allies were its enemies. The cause of the nation, which had hitherto been the war-cry of the parlements, was taken over by the Third Estate, and the advocates of its claims annexed the title of Patriots. Whether there was any organized control of their activities has been much debated. The alleged Masonic plot can be left where it belongs in the realm of legend. The Orleanist conspiracy has a little more substance. The duc d'Orléans certainly had his hireling faction, centred on the Palais Royal. He was quite prepared to be a Patriot king if Louis XVI could be eliminated, and would shrink from no means, however despicable, of achieving his ambition. But at most the Orleanist faction exercised a localized and minor influence. There was also the famous and mysterious Society of Thirty, which included leading members of the liberal *noblesse* such as La Fayette, Condorcet, La Rochefoucauld-Liancourt, and the bishop of Autun, better known as Talleyrand, and was attended also by the abbé Sieyes, who had made a name for himself by writing the most popular of all pamphlets against privileges, *Qu'est-ce que le Tiers État?*, and by Mirabeau. It met at the house of Adrien Duport, a young *parlementaire* who had thrown in his lot with the Patriots of the Third Estate. Many of its members had formerly advocated the cause of the American Revolution. There are no grounds, however, for attributing a decisive influence to the Society of Thirty: it was a symptom, not a cause, of a nation-wide movement.

The first objective of this movement was double representation of the Third Estate. When, on 27 December 1788, the royal council met to decide this question, Necker, faithful to his policy of never doing anything that might harm his popularity, proposed the doubling of the Third Estate. The Keeper of the Seals, who alone opposed the proposal, wrote that Necker's argument was that the royal authority had everything to fear from the two higher orders and everything to gain by allying itself with the people. This was, indeed, the way in which the declaration in favour of doubling the representation of the Third Estate was interpreted in the country: the king, it was believed, had thrown in his lot with the people. He became overnight a popular idol. Assemblies of nobles in the provinces issued protests, in Brittany *noblesse* and patriots came into armed conflict; but Necker and the council, with the acquiescence of the king, had by a stroke of the pen defeated the revolution of the privileged classes. A new and great weight had been thrown into the balance: at the very moment when the parlements and the *noblesse* thought themselves victorious, a new revolution, which was directed against them, had already begun.

6. VICTORY OF THE THIRD ESTATE

IT is natural to feel a disinclination to attribute great events to petty causes. The changes in French society and the revolution in ideas were perhaps bound to find their reflection in political and institutional developments sooner or later; but this is not equivalent to saying that the French Revolution was inevitable. What form the impending social and political changes were to take, and when they were to come about and how, were matters to be decided by circumstance. The Revolution was not a Niagara in the stream of national life, its incidence and situation determined by the presence of a single great fault in the social strata: it was rather the result of the confluence of a host of contributory currents, small and great, flowing together to swell suddenly into a mighty flood. Changes in the structure of French society and government might have been imposed from above or they might have been the result of a gradual evolution. In so much as it happened, a revolution was doubtless inevitable and this was necessarily the revolution that actually occurred. But to understand the way in which it came about, the end of the *ancien régime* must be studied almost on a day-to-day time-scale and in relation to the lesser as well as the greater forces: and since all these influenced the course of the Revolution, they also played their part in determining the society that should emerge from it.

The most realistic contemporary analysis of the factors which made the Revolution possible was that of Robespierre:

In states constituted as are nearly all the countries of Europe, there are three powers: the monarchy, the aristocracy, and the people, and the people is powerless. Under such circumstances a revolution can break out only as the result of a gradual process. It begins with the nobles, the clergy, the wealthy, whom the people supports when its interests coincide with theirs in resistance to the dominant power, that of the monarchy. Thus it was that in France the judiciary, the nobles, the clergy, the rich, gave the original impulse to the revolution. The people appeared on the scene only later. Those who gave the first impulse have long since repented, or at least wished to stop the revolution when they saw that the people might recover its sovereignty. But it was they who started it. Without their resistance, and their mistaken calculations, the nation would still be under the yoke of despotism.

The calling of the States-General was undoubtedly the critical step, for it meant the abdication of absolute monarchy. It was made necessary, as has been shown, by the financial difficulties, which were in essence the result of the resistance of the privileged classes throughout the century to the attempts of the king's ministers to introduce financial reforms. Without the parlements to act as the point of crystallization it is doubtful whether the *noblesse* and clergy could have made their resistance effective: the restoration of the parlements in 1774 was therefore the fatal moment for the monarchy. A far stronger king than Louis XVI would have been needed to crush the opposition of the privileged classes, which steadily grew during the next fifteen years, now spreading underground like a heath fire, now bursting into flames on the surface. Only when royal authority had been weakened, and the king humiliated and forced to refer the problem of governing France to an elected assembly, did the Third Estate enter into the struggle in its own right, put forward its own claims, and in so doing transform what had been an aristocratic Fronde into a revolution of a new kind, such as Europe had not witnessed before.

The parlements, *noblesse*, and upper clergy had certainly not desired or expected their revolt to be taken over and diverted to its own ends by the Third Estate. In its turn, the Third Estate also was to find that it had started something that it could not easily stop. As the forces of revolution swept onward in a destructive torrent, overwhelming faction after faction, which, while it was riding on the crest of the wave imagined it was leading and controlling the onward rush, it seemed to those who were being swallowed up by the advancing tide that some hidden hand must be at work; and so in a sense there was, but it was not the secret societies or the plots and conspiracies of legendary history. The hidden force at work, which provided a continual supply of inflammable material to feed the fire of revolution, was one which the eighteenth century, with its belief in the power of government and its predominantly political outlook, did not recognize, though it was plain enough to see. It was simply the supply and the price of food, which meant primarily bread, or grain of which bread could be made, for bread was truly the staff of life: it constituted the major element in the cost of living of every poor family, that is, of between three-quarters and four-fifths of the population of France. When other foods were unobtainable there was scarcity, only when bread was lacking was there famine.

Here is the hidden factor which explains why parlements, nobles, and Third Estate were in turn able to promote and profit by the revolutionary movement. If a chart of popular disturbances during the eighteenth century is drawn up, it will be found that they coincide fairly closely with periods of high bread prices. It seems probable that, while the condition of the people improved considerably in the first few decades after 1715, subsequently there was a drastic deterioration. I have suggested above that the main cause of this was the pressure of a growing population on an economy which, if developing rapidly in some sectors, in the essential productivity of agriculture and industry was progressing only slowly. The reign of Louis XVI was marked by a general economic regression, but French economy being so largely an agrarian one, the ultimate catastrophe occurred when, after a period of economic deterioration, there came the disastrous harvest of 1788. The worst time after a bad harvest was always the summer following, when the produce of the previous year's harvest was exhausted and the new harvest had not yet been brought in. The point of maximum distress was thus timed, as though by an unkind fate, to coincide with the opening sessions of the States-General.

Disturbances were spreading all over France in the spring of 1789. They were too widespread and disorganized to be regarded as other than a spontaneous expression of popular distress. From intendant after intendant, during April and May, were flooding in reports of bread and grain riots. These were particularly liable to break out when stocks of grain were being moved about the country, and of course the greater the shortage the more grain was liable to appear in transport, as towns and provinces tried to protect themselves from starvation by buying it wherever a supply could be found. Since the cheapest form of carriage for a bulk article, and indeed the main form of transport in the eighteenth century for anything, was by water, much grain was seen travelling down the rivers and canals or round the coasts. From this arose a popular belief that it was being exported to create an artificial shortage and so increase the profits of monopolists. Who were the villains of the piece was not quite clear, but it was evidently a plot to starve the people for the advantage of speculators. The owners of seigneurial rights, who were still taking their share of the diminished harvest and selling it at greatly enhanced prices, naturally did not gain in popularity. Finally, as well as attacks on convoys of grain, and an intensification of hostility to the seigneurial régime, there arose a nation-wide demand for the fixing of maximum prices, involving violent demonstrations against the local authorities, who were responsible for price control. The lower strata of the rural population, which had little or no land, provided recruits for bands of half-beggars half-brigands who terrorized the countryside. The reliance of many in the country on domestic industry, which normally helped them to make ends meet, now merely aggravated the distress, for bad harvests involved a general slackening of economic activity and so a great decline in the demand for industrial goods. Starving country workers fled to the towns to swell the ranks of the urban unemployed. From 1787 to 1789 there is evidence that unemployment in French industry rose to a general level of 50 per cent.

That the economic crisis was intense cannot be doubted, though it must not be exaggerated: we do not read of people starving to death. In 1789 there was a distressed but not a dying population. The great famine of 1709–10 seems in fact to have been the last in which there was a large death-rate directly from starvation. Was the change due to improved facilities for the transport of food, or – as is more likely – to the development of governmental efforts to provide food for the people in time of shortage? The correspondence of the intendants bears witness to the frantic efforts they were making to provision the distressed populations of their *généralités* and to the humanitarian spirit that had grown up in the course of the eighteenth century. The dangerous factor was the coincidence of food shortage with a period of intense political agitation: the distress of the masses made them malleable material for successive opposition groups. The bands of mountaineers who invaded Pau in June 1788 in support of the nobles and the parlement had been told that the king intended to impose new and yet heavier taxes on them. The legend of the '*pacte de famine*', which the parlements and *noblesse* had employed against Louis XV and Maupeou, was renewed against Louis XVI. Popular agitation was intensified and kept at fever-heat by the continuation of economic difficulties at a time when all France was being summoned to elect its representatives to the States-General.

The opinions that found expression in political form were, of course, not those of the most distressed sections of the population. The opposition of the privileged orders to the doubling of the representation of the Third Estate released the latter from its alliance with the privileged classes and enabled it to put forward its own programme; the drawing up of *cahiers* in the countryside opened the door to the expression of the grievances of the peasantry; but in neither town nor country did the masses of the population have much opportunity for the statement of their views, even if they had been coherent and articulate enough for expression. The *cahiers* of the towns put forward the claims of the well-to-do middle classes, and the parish *cahiers* those of the *laboureurs*, the better-off farmers. Summarizing the *cahiers* very briefly and inadequately, we may say that the bourgeois in the towns demanded equality of status with the privileged classes and the peasants in the country freedom from seigneurial dues, relaxation of royal taxation, both direct and indirect, the re-diverting of the tithe to its proper purposes, and the ending of what was seen as a general exploitation of the country by the town. There is much more in the *cahiers* than this, but only a lengthy discussion could do justice to the many problems involved in their interpretation. However limited their scope, discounting local peculiarities, such as protests from Lorraine against the bad breath of sheep being allowed to infect the pastures, against the growing of potatoes, which was said to spread diseases in the arable land, against *cabarets* which led the poor into dissipation, or against the introduction of textile machinery which robbed them of work, and some of the more abstract clauses, a programme could have been compiled from the *cahiers* of the Third Estate which would have made a practicable and effective scheme of royal reform. The monarchy might conceivably have been saved if some such programme had been put forward in the first place by the government. Necker, pressed to take the initiative, gave as the excuse for his inaction the resistance that such a programme would provoke from the nobles and the clergy. He was, after all, only a clever banker, and statesmanship could not be expected of him; but to suppose that an initiative was psychologically possible for the king and his ministers would be to forget both the persons concerned and the repeated humiliations inflicted on royal authority by the privileged orders in the course of the previous fifty years. In any case, an inert king, with a weak ministry, was not capable of striking out an independent line in opposition to the court, for which the interests of the privileged orders were paramount.

The drawing up of the *cahiers* and the choice of representatives thus went on with no control or guidance from above. The elections were an appeal to a France which the court never knew, the France of quiet market towns and small provincial capitals, of secluded manor-houses, modest vicarages, humble farms. Versailles, which had for so long been the voice of France, found that in the decisive hour France could speak for itself and choose its own representatives. Naturally, the elections being held in the provinces, it was men from the provinces who were chosen to be sent to represent them at Versailles. Paris was to reassert its supremacy in due course, but in 1789, for a short moment, the provinces had their hour. To the Second Estate, few of the court nobility were elected but many of the provincial *noblesse*, with rare exceptions bringing with them no contribution to the counsels of the state but their intransigent determination to defend their ancestral rights and their declining fortunes, so closely bound up with their privileges. For the First Estate, the lower clergy, aided by the system of election to their Order, sent to Versailles some 200 parish priests out of 300 representatives: for the first time the ideas of richerism on the government of the Church seemed within reach of achieving practical expression. The Third Estate, also, elected almost exclusively local men. These were, to the extent of over 40 per cent, the holders of minor offices in the juridico-administrative system of local justice and government. Lawyers, most of whom would have aspired to a similar office when they had acquired or inherited sufficient capital to purchase one, constituted one-fourth of the Assembly, and other professional men another 5 per cent; the world of commerce, finance, and industry was only represented by some 13 per cent of the deputies. Despite the overwhelmingly rural nature of the electorate, at most only 7–9 per cent of those chosen were agriculturists.

On 4 May 1789 the States-General met at Versailles and proceeded in procession to hear Mass at the Church of Saint-Louis. The next day they held their opening session. The order of proceedings, and even the garb of the participants, had been laid down by the court master of ceremonies with due regard to precedents. As these dated at latest from 1614, it is not to be wondered at if the Third Estate was somewhat restive at regulations which instructed them to be attired in their customary suits of solemn black, to keep their hats off when the nobles and clergy followed the king in donning theirs, to be received by the king in a different manner and room from those prescribed for the

first two Orders, and to enter the Assembly by a side door
after the clergy and nobles had walked in by the front.
Besides this, the royal officials in charge of the proceedings,
accustomed to dealing with the intimate etiquette of the
court, were overwhelmed when they had to organize a mob
of over a thousand provincials. At the opening session of the
States-General there was considerable confusion, long
delays, and when the voice of authority spoke, in the person
of the Keeper of the Seals, it was largely inaudible. Necker,
and, after his voice also gave way, a substitute, then droned
on for more than three hours in a speech full of complicated
financial explanations. He called on the privileged orders
to give up their exemptions from taxation, but made explicit
the royal capitulation to the aristocratic revolution by leaving it to the three orders to decide separately which subjects
they would be prepared to deliberate and vote in common.

The Third Estate, which had flocked to Versailles full of
enthusiasm, expecting and prepared to follow a strong royal
lead, was profoundly disillusioned. On what it rightly
regarded as the crucial issue the king had come down on the
side of the privileged orders. Only a union of the orders
would give the Third Estate – the nation as it regarded
itself and as Sieyes and other pamphleteers had taught it to
believe – a majority and the possibility of passing the
reforms it desired. This, then, became the first object of the
Third Estate, and the tactic it adopted to secure its end
was one of passive resistance; it refused to take any other
step until its demands in this respect had been satisfied.
At the same time it appealed to the king in the name
of the 'natural alliance of Throne and People against the
various aristocracies'. On 17 June, tired of waiting, it arro-
gated to itself the title of National Assembly, thus implicitly
asserting its possession separately of all the powers of the
States-General, almost implying that it was, as Sieyes had
claimed, everything, and the other two orders nothing.
Moreover, the Third Estate had the advantage, on this
question of the union of orders, of being united, whereas
the First and Second Estates were divided. Many of the

lesser clergy sympathized far more with their brethren of
the Third Estate than with their own aristocratic superiors,
and a group of democratic *curés* was working hard to secure
the adhesion of the clergy to the Third Estate. A small
group of liberal nobles also was sympathetic, though the
great majority of the *noblesse* had no intention of capitulating
to the demand for union.

When it became patent that only the king could break the
impasse it was decided to hold a joint session, though the
royal council was too divided to have any settled idea what
it proposed to do at this. On 20 June the large hall which the
Third Estate used was closed to facilitate the alterations in
accommodation necessary for the royal session. Through a
misunderstanding the members had not been informed, and
when they found a detachment of troops occupying the
building it seemed to them that their assembly was being
dissolved by force. Gathered in an indignant mob in pouring rain outside the closed doors, they followed their president, Bailly, the eminent astronomer who had taken liberty
for his pole-star, to a neighbouring indoor tennis-court, the
nearest large building that offered shelter. There, with only
one open dissentient, they took the oath never to separate
and to meet wherever circumstances dictated until the
constitution of the kingdom and public regeneration had
been established and consolidated. Two days later, their
hall still being closed, they assembled in the Church of St
Louis and were now joined by 149 members of the clergy.

The royal session was due to be held on 23 June. Necker
had at last resolved to do what should have been done at
the outset and to present the States-General with a royal
plan of reform. The strength of the opposition to this proposal in the royal council perhaps justifies his belief that it
would have stood no chance of acceptance earlier, but circumstances were even now hardly more favourable. The
elder son of Louis XVI and Marie-Antoinette had died early
in June. History does not pay much attention to private
grief, but the consequences of this loss were far-reaching.
The court went into retirement at Marly. There the king

was surrounded and indoctrinated by courtiers, headed by his younger brother, Artois. The parlement of Paris, now belatedly converted to the cause of royal authority which it had done so much to undermine, sent secretly to the king to call for the dispersion of the Third Estate by force. The result was that at the royal council which drew up the final instructions for the royal session, although the form of Necker's proposals was retained, their substance was drastically altered. At the eleventh hour the aristocratic revolution reasserted itself. The declaration drawn up for the king to read embodied its maximum concessions and minimum demands. It was an aristocratic and not a royal programme.

Necker absented himself on 23 June, when the three Orders assembled for the royal session amidst a considerable show of armed force, the Third Estate characteristically being kept waiting in the rain while the privileged Orders were being seated. The declaration of the king's intention that was read to the assembly provided the ground plan for the conversion of France into a constitutional monarchy and suggestions for a whole range of important reforms; but the vital fact was that it promised the royal sanction for the abolition of fiscal privileges only when the privileged Orders had agreed to this, and therefore presumably only on their own terms. The king was made to declare that the distinction of the three Orders should be preserved in its entirety and that the decisions of the Third Estate on 17 June were null and void. He ended by ordering the assembly to disperse and resume meetings in their separate chambers on the morrow.

If there were not so many fatal occasions in the revolution one would be tempted to say that it was in the royal session that the monarchy sacrificed the possibility of alliance with the nation and bound its fate to that of the privileged orders. In essence the royal session was the counter-revolution and it had already come too late. On 25 June a group of liberal nobles followed the majority of the clergy in joining the Third Estate. Now there were some 130 clergy and 241 nobles sitting separately, and 170 clergy and 50 nobles who had joined the Third Estate. What caused the king to reverse his policy drastically and to issue instructions, on 27 June, for the privileged Orders to join the Third Estate, has never been made clear. Perhaps the rumour, which prevailed at the time, of 40,000 armed brigands who were said to be preparing to march on Versailles, is the nearest we will ever get to an explanation. It receives support from the fact that orders were at the same time secretly issued calling up 20,000 troops from the provinces. The Janus deity of fear, with its other face of terror, was already unveiled: it was to preside over the destinies of the Revolution from beginning to end. Unwillingly, in obedience to the king's instructions, the recalcitrant nobles and clergy entered the assembly, in a deathly silence, on 30 June. The Third Estate had won its first battle. That night Versailles was illuminated. Crowds paraded in front of the Palace shouting '*Vive le Roi!*' '*Vive Monsieur Necker*'. The king and queen appeared with their children on the balcony but it was observed that the queen was in tears.

The court, however, had merely postponed the struggle. As troops steadily poured into the neighbourhood of Paris and Versailles, under the command of the Marshal de Broglie, it felt strong enough to show its hand. On 11 July Necker and his supporters in the council were dismissed and Necker himself was ordered to leave the country. The queen's favourite, Breteuil, was brought back to lead a government which would put an end, it was hoped once and for all, to this nonsense of the Third Estate. The constitutional struggle was about to turn into a civil war.

It would be tempting to declare that the court now took the initiative in an appeal to force, as the privileged classes already had in the disturbances of 1787 and 1788; but we could only say this by averting our gaze from what had been happening all over France in the course of 1789. The aristocratic Fronde had weakened or destroyed royal authority everywhere, and the power to keep a distressed populace under control no longer existed. In town and country disturbances were endemic. Paris itself was becom-

ing ungovernable. In April the rumour, an untrue one, that
a wallpaper manufacturer named Réveillon had advocated
a reduction in wages, started a riot which burnt down and
pillaged his house, and was only repressed with much bloodshed. What was very odd was that Réveillon was well
known for his good treatment of his own workers, none of
whom took part in the affair. In July mobs attacked and
burnt the customs posts surrounding Paris, which were a
natural object of hatred to a starving population; but there
is a curious report that two posts belonging to the Duke of
Orleans were spared. Both at the time and subsequently
such popular movements have been attributed to the
machinations of enemies of the régime, particularly to the
agitation of Orleanist agents. In the absence of proof all one
can say is that on the one hand Orleans and his agents were
certainly fishing in troubled waters, and on the other that
the misery of the populace was quite sufficient to explain
outbursts of violence without hypothesizing the operations
of any hidden hand behind the scenes. The alleged, and
probably exaggerated, Orleanist plot was provided with
some semblance of plausibility by the fact that the gardens
of the Palais Royal, which had been commercialized and
turned into a popular pleasure resort, with shops, cafés,
and entertainments, had become a centre for democratic
agitators. Some were doubtless in the pay of Orleans, but
his resources were limited and certainly not equal to
starting the widespread agitation that developed.

There was ample reason in the second week of July for
the Third Estate to feel itself threatened. The dismissal of
Necker, still the idol of the people, and the concentration
of troops, largely foreign, near Paris, were evidence of an
impending military *coup*. Orators at the Palais Royal called
the people to arms. Mobs formed daily, in an increasingly
feverish political atmosphere, ready to defend liberty and
their lives against the threatened military dictatorship. But
where could they obtain arms, for weapons were expensive
and few private individuals outside the ranks of the *noblesse*
possessed them? The rioting crowds turned to the municipal

authorities, who in face of the general disorder were helpless. Besieged in the Hôtel de Ville by a threatening mob,
the Provost of Merchants, de Flesselles, could do nothing
but try to divert them elsewhere, for example to the
Invalides, which on the morning of 14 July was raided by
a large mob seeking for arms.

Crowds were now surging everywhere about Paris, gathering round all public buildings, and not least before the Bastille, the frowning fortress whose guns were menacingly
directed on the poor quarter of the Faubourg St Antoine
which surrounded it. Rumour and pamphleteers had for
years been disseminating a picture of its dungeons packed
with wretched state prisoners. It was the obvious stronghold
from which the royal troops would sally forth to commence
their slaughter of the Parisians. It was in fact garrisoned by
eighty Invalides and thirty Swiss. The mob before it sent a
deputation to the Governor, de Launay, who promised not
to fire unless attacked. The outer courts, which had been
left unguarded, were filled by an agitated crowd. Across an
unguarded drawbridge they penetrated to the inner court,
and although they were still quite incapable of invading the
fortress itself, the defenders in panic fired on them, with considerable slaughter, arousing among the besiegers a spirit of
fury that could not easily be appeased. At this point a new
factor came into play. <u>A detachment of rebellious Gardes
Françaises marched to the Bastille with five cannon they
had taken from the Invalides. Under fire they got their guns
into position and trained them on the main gate.</u> The incompetent de Launay now lost his head metaphorically, in
advance of losing it literally, and surrendered, with a
promise of safe conduct for himself and his troops. As the
garrison emerged some were seized on by the infuriated
crowds and slaughtered, and the rest hustled off to the comparative safety of prison. De Launay himself was struck
down, and his head, cut off with a butcher's knife, paraded
round Paris on a pike. The Provost of Merchants, for his
efforts to prevent the arming of the populace, was seized by
another mob at the Hôtel de Ville and suffered a similar

fate. The prisoners who poured out of the dungeons of the Bastille consisted of four forgers, two lunatics, and a dissipated young noble. The people set about demolishing the fortress, but the task was taken over by professional housebreakers, who made a considerable profit out of the affair. The episode was a striking one, but the actual events have been greatly exaggerated by the romantic historians of the nineteenth century. Only some 800 individuals were able to justify their claim to the title of 'Conquerors of the Bastille' and these were a mere handful of the agitated crowds who were ranging Paris. The significance of the fall of the Bastille lies in its symbolic value. The important fact was that the king had lost control of Paris and even with the troops called to Versailles had no prospect of regaining it.

In the face of the Parisian revolution, what would be the reaction of the new ministry? Fear had set the populace of the city in motion and now fear dictated the varying responses of the court. The revolt of the Gardes Françaises seemed to spell doom: even the foreign regiments were of doubtful loyalty. Breteuil counselled a withdrawal of the court to Compiègne and the restoration of order by military force; Artois and Condé supported him; but Louis XVI was not the man for strong decisions. Did he even yet appreciate the seriousness of the situation? On the day of the capture of the Bastille he returned late from the hunt and wrote in his diary, '14 July, nothing'. Suspicious of the ambitions of his brothers, and even more of those of Orleans, he hesitated, but sent to the Marshal de Broglie to ask if he could guarantee an escort to Metz. De Broglie was discouraging: he was not sure of his troops, he said. What subsequent policy, he asked, did the king propose to follow when he had reached Metz? To this there was no answer. Since he feared to leave, Louis had no choice but to submit. He dismissed Breteuil, recalled Necker, and on 17 July went with fifty deputies to the Hôtel de Ville of Paris to receive from the hands of Bailly the national cockade of red and blue, the colours of the city, with white for the house of Bourbon in between, symbol that Paris had reconquered its king.

Artois, generally regarded as the inspirer of the attempted military *coup*, Condé, the Polignacs, Breteuil, and their adherents, could no longer safely stay in France, denounced by pamphleteers and mob orators as enemies of the people. They fled across the frontier and the emigration had begun. In the next two months some 20,000 passports were delivered. The privileged classes had proved themselves, at the first test, incapable even of defending themselves. The falsity of their position was revealed when it appeared that the authority of the Crown, which they had done so much to undermine, was the only bulwark for their own privileges. In the first two weeks of July the Third Estate, which they had ignored or treated as a dependent ally, had taken over the revolution from them. It now had the burden of maintaining the state thrust upon it, along with the twin problem of reshaping French society and government after a pattern closer to its own interests and ideals. The door was wide open to reform: but the identity of the figure that was advancing through the door seemed somehow different, its shape and size uncertain and vaguely menacing.

III

THE DECADE OF REVOLUTION

I. THE RISING OF THE MASSES

The revolt of Paris, in which culminated the nation-wide disturbances of 1789, and the general collapse of royal administration, confronted the members of the Third Estate with the problem of taking steps to protect property and restore some semblance of law and order to France. In their turn, like the privileged classes before them, they were to find that they had started something they could not stop, and that a movement which they had envisaged as one of moderate constitutional and social reform was to become a revolution of a very different nature and scope. Their response to the new challenge was dictated by circumstances. All through the Revolution we find that theory plays little part in determining policies, though it has played much in their subsequent interpretation. The actions of the revolutionaries were most often prescribed by the need to find practical solutions to immediate problems, using the resources at hand, not by preconceived theories.

The Parisian populace, which by its rising had frustrated the plans of the court and saved the Third Estate, was not moved solely by altruistic political emotion, it had its own grievance in the high price and shortage of bread. A week after the fall of the Bastille, Bertier de Sauvigny, intendant of Paris, and his father-in-law, Foullon, who were responsible for food supplies, were seized by a mob besieging the Hôtel de Ville and massacred. Their heads – it was an *ancien régime* custom – were stuck on the end of pikes. A man in the uniform of a dragoon, followed by a large crowd, pushed his way into the meeting of the municipal body with a chunk of bleeding flesh, saying, 'Here is the heart of

Bertier.' When it was proposed to bring in the decapitated head also, messengers were sent out to inform the populace that the council was engaged on important business and preferred not to have the head of its former intendant on the agenda. The electors, who had been chosen in the first place as secondary electors for Paris to the States-General but had never dissolved, now constituted themselves the municipal authority, appointed Bailly, the eminent scientist, as Mayor in place of the murdered Provost of Merchants, and took over such government as the city was capable of.

Events in Paris reflected those that had been taking place up and down the length and breadth of France. In some towns an understanding was reached between the old municipal authorities and the new revolutionary ones. Elsewhere revolutionary committees simply took control by main force. Before the changes were given legal sanction by the law on municipalities of 14 December, the municipal revolution was a *fait accompli* practically everywhere in France. The new authorities, however, required a means of restoring some degree of law and order. It was to their hand in the equally spontaneous growth of a citizen guard, which had been springing up everywhere for the dual purpose of protecting property from indiscriminate pillage and defending the Third Estate from suspected or real aristocratic plots. This also was given official recognition: it became the National Guard, and on the morrow of the fall of the Bastille the hero of the American expedition, La Fayette, was appointed to its command in Paris, which made him, as the royal army disintegrated, potentially the most powerful man in France.

Municipal authorities and National Guard represented the determination of the well-to-do Third Estate to take over the responsibility for government, local as well as national, that had fallen from the hands of the royal officials. In calling to its aid the people of Paris the Third Estate had let loose more dangerous forces than it realized, but it did not feel any strong remorse for the assassination of Bertier and Foullon. Was this blood, then, so pure, Barnave asked in the National Assembly, making himself, as so many others were to be, the apologist of terrorism before he became its victim. In the countryside, however, a different revolution had been taking place, and one which the Third Estate viewed in a very different light. If 1788 saw the last Fronde, 1789 saw the last Jacquerie.

It must be frankly admitted that the history of eighteenth-century France as I have given it up to this point has been, apart from a few sentences, the history of one-tenth of the French people. Glacier-like, the rural masses of most nations before the nineteenth century remain anonymous and concealed, even from contemporaries, beneath the surface. That France was suffering from the effects of rural over-population I have already suggested, and equally that, short of a great increase in production, for which the conditions did not exist, there was no remedy for the consequent distress. The result was an increasingly bitter struggle for the diminishing slice of cake – or rather of bread – that remained to go round. Land hunger was its most obvious manifestation. By 1789 peasant proprietors owned perhaps one-third of the land of France, though, in ignorance of what proportion of the arable this included, and knowing something of the great variations from district to district, such a statement tells us less than it seems to. Arthur Young, who continually complains that wherever there is the property of great nobles it is bound to be forest or waste, might have reflected that possibly this may have been because so much of the more cultivable land had already passed out of their possession. Round the towns the wealthy bourgeoisie and *noblesse de robe* had invested heavily in land, on which they put farmers, or *métayers* on a stock and land lease. The more prosperous peasants were also building up their properties with some success.

⟨Short of confiscating the lands of the Church, and although this suggestion had been made earlier it was not a practical one before 1789, the only land that might still be thrown into the market was the common land of the village communities.⟩A royal edict of 1767 established a procedure for the enclosure of these which was to the advantage of the possessors of seigneurial rights and the larger proprietors. There were, however, also complaints in the *cahiers* that enclosures gave patches of land to the poorer villagers and so made them less amenable as hired labour. The better-off peasant proprietors, the *laboureurs*, thought that they lost more than they gained by enclosure of the commons and therefore opposed it, and with considerable success, for they exercised the strongest influence in the rural communities. The bitterest struggle in rural France during the last years of the *ancien régime* was between the peasant proprietors and the possessors of seigneurial rights.

The seigneur might be a noble or a bourgeois, he might even be a prosperous peasant, for seigneurial rights were no more than, to quote a legal treatise of the time, 'a bizarre form of property'. Such rights were the *banalités*, the compulsion to use the lord's mill, bakehouse, or winepress, the *cens* or quit-rents, a kind of perpetual ground rent, *péages* or tolls on the road or river, the right of keeping pigeons or rabbits to feed on the peasants' crops. Innumerable local dues, in kind or money, were added to such more general ones. The seigneur himself in his court, through some petty local attorney appointed to act as his judge, adjudicated on disputes over his own rights. Appeals were to the parlements, which, as the magistrates were themselves large purchasers of seigneurial rights, had no doubts on which side the scales of justice should be tilted. Indeed, without the juridical backing of the parlements the whole system of seigneurial rights might have collapsed, for the royal officials had no interest in the maintenance of a system which removed income from those who were taxable into the hands of those who could not be taxed. In the course of the eighteenth century, perhaps partly owing to the purchase of seigneurial rights as a form of investment, they came to be exacted with increasing severity. A class of professional *feudistes* took over the task of drawing up and revising the *terriers* in which the dues were recorded, resurrecting long-forgotten claims from old manorial rolls. A skilful *feudiste*, working on a commission basis, could secure a greatly increased return to the seigneur, and – since the latter possessed all the documents – without much danger of the claims being disproved, though legal cases over them were endless.

Seigneurial dues were an anachronistic relic, a survival of feudal lordship which the peasant proprietors resented all the more because they were now the real owners of the land on which the dues were imposed; but the spirit of the push for increased seigneurial dues that was the main feature of the so-called 'feudal reaction' that preceded the Revolution was much more commercial than feudal. *Mainmorte*, retaining some of the features of personal servitude, and the *capitaineries*, or hunting rights in forest areas, were more truly feudal, but they were restricted in their incidence to certain areas. They were regarded as incompatible with the ideals of a century of enlightenment, and moreover non-nobles normally did not possess them, so they were generally condemned. On the other hand the Third Estate in the towns had little quarrel with the seigneurial dues. Their *cahiers* said little on the subject until they were faced with the demands of the peasants. Demands for the abolition of seigneurial dues were subsequently inserted in the more general *cahiers* of the Third Estate, though usually with a provision for compensation.

The deputies of the Third Estate evidently did not contemplate dealing in a hurry with a grievance which did not affect them personally. Moreover, seigneurial dues were a form of property. To denounce 'feudalism' in the abstract was all very well: to attack a widely owned property right was another matter. In fact the Third Estate did not launch the attack: the decision was taken out of its hands. Just as the parlements and *noblesse* found that they had started a movement among the bourgeois which went far beyond their own aims, so the bourgeois were to repeat the experience with the peasants. The bread riots of the spring and early summer of 1789 prepared the way for a general breakdown of social discipline in the countryside. Here and there, throughout France, abbeys and manor-houses were attacked, game was trapped illegally, the peasants ceased to pay their dues. The break-down of royal authority in the towns intensified rural unrest. Belief in an aristocratic plot – and there were in fact little local aristocratic plots, apart from what was going on at Versailles – spread like wildfire. In the third week of July there were risings in the Norman *bocage*, in Franche-Comté, the Mâconnais, and Alsace.

Towards the end of July these sporadic risings were caught up in a different and more extensive movement which has come to be known as the Great Fear – a panic terror of brigands who were supposed to be descending on the peaceful villages of France. Over large areas the Great Fear raged like a forest fire. The legendary brigands were never clearly identified. In the north-east, where there had been the troubles of the Fronde, they were called the Mazarines, and in the centre *la bande anglaise* – shades perhaps of the Black Prince and the White Company still surviving in the age-old peasant memory. The association of an aristocratic plot with the menace of nameless brigands set a pattern that was to be repeated more than once in the Revolution. At the time of the September massacre it was the criminals of the Paris prisons who were expected to be let loose by the aristocrats on the wives and children of Patriots. Given the picture of the Revolution as a rising of the riff-raff of the towns and the landless proletariat of the country, such fears are meaningless. When it is realized that the revolutionary masses were not these, but rather the master craftsmen, shopkeepers, and the like in the towns, and the peasant proprietors in the country, they become easily explicable.

The prosperous professional men and officials of the Third Estate, who had seized control of the Revolution from the privileged classes, had no intention of letting it slip from their hands, but the game they were playing, even if unconsciously, was a dangerous one. After the affair of the Bastille they regained control of Paris with the aid of the new municipal authorities and the National Guard. The countryside presented a more difficult problem. The peasants rarely attacked individuals, their objective was usually to burn the manorial rolls, overthrow enclosures and restore common lands, kill game, and 'have fires out of the Grand Duke's wood'. Regular troops and National Guards were sent out from the towns to repress such disturbances and protect property rights. Where effective action was possible the rioters were seized and, after trial before summary courts, hanged. In most areas, however, the authorities were powerless before the resistance of the peasantry. Unless something was done rapidly to remedy the situation, it was evident that it would soon be completely out of control. But from what quarter could a lead be given?

There was one more or less organized political body at Versailles. A group of deputies from Brittany had formed the plan of meeting daily in a café for the purpose of concerting their policy. They were joined by deputies from other provinces and by some who were not deputies. The Club Breton – only after it had followed the Assembly to Paris and hired a hall from the Jacobin convent in the rue St Honoré was it to be known as the Jacobin Club – became a rallying point for the Patriots, as those who aimed to complete the victory of the Third Estate called themselves. It was probably in private discussions at the Breton Club that the conclusion was reached that only by swift and drastic concessions could peace be restored to the countryside, and that the only hope of passing the necessary laws was to take the National Assembly by surprise and rush them through in a night session. The duc d'Aiguillon, peer, commandant of the King's Light Horse, a great landowner, and one of the liberal nobles who had led the secession to the Third Estate, was chosen to put the manoeuvre into effect on the night of the fourth of August; but, perhaps because he had learnt of the scheme and saw a personal advantage in anticipating d'Aiguillon, the initiative was seized from him by another liberal noble, the vicomte de Noailles, nicknamed for his lack of lands *Jean sans-terre* and therefore perhaps all the more ready to give away the property of others. D'Aiguillon followed him, and then a fury of renunciation swept the Assembly. The privileges of nobles, tithe-holders, provincial estates, cities, corporations, were hurled on the bonfire. At two o'clock in the morning, exhausted but triumphant after its orgy of self-sacrifice, the Assembly decreed a solemn *Te Deum* and adjourned.

Second thoughts brought a measure of repentance. The next week was spent in tidying up and whittling down the concessions of the night of the fourth of August. The Assembly had gone much farther than had perhaps originally been intended. An attempt was made, in drawing up the definitive legislation, to rescue what could be saved from the holocaust by inventing a distinction between those rights which were 'feudal' in origin, that is, derived from personal servitude, and those which were of the nature of property, derived from a contractual relationship. The former were to be abolished without compensation and the latter to be made redeemable. The distinction was a difficult one to draw in law and impossible in practice. The peasants simply disregarded their former obligations and stopped paying their dues, and no Assembly in Paris had any means of forcing them to do otherwise. When, finally, in July 1793, the Convention decreed the suppression of all remaining 'feudal rights' without compensation, this was merely the recognition of a *fait accompli*. The peasant proprietors won their victory in 1789. So far as they were concerned the Revolution was over: their role for the rest of its history was a purely passive one, except where, as in Brittany and the Vendée, they turned into active opponents.

For the National Assembly the unrest of the towns and the peasantry was a diversion from its proper task, which was to give France a new Constitution. Royal cooperation in this task was still less than half-hearted, and aristocratic opposition vigorous and vocal. The king, it was feared, had not drawn the necessary lesson from the fourteenth of July and the Patriots came to think that only another dose of the same medicine would make him fully amenable to their wishes. In Paris, popular agitators and journalists were keeping the people in a fever of political excitement with denunciations of aristocratic plots. Neither the respectable leaders of the Patriot party in the Assembly, nor the less respectable agitators in the streets, could have taken effective action, however, if it had not been for the continuing and even increasing economic distress of the populace. The incident which set fire to this inflammable material was so petty as to give ground for the suspicion that it was merely the occasion and not its cause.

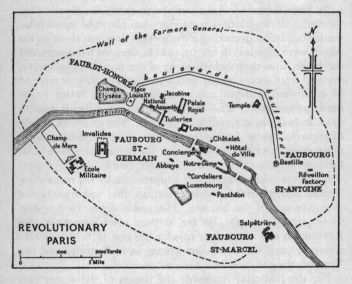

On 1 October a dinner was held at Versailles for the officers of the Flanders Regiment newly arrived there. When the king and queen appeared, to acknowledge their loyal acclamations, Blondel's song '*O Richard, O mon roi, l'univers t'abandonne*', from Grétry's opera, was sung amid enthusiastic demonstrations. Nothing happened for four days, which is odd if this episode is to be regarded as the provocation which led to the October Days, but indeed the

whole story of what did happen is an odd one. On 5 October women gathered before the Hôtel de Ville demanding bread: this was quite normal. Getting no satisfaction the cry was raised – by whom? – that they should make their way to Versailles to appeal to the king. Several thousands set out, gathering numbers as they went. It was a gloomy, wet October day, hardly the best one for a spontaneous demonstration. Now, however, the tocsin was being rung through Paris, district assemblies were meeting, National Guards and others were gathering, especially before the Hôtel de Ville, where La Fayette, on horseback, was trying unavailingly to control the situation. The watchword still seemed to be to march on Versailles. At four o'clock in the afternoon the Municipal Council authorized La Fayette to move off with the National Guard, and now there appeared for the first time a definite objective: the king was to be brought back to Paris. With a mixed body of National Guards and others La Fayette set out. At Versailles Louis XVI, who as usual had been out hunting, returned in the afternoon, interviewed a deputation of the women who by now were congregated before the palace and promised them a supply of bread for Paris. That evening the main body of the Parisians arrived, settled down for the night as best they could or ranged about the streets of Versailles and the courts of the palace. At early dawn on the next day a few hundred of the demonstrators found a way into the palace, slaughtered some of the royal bodyguard whom they encountered and penetrated nearly to the queen's apartments before they were repulsed.

Morning saw serried masses in the courtyard before the palace, now with one cry, 'To Paris!' Was resistance to an armed mob of some 20,000 possible? It seems not to have been contemplated. The idea of flight had again been urged on the king and queen, only to be rejected by them, perhaps for fear of leaving the throne vacant for Orleans, whose inspiration was suspected behind the march on Versailles. The only course left was to yield as graciously as possible in the circumstances. In the afternoon of 6 October the triumphal procession set out on the muddy march back to Paris – National Guards armed and royal bodyguard disarmed, wagons laden with corn and flour lumbering, market men and women straggling along, Regiment of Flanders and Swiss Guard, La Fayette riding alongside the carriage bearing the royal family, also beside them the heads of two of the Royal Guards on pikes, a hundred deputies in carriages as evidence that the National Assembly would keep the king company, and trudging along in the rapidly failing twilight the dark shapes of thousands of nameless Parisians. At ten o'clock on a gloomy autumnal night the royal family, having first for two hours listened to speeches before the Hôtel de Ville, at last reached the Tuileries, whence Louis XIV had departed for Versailles 118 years earlier, and camped down in hurriedly cleared rooms as best they could for the night.

In the October Days the capital took possession of king and Assembly. For the next five years Paris was to dictate the course of the Revolution, and the Paris mob, which the Patriots of 1789 had used for their purposes, was to prove, as they were to discover in due course, a weapon that could be employed by more than one party and to more than one end.

2. FRANCE UNDER THE CONSTITUENT ASSEMBLY

It is easy in retrospect to see the fatality of the situation that had been created by October 1789 and the price at which the Third Estate had bought its victory. At the time few appreciated the full implications of what had been done and none knew if the victory was final. For that reason the triangular conflict of monarchy, aristocratic reaction, and democratic revolution continued. The king, having lost the initiative from the beginning, was doomed henceforth passively to follow circumstances, always their victim and never their master. The opposition to the Revolution was to come not from the monarchy but from the aristocratic revolution, the leaders of which had taken flight and were already preparing to instigate a counter-revolution from abroad, having given up hope of successful resistance within France. Their belief was that it would be easy to reconquer their privileges by an invasion with the aid of foreign powers: what this might imply for Louis XVI and Marie-Antoinette did not much concern them. They followed from the beginning, therefore, a wrecking policy: the worse the excesses into which the Revolution fell, they thought, the sooner it would be over.

The Third Estate itself could not believe in the completeness of its victory. The Patriots continued to attack the crown, though they had no practical alternative to royal government to propose. In spite of their suspicions, they could not rid themselves of the idea that government was the function of the king and his ministers. On the other hand, distrusting the court and the queen profoundly, they could not trust Louis XVI's ministers to govern. Obviously the result was to make all government impossible, but this practical consequence was only gradually to be revealed. Meanwhile the National Assembly, though it continually interfered with the administration through its committees, assumed that its task was not to rule but to draw up a constitution. It was literally a Constituent Assembly. Since this was the eighteenth century, the first step inevitably was to lay down general principles in the form of a Declaration of Rights, which was accepted by the Assembly on 26 August 1789.

A whole book could be written – indeed books have been written – on the Declaration of Rights. Little need be said here about the confused debate over its origins. American precedents are obvious but not fundamental, for even without these the same intellectual influences which produced the American Declaration would have operated in France. What were these influences? Not the little read and less understood *Social Contract* of Rousseau, nor the writings of the *philosophes*, so little concerned with political theory. If a source in eighteenth-century France is looked for, it will be found in the Remonstrances of the parlements, and behind these in the ideas of the Natural Law school of thought, which provided the basic content of current political thinking. The Declaration begins with the assertion that men are free and equal in rights. This was not intended to eliminate social distinctions, but their justification henceforth was to be utility. The object was to abolish distinctions based on privilege, and break the monopoly still retained by the privileged orders of the higher posts under the government, which was already a social anachronism. All careers are henceforth to be open to talent equally, but this is where equality stops. The right of property is recognized as natural, inalienable, sacred, and inviolable. Freedom from arbitrary arrest and imprisonment, freedom of opinion 'even religious', freedom from taxation without consent, are recognized as political rights. Law is the expression of the general will, by which is meant the will of a representative assembly, for the idea of the general will was common in eighteenth-century political thought and is not to be interpreted in the subtle philosophical sense given to the term by Rousseau.

The Declaration of Rights was the death-warrant of the system of privilege, and so of the *ancien régime*. In this respect it inaugurated a new age. Yet in the history of ideas it belonged rather to the past than to the future. The age of individual rights was not beginning but ending. The Declaration was the conclusion, not the commencement, of a great intellectual development and is far from summing up the revolution in political ideas that the democratic movement of the later eighteenth century brought about. A shorter and often unnoticed decree of the Constituent Assembly, passed after the forcible removal of the king to Paris, tells us more. This decree changed the royal title from 'Louis, by the grace of God, King of France and Navarre' to 'Louis, by the grace of God and the constitutional law of the state, King of the French' – *roi des Français*. It was a recognition that divine-right monarchy belonged to the past. It was more than this: it meant that the state had ceased to be simply a territory, or collection of territories, under a single authority; it had become a people, a nation, and as the Declaration of Rights said, 'The source of all sovereignty resides essentially in the nation.'

To understand fully the significance of this change in political ideas we must look back to the treatise which expressed in the clearest language the political ideals of the Third Estate on the eve of the elections to the States-General. Sieyes' famous *Qu'est-ce que le Tiers État?* was primarily an attack on the privileged orders and an assertion that the Third Estate was the nation; but Sieyes did not stop at this, he went on to tell the nation what its powers were:

The Nation exists before all things and is the origin of all. Its will is always legal, it is the law itself ... Nations on earth must be conceived as individuals outside the social bond, or as is said, in the state of nature. The exercise of their will is free and independent of all civil forms. Existing only in the natural order, their will, to have its full effect, only needs to possess the *natural* characteristics of a will. In whatever manner a nation wills, it suffices that it does will; all forms are valid and its will is always the supreme law.

In the ideas of Sieyes, and in the practice of the Revolution, a national sovereignty far more extensive in both theory and fact than the monarchical sovereignty of the *ancien régime* was let loose on the world. This national sovereignty was not, like the sovereignty of the people in Rousseau, confined to the drawing up of general laws by an assembly of the whole people, such as was conceivable only of a little state hardly as big as the smallest Swiss canton. For Sieyes, as for the French Revolution, the full power of the absolute and unlimited sovereignty of the people was attributed to a representative assembly, which, it was assumed, being the embodiment of the people, was not susceptible of any limitations, nor of needing any, for the people could not be supposed to be capable of exercising tyranny over itself. At the very moment, therefore, when restrictions on the exercise of political power were being laid down with an eye to the authorities of the past, a new political authority was set up which was by its very nature emancipated from all such restrictions.

The contradiction was crystallized in the opposition between the two leading political ideas of the revolutionaries. The idea of the separation of powers, incorrectly attributed to Montesquieu, who had argued for a balance and not a rigid separation, was employed to exclude executive influence from the legislature; on the other hand, the principle of popular sovereignty justified the legislative assembly in any invasion of the sphere of the executive. Although the full effects of the emancipation of sovereignty from all restraints were not to be seen for another century and a half, the revolutionary and Napoleonic quarter of a century in France provided some indication of what they would be. At the same time it must not be supposed that the Constituent Assembly was conscious that it was inaugurating anything other than a liberal and individualist régime.

Two years of discussion in committee and of debates in the Assembly were required before the Constitution was completed. Much of this discussion was too detailed and technical to arouse public interest, but one of the issues which provoked a major controversy arose at an early stage. The first constitutional committee of the Assembly proposed, towards the end of August 1789, that the king should be given an absolute veto on legislation. The patriot orators and journalists started a popular agitation against the proposal. As one revolutionary journal put it, presumably not in irony, the speed with which the populace became instructed on this 'truly delicate and profound question' was incredible. Who could have guessed, in the summer of 1789, how little it would matter whether the king had an absolute or a suspensive veto, or no veto at all? The episode is of significance, coming between the fall of the Bastille and the October Days, as an indication of the interplay between the Patriot party in the Assembly and the Parisian agitators.

The threat of a popular rising was a form of blackmail

that the more advanced section of the Assembly continually used against its opponents. But mobs require leaders, and to provide this intermediate leadership an underworld of political agitators and journalists grew up which was capable of being used, when the revolutionaries themselves split, by one faction against another, and in the end of becoming a power in itself. This is to look ahead. The Constituent Assembly, even if it was ready to make use of popular unrest to put pressure on the king, had no intention of sharing its political authority with the lower social strata, as it made clear in the debates on the franchise. It was, of course, difficult to talk grandly about the sovereignty of the people in theory and at the same time refuse political rights to a large section of the sovereign people – difficult but not impossible. Sieyes provided the necessary formula in the shape of the distinction between active and passive citizens. All adult males were citizens, but only those who paid a direct tax equivalent to the value of three days' labour in the year were active citizens with the right of voting. A much higher qualification was required for membership of the electoral assemblies: the qualification for sitting in the Legislative Assembly was to be the payment of a tax of a *marc d'argent*, about 52 livres. In this way it was hoped that the principle of democratic sovereignty might have the sting taken out of it and effective power remain in the hands of the propertied classes. This was the issue which produced the most violent division in the ranks of the Third Estate. A few members of the Assembly, including particularly the deputy from Arras, Robespierre, and a large body of agitators and journalists in Paris, denounced these proposals as creating, in the words of one of them, Marat, an 'aristocracy of wealth'. In the end, before the Constitution was finally passed into law in 1791, the qualification of the silver mark was dropped, though the other property qualifications remained.

The year 1790, following on an improved harvest in 1789, was, apart from some mutinies and a good deal of scattered unrest, a comparatively peaceful year. The optimism and idealism of the early phase of the Revolution still set the prevailing tone, and the rosy light with which France was suffused seemed the promise of dawn rather than the darker hues of sunset. The Revolution, perhaps for most of the nation, was something won, not something yet to be fought for, and as such it was celebrated, in the summer of 1790, all over the country. Out of many possible illustrations may be chosen the civic fête of 20 June, held by a society formed at Paris for the purpose of commemorating the tennis-court oath. Arranged in a procession the participants march from Paris to Versailles, in their midst four victors of the Bastille bearing a tablet of bronze with the tennis-court oath inscribed thereon, and four other victors carrying stones from the demolished fortress. At Versailles the municipality welcomes them and a guard of honour from the Flander regiment presents arms. The procession proceeds to the tennis-court, where all present renew the oath '*dans un saisissement religieux*'. After speeches, in the course of which one orator tells them that their children will flock to that sacred spot as the Muslims to Mecca, four aged men seal the tablet in the walls. With mutual embracings the municipality, the National Guard of Versailles, and the Flanders regiment escort them to the gates of the town. On the return journey a halt is made in the bois de Boulogne, where a repast for 300, 'worthy of our ancestors', is served by young patriotic nymphs on tables decorated with the busts of the friends of humanity, Rousseau, Mably, Benjamin Franklin. For grace the first two articles of the Declaration of Rights are read. A toast is proposed by Danton to the liberty and happiness of the whole world: Robespierre, Barnave, and other prominent revolutionaries follow with equally appropriate toasts, and women dressed as shepherdesses crown the deputies present with oak leaves. Now the four victors of the Bastille bring on a model of it, which they place on a table. National Guards surround it and destroy it with their swords, one hopes carefully, for in the midst is found, O joy, O ravishment of the spectators, a baby dressed in white, symbol of oppressed innocence and new-born liberty; also a red Phrygian cap, which amid applause is placed on the baby's head, and several copies of the Declaration of Rights and extracts from the works of Raynal and Rousseau, which are scattered among the spectators. With this final gesture the celebration is ended. It seems all very fresh and innocent and even naïve, but unless we can recapture some of the spirit in which such fêtes were held and trees of liberty were planted, and judge them without undue cynicism or wisdom after the event, we shall fail to understand an essential element in the revolutionary victory. This spirit was what Wordsworth recalled when he looked back to the days when he was a companion of the young republicans of Blois.

> Bliss was it in that dawn to be alive,
> But to be young was very Heaven! O times,
> In which the meagre, stale, forbidding ways
> Of custom, law and statute, took at once
> The attraction of a country in romance!
> When Reason seemed the most to assert her rights
> When most intent on making of herself
> A prime enchantress to assist the work,
> Which then was going forward in her name!
> Not favoured spots alone, but the whole earth,
> The beauty wore of promise – that which sets
> (As at some moments might not be unfelt
> Among the bowers of Paradise itself)
> The budding rose above the rose full blown.

In this idyllic landscape, or cloud-cuckoo land of political ideals, the ardent revolutionaries dwelt, while the Constituent Assembly laboriously debated the constitutional proposals, and the king's government continued its decline into ever-increasing impotence. Urgent problems demanded attention. Something had to be done to restore local government. Since there could be no question of abolishing the communal councils which had sprung up spontaneously all over France, they remained the basic element in the new system of local government. In place of the thirty or so *généralités* France was divided into eighty-three departments. The essential object of this change was to destroy the

The provinces of France varied in size from the huge area of Guyenne and Gascony to the petty Boulonnais or Aunis. Some of them, for example Brittany, Normandy, Alsace, Dauphiné, retained a strong provincial feeling. Others had been from the beginning artificial agglomerations of territory. By the eighteenth century they had lost practically all their administrative significance. Only in a few cases did the généralités correspond to them. Yet provincial tradition must have counted for something in 1789, for the map shows how often the new departmental frontiers did in fact follow provincial boundaries.

provincial spirit, so bound up with the traditions of the *ancien
régime* and the system of privilege. At the same time the
electoral principle, with a property qualification, was sub-
stituted for the monarchical principle of nomination. Before
1789 local government had been controlled almost exclusively by officials appointed from above; after 1789 it was
entirely in the hands of committees elected from below. In
the long run, with its system of municipalities or communes,
and departments, the Constituent Assembly had laid sound
foundations, as a century and a half of subsequent history
was to show; but immediately its legislation was vitiated by
two glaring gaps. The new local authorities were given considerable powers, but no provision was made for financing
their activities. Naturally, within a year they were bankrupt. Further, no administrative machinery was created to
connect the local and central government. If it is added that
a natural conflict of interests rapidly developed between the
departmental directories, representing the wealthier classes,
and the communes, in which a poorer though still propertied section of the population was represented, it is evident
why the disintegration of central government was to be accompanied, and indeed partly caused, by a parallel collapse
of local government.

Apart from the reorganization of local government, the
most urgent problem before the Constituent Assembly was
finance. In the spring and summer of 1789 the collection of
the taxes, both direct and indirect, had broken down. Fiscal
equality was achieved at a bound in a situation in which nobody paid any taxes at all. At the same time the National
Assembly demonstrated its financial orthodoxy by ordering
the resumption of payments of interest on the royal debt.
The financial burden was also immensely increased by the
achievement of a reform which the controllers-general of the
past had never dared to introduce. All venal offices were
abolished. This was undoubtedly the removal of one of the
greatest abuses of the *ancien régime*, and, more remarkable, it
was the work of an assembly composed, so far as concerned
the Third Estate, of venal officers in the proportion of some

43 per cent. The explanation of what might otherwise seem an act of extraordinary self-abnegation on their part is that before 1789 at least some of the offices had already been declining in value, and that it was not abolition without compensation.

The solution to the fundamental financial problem was a simple one. It had been commonly held that the property of the Church was in some way different from other property. As early as August 1789 left-wing deputies were asserting that ecclesiastical property belonged to the nation. Occasional outbursts of anti-clerical feeling appeared during the summer of 1789 and the upper clergy were the objects of attack along with the *noblesse*. On 10 October the secular-minded and ambitious Bishop of Autun, better remembered as Talleyrand, whose life, declares a biographical dictionary of the time, 'would be the secret history of our epoch', proposed the nationalization of ecclesiastical property, on condition that the state took over the financial responsibilities of the Church. The sale of Church lands, he declared, would bring in two milliards of livres, and the upkeep of the clergy would cost only 100 million a year. It seemed, if one may put it so, a heaven-sent solution to an otherwise insoluble problem. That so much valuable land had been kept out of the market in the dead hand of the Church had long been a grievance to the land-hungry bourgeois and peasants. The lower clergy, who were promised an annual salary of not less than 1,200 livres for a curé, apparently stood to gain materially by the proposals. With very little opposition, on 19 December, the sale of the first 400 million livres of Church properties was decreed. Among those who negotiated for their purchase was Marie-Antoinette. That it was to be the first step in the secularization of the state and the commencement of a still unfinished war between the Church and the Revolution hardly anyone guessed.

Backed by the proceeds of the sale of Church lands, paper money, in the form of assignats, was issued. It was to be bought in and destroyed as money returned to the Treasury from the sales, and thus the fear of inflation, which had haunted France since the time of John Law, was dissipated. With the aid of the assignats the interest on the *rentes* could be paid, the bottomless budget plugged, and a breathing-space ensured in which the Assembly could bring into operation a new and reformed fiscal system. In fact, instead of stabilizing the situation, as it supposed, the Assembly had primed the pump of continued revolution. Inflation was to be the root cause which perpetuated economic distress and so provided the raw material for future upheavals; but this consequence must not be pre-dated. There had been, before 1789, a shortage of currency in France, and therefore a certain amount of slack existed to be taken up before the rope began to tighten. The assignats, which were at a slight discount of 5 per cent when they were issued, had only fallen from 95 to 91 per cent of their face value by January 1791 and to 87 per cent in July. It is after this date that the catastrophic fall begins. The Constituent Assembly, by confiscating the lands of the Church, had given itself two years in which to complete its work.

While the nationalizing of Church lands aroused little opposition, the imposition of the Civil Constitution on the Church, by a law of July 1790, was to have a very different reception. In the new organization, bishops and curés were, on the best democratic principles, to be elected by those on the roll of active citizens. The religious orders were dissolved, except provisionally for those engaged in teaching and charitable work. In these laws for the first time we come to a development which was determined mainly by ideological considerations rather than by pressure of circumstances. The anti-clericalism of Voltaire and the *philosophes* had bitten so deeply into the minds of those who represented the Third Estate at Paris that the extent of the opposition their reorganization of the Church was to provoke was hidden from them. Unknowingly, they had added religious schism to the other causes of political and social unrest. Open opposition was slow to develop, however. The clergy themselves, to begin with, were at a loss to know what to do. The king, after some months' delay, ratified the Civil Constitution. The oath of loyalty to the Constitution, which was imposed on all clergy, was taken only by seven bishops out of 160; but of the lower clergy possibly about one-third took the oath. In the local variations the religious map of nineteenth-century France was already sketched out, with four main centres of opposition to the Civil Constitution, in the north-east (Nord and Pas-de-Calais), Brittany and its environs, part of the mountainous region of the centre (Lozère and Haute-Loire), and an area in the east (Bas-Rhin and Moselle). Divided and hesitant, the Church waited for a lead from the Pope, who, anxious not to do anything that would imperil the Papal possessions of Avignon and the Venaissin, postponed a decision as long as he could. Only in March 1791 did the Vatican take the plunge, declare the Civil Constitution destructive of the Catholic religion, and denounce the 'monstrous right' of liberty of thought and writing. Soon after, when the Vatican suspended all priests who did not withdraw their acceptance, a movement of retraction began among the clergy who had taken the oath. The Constitutional Church, in spite of a great shortage of qualified clergy, was to survive for a decade. The war that had been started between Church and state was to continue to the twentieth century.

To catalogue the laws, most of them of a more permanent nature than the ecclesiastical legislation, in which the Constituent Assembly continued the great age of reform inaugurated before 1789, would be a long task. Their key-note was liberty. All offices were opened to Protestants in 1789; there was opposition from Alsace and Lorraine to the granting of rights of citizenship to Jews but this was finally voted three days before the Constituent Assembly dissolved. The attempt, when the States-General met, to prevent the publication of reports of its meetings was frustrated by Mirabeau, who adopted the device of turning his journal into the form of a periodical report to his constituents. Until the revolution of 10 August 1792 the press enjoyed the most absolute liberty. The theatre was equally freed from control and became, like the press, a medium of political propaganda.

The proposal to abolish slavery in the colonies, put forward by the *Société des amis des Noirs*, met with opposition from the strong vested interest of the plantation owners, many of whom were resident in France, and from the merchants engaged in the Atlantic trade. The Declaration of Rights was a little difficult to reconcile with slavery, but the Constituent Assembly gallantly swallowed its principles, which, however, having penetrated to the Antilles, were to provoke a devastating revolt there. The principle of liberty also ran into difficulties in its application to the traditional authority of the father of the family. This was henceforth restricted to children under the age of twenty-one and the powers of imprisonment it carried with it were limited, though not abolished. The secularization of marriage was a logical corollary of the anti-clerical ideology, but the Constituent Assembly only reached the point of proclaiming the principle that marriage was a civil contract. Civil marriages and secular registrations of births and deaths were to be established by law in 1792, when a system of civil divorce was also introduced. The laws of inheritance, which varied from province to province, presented too controversial a problem for the Constituent Assembly to solve. The principle of equality of inheritance between children was generalized in 1790, but specific prohibitions against willing property unequally were only introduced in 1793.

That the criminal laws and the law courts, both civil and criminal, needed drastic reform was generally agreed by enlightened opinion before the Revolution. On the future of the parlements, which clung to the use of torture and the good old ways, there were no two opinions in the Third Estate; they were first put on permanent vacation and then abolished, a new system of courts being set up in their place. 'Imaginary crimes' – heresy, lèse-majesté, and magical practices – were no longer recognized. Mutilations and all forms of torture were removed from the list of punishments, leaving only deportation, imprisonment, and death. The aristocratic privilege of decapitation was extended to the whole nation, with the aid of a new invention, incorrectly attributed to Dr Guillotin. What all this meant in the way of humanitarian progress cannot easily be overestimated.

Along with liberty and equality the National Assembly proclaimed the sanctity of property, though this did not include 'feudal' privileges or the lands of the Church. What it meant was the free exploitation of recognized property rights; it therefore implied the extinction of the system of state control of trade and industry. The corporations were suppressed; but when the workers of Paris assumed that liberty meant the liberty to strike, the Assembly replied with the law Le Chapelier, prohibiting associations of workers. Even the left-wing in the Assembly did not oppose this law. In the country a major issue was that of enclosures. In spite of rural hostility, which had been manifested before 1789 and was expressed in the parish *cahiers*, the Assembly went as far as it dared, in the face of this opposition, in authorizing and encouraging them. Finally, all internal restrictions on the free passage of goods were abolished, the long-elaborated plans for a single tariff at last emerging from the bureaux of the *Contrôle général* and being put into effect by the officials who had struggled unavailingly for their acceptance before 1789. On the other hand the protective system of tariffs on goods coming into France was strictly preserved, for the free-trade treaty of Vergennes with England had aroused a torrent of opposition and the economic crisis was attributed, however incorrectly, to it. Similarly, the monopoly of colonial trade was maintained. Altogether, the National Assembly cannot be charged with slavish adherence to theoretical principles of liberty in its economic legislation.

While the foundations were thus being laid for the future, the present had been forgotten and France was fast sliding into a state of anarchy. The collapse of the civil administration was serious, but even worse was the spread of indiscipline among the armed forces of the Crown. Revolutionary committees of soldiers and sailors were formed, which came into conflict with their officers. The most notorious among many outbreaks was that in August 1790 at Nancy, where the regiment of Châteauvieux, after the cruel punishment of the *couvroies*, a kind of running the gauntlet, had been inflicted on two insubordinate soldiers, mutinied and with the aid of the mob took control of the town. The marquis de Bouillé, in command of the army of the East, stormed Nancy with heavy loss on both sides; several of the mutineers were sentenced to death and some forty-one to the galleys. Though the National Assembly voted thanks to Bouillé, political agitators were able to make good use of the episode for propaganda purposes.

Revolutionary clubs played a leading part in such disturbances, and indeed in a state in which the old authorities had collapsed and the new ones had hardly begun to function it was inevitable that such revolutionary groups should become the real centres of power. The establishment at Versailles of the Breton Club, later to become the Jacobins, has already been mentioned. The deputies who belonged to the club constituted an influential left-wing pressure group in the Assembly. By such forms of social assistance as the distribution of vouchers for cheap bread, and by giving pecuniary or legal help to poorer patriots in distress, they acquired a popular clientèle, though not until October 1791, when additional galleries were constructed and their sessions thrown open to the public, could they be said to have fallen under the influence of the mob instead of influencing it. The prestige of the club was so great that it was able to survive extensive secessions. It far surpassed in influence the other political clubs, such as the right-wing Club des Valois and the left-wing club of the Cordeliers, which was led by extra-parliamentary agitators like Danton, Camille Desmoulins, Anacharsis Clootz, friend of humanity, and the poetically self-named Fabre d'Eglantine.

All over France similar political clubs were formed by local revolutionaries. Establishing a system of correspondence with the Paris Jacobins, many of them came to adopt its name and look to it for leadership. By 1793 there were probably between five and eight thousand such clubs, with a nominal membership of perhaps half a million, though the active membership may have been much smaller. The Jacobin Clubs gradually came to usurp the powers of local government, and later, under the Committee of Public Safety, became in effect auxiliary administrative bodies as well as centres of propaganda and electoral influence. The role of the clubs in revolutionary France is yet one more example of the victory of practical considerations over theory, for in theory any kind of party organization was regarded as factious and held in disrepute. The very idea of concerted action among the deputies in the Assembly was looked on with suspicion. The justification for the part played by the clubs was given by a speaker at the Jacobin Club of Paris in April 1793: 'Patriots do not form a party,' he declared, 'that designation can only be applied to the intriguers of the Convention.' It was through the Jacobin Clubs that the more advanced revolutionaries were gradually able to impose their rule on France. The pattern remained to the end what it had been in the beginning: the exploitation of popular discontent and the stirring up of mob passions, whether against aristocrats or priests, or simply political opponents.

The Jacobins, of course, were not the mere '*vauriens*' of royalist legend. At the commencement the high subscription of 36 livres, with 12 livres entrance fee, as well as the level of the debates, were sufficient safeguard against this. Although the membership of the Jacobin Clubs was broadened later, it has been shown that even under the Terror they remained largely middle class in composition: the tax assessments of the Jacobins were well above the average. They were opposed both to the rich and to the propertyless. They came from the cities and small towns: though there were clubs in villages they seem to have exhibited little activity, and the rural masses, after the summer of 1789, were either passive or hostile to the Revolution. What held the Jacobins together was less class interest than a common ideology, which became increasingly narrow with the development of ritual, tests of orthodoxy, purges, and public confessions. Being only a small minority in the whole nation they came to think of themselves as a chosen body, an élite, 'the very small number,' Camille Desmoulins put it in 1791, 'of those to whom only the witness of their conscience is necessary, the small number of men of character, incorruptible citizens.'

If we want to understand the revolutionaries we must remember above all that they had been nurtured on a classical education. Robespierre, asked what constitution he wanted, replied 'That of Lycurgus'. Plutarch, Livy, Tacitus were their teachers; Brutus the consul, Brutus the tyrannicide, and Cincinnatus their models. They wore Phrygian caps, built triumphal arches, and erected statues – usually of not very durable plaster – to all the classical virtues, crowned their heroes with laurel wreaths, converted the appropriately classical church of Ste Geneviève into a Panthéon to hold the mortal relics of their prophets and martyrs, and if they had to die, did it when they could in the old Roman fashion. They were to have senates and councils of ancients, bearers of the fasces, consuls, and in due course an emperor. But even their classicism, as I have already implied, was not an invention of the Revolution. In the plastic arts its triumph was already manifest before 1789. Hubert Robert's landscapes, with ruined temples and fallen columns, earlier in the century testified to the interest in the antique. The French Academy at Rome was the centre from which a more rigorous classicism spread and the crucial moment was when the most brilliant of the rising young artists in France, David, went there with the Prix de Rome in 1774. The new style won its decisive victory with David's *Oath of the Horatii*, exhibited in the Salon of 1785. When the Revolution came it merely set the seal on his artistic triumph. While Vigée Le Brun emigrated and Fragonard for a time took refuge in Provence from the new hard climate, David became the unchallenged leader of revolutionary art. He put his already great reputation and his artistic genius to the service of the Revolution. The Jacobin Club, of which he had become a member, commissioned him, on the first anniversary of the tennis-court oath, to immortalize it in paint. His drawing for this, exhibited in 1791 and widely reproduced, is, of course, an imaginative reconstruction, influenced by subsequent political events, and not a contemporary record. It was destined never to be finished, for the artist entered the Convention, and politics, or political art, made increasing demands on him until Thermidor. He was to be, for a time, practically the artistic dictator of France. Contrary to an old story, he used his influence, as a member of the Commission of Monuments, to save the artistic treasures of France and he protected Fragonard. If his huge canvases won him his contemporary fame and made him the official artist of Jacobinism, however, it is by his magnificent portraits that he survives as one of the greater painters of France. In modern times, at least, official art is generally bad art. David's contribution to the propagation of Jacobin ideology must be spoken of in its place.

All this is to anticipate. Between 1789 and 1791 such consistency as the Jacobin Clubs were later to give the Revolution was lacking. Agitators and journalists were stirring up trouble and the Constituent Assembly was unable to control the rising tide of anarchy. To condemn the Assembly, in the language of Burke, as a collection of country curates and petty provincial attorneys is absurd. Though a majority of the members were, naturally, local notabilities who as individuals have left no mark on history, there has perhaps never been an assembly in French history which contained so much talent. What its members lacked was what in the nature of things they could not have acquired – political experience. If in this respect one man stands out in contrast to almost all the other members of the Constituent Assembly, it was not because he was wiser or better than the rest, but because he, almost alone, recognized as if by a native instinct the necessary conditions of the parliamentary régime.

Mirabeau, younger son of the physiocratic marquis, won notoriety before the Revolution for his amorous adventures.

He published works of varying degrees of scurrility and obscenity and attempted to break into public life by way of the back-stairs of diplomacy and shady finance. The Revolution provided the opportunity for him to turn to a better use the energy and ability which had gone to waste under the *ancien régime*. Even before his election to the States-General, Mirabeau had written to the Foreign Secretary warning him of the need for the ministry to adopt a plan of action in order to remain in command of the situation and avoid the dangers of aristocratic plots and democratic excesses. No notice was taken of his advice and the government was to fall a victim to both in turn. Elected a member of the Third Estate, Mirabeau, with his stentorian voice, massive build, lion-like mane, and domineering countenance, its natural ugliness accentuated by the ravages of smallpox, at once became a leading figure. For the Assembly itself, filled with worthy and high-minded characters amongst whom he was as out of place as Gulliver among the Lilliputians, he had the utmost contempt. But he concealed this. I have never known any man who, when he wished, could be more seductive than him, wrote the young Genevan Dumont, one of the group of experts who prepared Mirabeau's speeches and whose backroom services enabled him to speak, as no other member of the Assembly could, with authority on any and every subject. Mirabeau at the outset made himself the voice of the Third Estate against the privileged Orders, to which he belonged by birth, but it was for the purpose of strengthening, not destroying, monarchical authority. ' I am the only one in that patriotic horde,' he said on one occasion, defending in private the need for royal authority, 'who can speak thus without performing a volte-face. I have never adopted their romance, nor their metaphysics, nor their useless crimes.' Necker he despised as only a strong, ruthless man can despise a weak-minded sentimentalist. While maintaining his reputation as a staunch revolutionary by violent-sounding, though often moderate in content, speeches, he established secret relations with the court. Marie-Antoinette was willing to pay him, but not to trust him. 'We will never be so wretched, I believe,' she wrote, 'as to be reduced to the painful extremity of having recourse to Mirabeau.' The king and queen never understood the reason of his demand for a ministry responsible to the Assembly, a principle, he rightly declared, 'more important even, if possible, to the king than to his people.' With the man who should have been his natural ally, La Fayette, head of the National Guard and a popular idol, mutual dislike made it impossible for him to work. Even apart from such personal difficulties, Mirabeau's plan of action could hardly have achieved success. His position was essentially false, fated as he was to arouse the distrust of the court by demogogic speeches in the Assembly, and of the revolutionaries by his attempts to preserve the authority of the Crown. In January 1791 he still wielded enough influence to be elected president of the Assembly. In April he died, worn out by toil and excesses, at the age of forty-two. 'O people,' wrote Marat, 'render thanks to the gods, your most formidable enemy has fallen.' To Mirabeau himself was attributed the dying phrase, 'I carry in my heart the funeral knell of the monarchy.'

Only after Mirabeau's death, and two years too late, did Louis XVI and Marie-Antoinette put into effect the advice that he had consistently given them to fly from Paris and set up the royal standard, with all who would support it, in a provincial capital. Mirabeau's advice had been to go to Rouen, in conservative and phlegmatic Normandy, flanked by the Catholic and royalist forces of Brittany and the Vendée. The king and queen, when at last they saw no hope but in flight, chose the destination they had contemplated in 1789, Metz, where Bouillé, after the suppression of the mutiny at Nancy, still maintained some kind of discipline among his troops, and from whence the frontier could easily be gained. The devoted Fersen made the arrangements for the escape. At half-past ten at night, on 20 June 1791, by an unguarded door, the king and queen, with the king's sister, Mme Elizabeth, the two royal children and their governess, left the Tuileries in a waiting carriage. At the gate of Saint-

Martin they changed into a heavy berline prepared for the journey and at a slow pace took the road. Meaux, Châlons, Ste-Menehould were passed and the little town of Varennes – fatal name – was reached between eleven and twelve o'clock on the night of 21 June. More than once in their slow progress the royal family had been recognized but allowed to pass unchallenged. At Varennes they met with a stauncher patriot and were stopped. The squadrons sent by Bouillé to safeguard his sovereigns, ranging in what seems a rather confused fashion about the countryside, missed them, and were unable to rescue them from the bands of peasants gathered at Varennes. The tragic journey back to Paris, far longer and more pitiful than that of October 1789 from Versailles, was accompanied by the shouts and threats of hostile crowds, only prevented from inflicting personal injury on the royal family by the presence of an escort of National Guards and the arrival of Barnave and two other deputies.

The king and queen re-entered the Tuileries on 25 June as prisoners, yet prisoners whom the Assembly would not or could not do without; for it was on the point of completing its task and presenting for the royal signature a monarchical constitution. Voices outside the Assembly, in the journals and on the streets, were now openly calling for a republic, but the members of the Constituent Assembly were not prepared for such a revolutionary step: even Robespierre believed that a monarchy was necessary. Therefore they had to pretend that the king had never fled: he had been kidnapped.

The popular agitation was not to be so easily diverted. A great demonstration was organized in the huge open space of the Champ de Mars, where a petition calling for the king's abdication was drawn up. After a preliminary meeting on 16 July 1791, the meeting on the following day was inaugurated by the lynching of two men found hiding under the steps leading up to the platform. Serious proceedings began with the signing of the petition. Meanwhile Bailly, Mayor of Paris, and the Municipal Council, along with La

Fayette, had decided that precautions must be taken. Martial law was proclaimed for the first time, the red flag hoisted, and a detachment of National Guard sent to the Champ de Mars. There a shot rang out, from which side is not known. General firing broke out, some fifty of the crowd as well as two National Guards were killed, and the demonstrators were dispersed. The use of force against a popular movement was followed by measures against its instigators. Leaders of the popular clubs were arrested or went into hiding and the more extreme journals were suppressed. A secession to the Feuillants threatened to extinguish even the Jacobin Club. In the face of this unexpectedly strong action the agitation collapsed. For the first time it seemed that authority was capable of asserting itself.

In the summer of 1791 the Constitution was, considering its slow progress during the previous two years, fairly rapidly completed. A last-minute move to strengthen the monarchical element in it might have succeeded if it had not been for irresponsible opposition from the right. As it was, Barnave, who had entered into a secret correspondence with the queen after conversations on the road back from Varennes, wrote to her, 'The constitution is a very monarchical one'. The king formally appended his signature on 14 September and on 30 September the Constituent Assembly was dissolved. Before this it had taken one decisive and fatal resolution, in voting the self-denying ordinance by which its members disqualified themselves from membership of the new Legislative Assembly. The motives of Robespierre, who proposed this decree and thus at a single stroke eliminated all the moderates who at last were showing signs of realizing the need for government in France, are obvious; but he could not have secured its acceptance without the support of the right, whose hatred for the constitutionalists led them to deal this last blow to their enemies even if it was to prove fatal to themselves and to the king. As the moderate marquis de Ferrières wrote, 'The Great Aristocrats and the Wild Men combined to pass the decree.' By it, all those who had learnt painfully something of the conditions of parliamentary government were to be eliminated temporarily from the scene. New men, in a new Assembly, were to take over the task of consolidating the gains of the Revolution and restoring a stable government to France.

3. FALL OF THE CONSTITUTIONAL MONARCHY

'THE Constitution,' wrote Mirabeau's disciple Dumont, 'was a veritable monster: there was too much republic for a monarchy, and too much monarchy for a republic. The king was an hors-d'oeuvre.' Such a judgement was obviously written after the Constitution had failed. The Legislative Assembly that met for the first time on 1 October 1791 had no such forebodings of disaster; despite the flight to Varennes it intended to make the constitutional monarchy work. Although some 136 of its members joined the left-wing Jacobin or Cordeliers clubs, many more, about a third of the total number of deputies, put their names down at the more moderate Feuillants, formed as a break-away from the Jacobins. The leadership of left-wing opinion in the new Assembly was taken by the small but active group who were called, from the name of their most prominent member, the Brissotins. Brissot, son of a restaurant proprietor of Chartres, came from a lower social stratum than even the most advanced of the members of the Constituent Assembly. He had left school at fifteen to become a lawyer's clerk and subsequently graduated in the underworld of literature; he wrote propaganda for financial speculators trying to rig the markets, possibly joined the London factory which was publishing pamphlets against Marie-Antoinette for the purpose of having them bought up and suppressed by the police, and associated with the more advanced and idealistic leaders of the Third Estate. In 1786 he entered the service of the Duke of Orleans, to which so many political adventurers gravitated. After the meeting of the States-General he founded the *Patriote française*, which became one of the chief journals of the extremer revolutionaries. He played a part in the organization of the Champ de Mars demonstration of July 1791 and was elected in September 1791 for Paris. The charges of dishonesty which the royalists in the earlier part of his career, and the Jacobins subsequently, directed against him, have little more justification than the fact that he was a poverty-stricken adventurer always short of funds. He died poor, which is a good if not a decisive defence. He was sincere in his way, yet a born intriguer, full of plans, facile, optimistic, ambitious, and above all a light man. His febrile activity gathered a brilliant group round him in the Legislative Assembly, including Vergniaud, one of the greatest orators of the Assembly, who as a leading light of the bar at Bordeaux was elected by the department of the Gironde, and other members of the same deputation.

Those who were labelled Brissotins were not a party – they were too few – but at most a faction, held together by ties of personal friendship, a common rather sentimental idealism and a vague republicanism. They took the lead in pressing for decrees against the émigrés and the refractory priests who had not taken, or had withdrawn, the oath to the Civil Constitution. In doing so they were necessarily provoking an open conflict with the king, for Louis XVI, so weak where his own interests were concerned, was sincerely religious and at the same time could not easily sanction positive measures against the émigrés, including so many of his own friends and relations. What the Brissotins wanted, apart from power, it is not easy to say. In their attempt to achieve this, however, they were to prove more unscrupulous, if less ruthless, than their enemies of the Mountain were to be later. They had one trump card: war, they rightly thought, would play into the hands of the left-wing and enable it to rally popular passions behind it. Brissot and his friends therefore set to work to bring war about.

On the other hand, the outbreak of war between revolutionary France and Europe can only be presented as the result exclusively of a Brissotin intrigue by taking the immediate occasion for the cause. Brissot had the war card in his hand, but if he had not, there can be little doubt that someone else would have played it instead. To treat the outbreak of war as the mere result of a faction struggle is to forget the history of the previous half-century, during which France had known in foreign affairs nothing but defeat. In 1787, when British and Prussian intervention forced the government to abandon the Franco-Dutch alliance in humiliating conditions, Arthur Young had found everywhere an outcry for war with England. When the States-General met, the desire for national unity was the earliest form taken by the patriotic spirit. The first measure to this end could be regarded as a mere formality: Corsica, already a French *généralité*, was declared part of the French Empire. It was not until September 1791 that Avignon and the Venaissin, after a bloody struggle between revolutionaries and the adherents of the papal authorities, were annexed. In the independent enclaves of the German princes on the left bank of the Rhine the laws against feudal dues were applied and protests rejected 'in the name of the sacred and inalienable rights of nations'.

It must not be supposed that the Constituent Assembly was bellicose in sentiment. On the contrary, it was imbued with the profoundly pacific ideals of the great writers of the eighteenth century. War, the revolutionaries believed, was a wicked habit of despots: a nation could not be aggressive. When, in 1790, the Anglo-Spanish conflict over Nootka Sound seemed about to develop into open war and Spain called for French support under the terms of the Family Compact, the Assembly insisted that the right of declaring war belonged to the nation and not to the king, and added the famous declaration renouncing all wars of conquest and pledging the French nation never to employ its forces against the liberty of any people. Such sentiments represent fairly the idealistic pacifism of the opening stages of the Revolution, but in this as in so many other respects circumstances were to be more influential than ideas.

Old Europe resounded with denunciations of the Revolution, which found their most fulminating expression in Burke's *Reflections on the Revolution in France* in November 1790. Round the frontiers of France gathered little congregations of émigrés, the king's younger brother, Artois, with Calonne to direct his tactics, at their head, stirring up counter-revolutionary movements in France and urging the powers to launch an attack for the purpose of restoring the *ancien régime*. The French Patriots could hardly have been expected to know that the powers had no intention of doing anything of the kind. In Great Britain the government of the younger Pitt was wedded to peace and quite content to see France, as Windham put it as late as 1792, 'in a situation which, more than at any other period, freed us from apprehension, on her account'. Austria and Prussia, chiefly concerned with the dangers arising from Russian policy and looking to the possibility of further spoils in Poland, were also not regretful to see French military power eliminated, or so they thought, from the map of Europe; while Catherine of Russia was only urging them to strike at France for the purpose of ensuring a free hand for herself to pursue further annexations in Eastern Europe. The appeals of the émigrés to the courts of Europe were therefore met everywhere with expressions of sympathy combined with a determination to do nothing to put it into practice.

The counter-revolution was not even united. Marie-Antoinette, with Breteuil to represent her and the king abroad, was profoundly, and not without reason, suspicious of Artois and his party; but at the same time was sending secret letters to her brother, the Emperor Leopold, denouncing the Constitution and the Assembly and calling for armed intervention. 'We have no longer any resource,' she wrote, 'but in the foreign powers: at all costs they must come to our aid.' The famous manifesto of Pilnitz, on 27 August 1791, showed how little they intended to respond to her appeal. Leopold and the king of Prussia satisfied their elastic consciences and their convenience at the same time. They proclaimed the common interest of all the sovereigns of Europe in the fate of the king of France, and declared themselves ready with the cooperation of these sovereigns to restore the king to a situation in which he would be free to strengthen the foundations of monarchical government. This was a formidable threat in appearance: in substance it amounted to nothing, for the signatories well knew that the other powers were not willing to join them. Marie-Antoinette's disappointment was bitter: 'The emperor has betrayed us,' she wrote. The revolutionaries did not see it in this light and anticipated at any moment a descent of foreign armies, spearheaded by the corps of émigrés and supported by an aristocratic rising inside France. It was not far from this fear to the idea of a preventive war to anticipate the attack.

The apparent threat from without met and intensified a growing bellicose trend within France. Austria was the hereditary enemy and the Austrian alliance had long been denounced by court factions as the source of all evil. Moreover, the Revolution was already an international revolution, not merely because of the universal applicability of its ideas, but in actual fact. The democratic movement of the second half of the eighteenth century, as I have said, had not been peculiar to France. America, England, Ireland, Geneva, the United Provinces, Liège, and the Austrian Netherlands witnessed similar movements, though only in America had the revolution achieved success. Democratic refugees from abroad flocked to France, some of the more distinguished to offer their advice and cooperation to the leaders of the French Revolution, even to be elected to the Legislative Assembly, others to join the underworld of agitators and journalists in Paris. They exercised a continuous pressure for French intervention in their homelands, which they represented as only waiting the signal to rise, overthrow their feudal and despotic rulers, and cast in their lot with France. The Brissotins formed the point of crystallization for all the tendencies leading France in the direction of war, and Brissot launched the campaign in a speech of 20 October 1791, which denounced the émigrés and called for their expulsion from the territories around France. 'In the event of a refusal,' he told the Assembly, 'you have no choice, you must yourselves attack the powers which dare to threaten you. The picture of liberty, like the head of Medusa, will terrify the armies of our enemies.' In November another member of the Brissotin faction, Isnard of the Var, invented the formula 'a war of peoples against kings'.

The agitation for war was now reinforced unexpectedly from within the government, and by the Minister for War who had been put into office by the influence of the moderates. This was the comte de Narbonne, commonly regarded as an illegitimate son of Louis XV, current lover of Mme de Staël and later to be an aide-de-camp of Napoleon. A noble and officer, Narbonne had thrown in his lot with the Revolution, but his aim, except that they both saw in a war the opportunity for political power, was precisely the opposite of that of Brissot. Narbonne shared the views of that section of the right which regarded a successful war on a limited scale as a means of restoring the power of the crown. Their calculations were not unsuspected among the revolutionaries, but few of the latter dared to criticize the war fever and only one opposed it with consistency and force. This was Robespierre, who, at first favourable to the idea of a declaration of war, had rapidly seen the possibility that it might play into the hands of the king. In a series of great speeches at the Jacobin Club, early in 1792, he attempted, practically single-handed, to stem the tide of war. Crush our internal enemies first, he said, and then march against foreign ones; in an even more striking phrase, 'No one loves armed missionaries.' Europe, he declared, with true insight, wants peace; the émigrés are powerless; the immediate threat to the Revolution is entirely within France.

The duel at the Jacobin Club between Robespierre and Brissot over the question of war was to weigh heavily on the future of the Revolution, for it was at the root of their subsequent discord. At the moment the forces on the side of Brissot and the war party were overwhelming, and Robespierre was left for the time being defeated and practically isolated. The Brissotins, with the almost unanimous support of the Assembly, forced the ministry to resign in March 1792. Narbonne did not reap any reward from his advocacy of war for he had lost office shortly before this in consequence of a quarrel within the ministry; but the leading figure in the new government was an even more determined advocate of war. Dumouriez was a professional soldier who, although not a noble, had risen to the rank of maréchal de camp before the Revolution, when he had also played a minor diplomatic role in the service of the anti-Austrian faction. After the outbreak of the Revolution he built up a reputation for himself as a patriot and established contacts with Brissot and the deputation from the Gironde. At the same time he maintained an indirect connexion with the king and was sending him secret memoirs through an intermediary. Intelligent, active, intriguing, and ambitious, Dumouriez saw fame and fortune in a successful war directed by himself. The Brissotins could feel that in him, unlike Narbonne, they had an ally who would play the same game as themselves. Along with Dumouriez, a group of ministers loosely connected with the Brissotins came into office, the king's advisers having now decided that the best way to disarm the opposition was to give it the responsibility of government. This was not necessarily a mistaken idea and it might have succeeded had the new ministers possessed more of the raw material of statesmanship. After Dumouriez, the most important ministers were Roland, a worthy civil servant and husband of Mme Roland, and the Genevan financier Clavière, of whom Mirabeau, whom he had provided with a financial policy and most of the speeches with which to defend it, said that he had the intelligence of a man and the emotions of a child.

With Dumouriez the ideas of the anti-Austrian party at the French court, so long frustrated, were at last carried into effect. His plan was to isolate Austria by ensuring the neutrality of the other powers, for which purpose the young marquis de Chauvelin, with Talleyrand to advise him, was sent to the court of St James, and the comte de Custine, who had fought with distinction in the American War, to Berlin.

The emperor was summoned to reduce his armaments, which were said to be threatening France. When this demand was rejected, Dumouriez persuaded his colleagues to propose a declaration of war. Louis XVI and Marie-Antoinette, seeing their salvation in the chance of French defeat, accepted the proposal, and on 20 April 1792 the king presented it to the Legislative Assembly. The only member who dared to speak against it was shouted down. In a transport of acclamation from Assembly and galleries the declaration of war was carried with only seven opposing votes.

Nothing was ready for the war on which France had so light-heartedly launched. The Legislative Assembly had not even made the preparations for which Narbonne had asked while he was minister. The army was in a deplorable condition. Out of some 9,000 officers about 6,000 had abandoned their commands. Whole regiments had disintegrated. Arms and all other provisions of war were lacking. Battalions of volunteers, the famous 'blues', so-called from the colour of their uniforms as contrasted with the white coats of the old royal army, had been raised by the Constituent Assembly, but though full of enthusiasm they fell short of what had been hoped for in numbers. With this inadequate and ill-supplied army it was proposed to wage war on Europe; but the Brissotin faction was counting on a general rising of the neighbouring populations in their favour and Dumouriez shared this expectation. Since, to enable such risings to take place, the presence of French armies was necessary, a general offensive was planned. La Fayette, in command of the French forces, starting from Metz was to move to Givet, that salient of French territory pointing like a spearhead at Liège, where, as in the Austrian Netherlands, there had already taken place a democratic revolution which the Austrians had repressed by force. From Liège, Brussels would be within short marching distance. It all sounded simple in Paris, so simple that the date for the offensive was advanced at the last minute. La Fayette was given a mere six days to move his army to Givet, an adequate time if logistics were entirely ignored.

The first encounter with the enemy proved how mistaken were these facile calculations. A small body of 3,000 men, which crossed the frontier in the direction of Tournai, was halted by a few cannon shot and the order was given to withdraw. Panic seized the French and they fled in disorder back to Lille, where they massacred their general and some Austrian prisoners they had taken. Similar episodes occurred elsewhere, and the offensive had to be abandoned almost as soon as it had begun. France lay open to the enemy and was only saved by the scholarly and traditional generalship of the aged Duke of Brunswick, who was not prepared to advance until all conceivable preparations had been made and all precautions taken.

The hopes of Brissot and his friends had proved false at the outset. Instead of reaping the fruits of an easy victory they found themselves saddled with the responsibility for military disaster. Nor was this their only concern. Economic difficulties, endemic throughout the revolution, were becoming more acute, partly indeed as a result of the strain imposed on France by the war. The assignat fell to 47 per cent of its face value in March 1792. Although the harvest of 1791 had been fair the food crisis reappeared, for the peasants were unwilling to sell their produce for a rapidly depreciating paper currency. Grain riots once again became widespread. In consequence of a negro revolt in St Domingo, in August 1791, the supply of sugar was cut off from France. In January 1792 shops with stocks of sugar were sacked in Paris and the populace helped itself to other foodstuffs as well. The Assembly, tied to progressive economic as well as political ideas, did not contemplate abandoning the principle of internal free trade and made no attempt to remedy the shortage of grain. For the Brissotins there were two possible courses of action: to join with the moderates in repressing disorder, or to throw in their lot with the more advanced revolutionaries. The dilemma was to haunt them until it finally brought them to the guillotine, for they could make up their minds to follow neither course of action consistently. For the time being they fell back on their well-tried tactic of denouncing the treachery of the court and aristocratic plots. That there were such plots and that the court was hoping for defeat is true, but they were not the cause either of the actual defeat or of the economic distress. This did not deter Brissot, who had confessed earlier, 'We have need of some great treachery'. The secret manoeuvres of Marie-Antoinette and the court were not so secret but that suspicions of them had been aroused. Backed by these, the theme of an 'Austrian committee', planning an invasion of France to restore absolute monarchy, was put into circulation and successfully exploited.

For once Paris was not the chief centre of disturbance. The outbreak of war had stimulated counter-revolutionary movements all over France and particularly in the south, against which the revolutionaries reacted with vigour. The Jacobins of Marseille, having won their victory in the great port, sent out flying columns to Aix, where they disarmed a regiment of Swiss, to Arles where they forced the royal troops to evacuate the town, and, under the leadership of the famous Jourdan Coupe-Tête, to suppress the counter-revolutionary movement at Avignon. The same kind of spontaneous revolutionary action was taken elsewhere, not without an occasional massacre, and the Brissotins conceived the idea of calling on the militant revolutionaries of the provinces to swing the balance in their favour at Paris. Contingents of National Guards were summoned to the capital to defend the Revolution. In this way, with that genius for political miscalculation which seemed natural to them, the Brissotins called into existence the very force that was to prove fatal to themselves.

The war having proved thus far such an unhappy speculation, they could find no better way of diverting public indignation from their own failure than to continue to stir up popular feeling against the monarchy. Their ally, Roland, the ineffective Minister of the Interior, on 10 July addressed a letter, drawn up in fact by Mme Roland, to the king, indicting him for his veto on the decrees penalizing refractory priests and creating the camp of provincial National Guards at Paris. The letter was written in terms of a severe and priggish reprimand. 'I know,' wrote Mme Roland, 'that the austere language of truth is rarely welcomed near the throne.' It conveyed a barely veiled threat of revolutionary measures. Even Louis XVI could not swallow this from his own government. He dismissed Roland and his two chief supporters in the ministry and replaced them with obscure Feuillants.

All that the Brissotins and Roland had succeeded in doing was to pour oil on the flames of popular unrest, already growing dangerously fierce. The leadership and organization of the revolution of 1792 are rather better known than those of the similar movement in 1789, but much still remains obscure. Marat, in the *Ami du peuple*, was waging a campaign of general denunciation, in which he did not spare Brissot, who, he wrote, 'apprenticed to chicanery, became a would-be wit, a scandal-sheet writer, an apprentice-philosopher, a fraudulent speculator, a crook, a prince's valet, a government clerk, police spy, publicist, municipal inquisitor, legislative senator, faithless representative of the people, abettor of the ministerial faction and finally henchman of the despot'. Hébert, in the *Père Duchesne*, poured out similar denunciations, larded with obscenity in a would-be popular tone, and other revolutionary sheets joined in the outcry. With the raw material of distress among the people to work on, a rising was prepared in clubs and secret committees by agitators drawn from varied ranks of society. Such were Santerre, the brewer of the faubourg St Antoine, and the butcher Legendre, both well-to-do tradesmen; the marquis de Saint-Huruge, a de-classed noble adventurer; Alexandre, a former *agent de change*, now commander of a company of National Guard gunners; Rossignol, a jeweller's workman; and Fournier, son of a respectable bourgeois family, who was called 'the American' because he had been in America at the time of the American Revolution. The considerable number of foreign agitators on the fringe of politics included Lazowski, a Pole and former prosperous Inspector of Manufactures whose post had been suppressed early in the Revolution, and Rotundo, an Italian teacher of languages and a crook. Whether more substantial political figures can be detected in the shade behind these agitators of the streets, or whether it was purely a group of such men who prepared the manifestations of 20 June, remains uncertain. On that day, in the face of rather feeble opposition from the municipal authorities, an armed procession was formed which demanded admission to the Assembly. For an hour National Guards, women, citizens with *bonnets rouges* and pikes, singing the revolutionary song, *Ça ira*, one with a calf's heart on the end of a stick and the inscription 'Aristocrat's heart', filed through the hall. The mob then moved to the Tuileries, penetrated into the palace, and even reached the royal apartments. For two hours they flowed round the king shouting and demonstrating, sticking a red cap on his head and giving him a glass of wine to drink with them. He put up with it all with great courage. His demeanour, and perhaps an element of good temper in the crowd, prevented any bloodshed. As evening fell the demonstrators melted away. Whatever had been intended by the demonstration, it had failed.

Despite this warning, Brissot and his friends continued to play with fire. Their object was to use the threat of mob violence to intimidate the king into restoring Roland and the other Brissotin ministers to office. On 3 July Vergniaud delivered a speech which was a general indictment of Louis XVI, in whose name, he said, foreign armies were descending on France. Yet shortly after, Vergniaud himself was one of the authors of a secret letter to the king, calling on him to restore the patriot ministers to office and promising to save him if he did so.

The general unrest was not diminished by the issue, on 25 July, of a Manifesto by the Duke of Brunswick threatening Paris with military execution and total subversion if there were the least violence offered to the royal family. On 8 July the National Guards summoned from the provinces, the famous *fédérés*, began to arrive in Paris. Though 25,000 had been called for, only 4,500 came, and some of these were subsequently diverted to a camp at Soissons; but what they lacked in numbers they made up in revolutionary ardour. The Brissotins soon discovered their miscalculation, for the *fédérés* were seized on and indoctrinated by the more advanced revolutionaries of Paris. Even more ominous was the fact that Robespierre, who had regained his influence in the Jacobin Club and whose reputation was higher than before, since events had justified his opposition to the Brissotins earlier in the year, now abandoned his defence of the Constitution and advocacy of legal methods.

The situation in Paris was all the more alarming because of the equivocal attitude of the municipal authorities. As was the case elsewhere, a cleavage had developed between the conservative departmental council and the more revolutionary Commune. Bailly resigned his office as Mayor of Paris in November 1791, and in a contest between La Fayette and Pétion, a lawyer from Chartres who had made a name for himself in the Constituent Assembly as an advocate of the popular cause, the latter was elected. It is noteworthy that only 10,300 voted in the election and that the court, to vent its spite on La Fayette, supported his more radical opponent. Pétion's partisans called him Aristides and Mme Roland said that he was incapable of the slightest evil action. He was to render the insurrectionaries an essential service by sanctioning the distribution from the arsenal of up to 50,000 arms, lacking which the popular rising could hardly have succeeded. Full of good intentions, his strongest passion vanity, he was a weak man, a fitting fellow-traveller of the Brissotins and, like them, quite unequal to the task of controlling the popular movement they both played their part in provoking. Lower in the ranks of the municipal hierarchy was a more formidable figure, the Deputy Procureur Danton. The Commune included advanced revolutionaries among its members and by opening its galleries to the public in March 1792 it was exposed, like the Assembly and the Jacobin Club, to the direct pressure of popular passions. Below the Commune there were the Sections, the meetings of the local constituency divisions of Paris, which on 25 July were declared permanent. Meeting at any hour, and if necessary without break, they provided forty-eight centres from which the leaders of insurrection could conduct their campaign.

The Brissotins were still not clear whether they were for or against the revolt that was evidently brewing in Paris, and perhaps did not even know whether it was for or against them. By a decree of the Legislative Assembly, pikes were distributed to all citizens and the ranks of the National Guard were opened to members lacking the tax-paying qualification for active citizenship. In a speech to the Jacobin Club on 29 July Robespierre, who had slowly been aligning himself with the revolutionary movement and establishing contact behind the scenes with its leaders, gave it a more specific programme than it had hitherto possessed. He called for a complete renewal of political personnel by the election of a National Convention based on universal suffrage. Thus the agitation now had the support of one of the unquestioned leading figures in revolutionary politics and the Brissotins had been by-passed by the movement they had started, to the advantage of Brissot's most bitter personal enemy. Robespierre was well on the way to revenge for his defeat in the debates at the beginning of the year. There are signs in their journals that the Brissotins were now trying to hold back the revolt they had done so much to provoke, but it was too late.

Political excitement continued to increase until, on the night of 9 August, the Section of the faubourg St Antoine, where lived the master craftsmen, who, followed by their journeymen, had won a reputation as the stalwarts of revolutionary action, summoned three representatives from each Section to the Hôtel de Ville. There they set up a revolutionary Commune side by side with the legal one. The night was a hot one, doors were open, many of the populace in the streets, crowds gathering here and there and excitement mounting. Towards eight o'clock in the morning a column left the faubourg St Antoine under the command of Santerre. Among the *fédérés*, the Bretons and Marseillais had already begun to march on the Tuileries. The king, who had decided to review the National Guard on duty before the palace, was greeted with cries of 'Vive la Nation' and hostile demonstrations. Finally, seeing the peril of their situation, the royal family fled for protection to the Legislative Assembly. The Marseillais and Bretons, who had now reached the Tuileries, penetrated into its forecourt and fraternization with the Swiss commenced. Suddenly firing broke out from the windows, at whose order and whether by the Swiss or the gentlemen of the king's guard is not clear. Some seven Marseillais were killed and the firing became general on both sides. Now arrived the column from the faubourg St Antoine, bringing cannon with which they drove the defenders to take cover within the palace. The king sent orders to the Swiss to cease fire and retire to their barracks, after which their resistance disintegrated and the fighting turned into a massacre. Altogether the attackers lost 373, while some 800 nobles and Swiss were killed in the fighting or massacred subsequently. If, as Karl Marx says, each historical event is enacted twice, the first time as tragedy and the second time as farce, the tenth of August followed the pattern of the attack on the Bastille with extraordinary fidelity, but it was far from being a farce. It was a new revolution in its own right; but just as the fall of the Bastille had to wait until the October Days for its logical conclusion to be drawn, so the tenth of August remained for a time an unfinished revolution.

The Legislative Assembly had now lost the initiative. It could only register the results of the struggle at the Tuileries. It suspended Louis XVI from his functions, but it was as much the victim of the new revolution as he was. The Brissotins tried to save what they could from the wreck of their policy. The monarchical constitution clearly being dead, they summoned a National Convention, to be elected by universal suffrage, for the purpose of framing a new constitution. Roland and his friends returned to office in a provisional executive council, but they had to offer a pledge to the victorious insurrection in the form of the appointment of

Danton to the Ministry of Justice. He, as well as Marat and Robespierre, had kept in the background during the fighting of the tenth of August, but they were the real victors, though months of political struggle were to follow before their victory was consolidated.

4. THE FAILURE OF THE BRISSOTINS

THE revolution of the tenth of August succeeded in destroying the authority of the Legislative Assembly and overthrowing the monarchical constitution, but it solved none of the problems which had brought about their collapse. Indeed, by intensifying internal cleavages it made the military situation of France more desperate. The revolutionaries were saved in the event less by their own efforts than by the slowness of Brunswick's preparations and the weakness of the forces which Austria and Prussia, counting on a general disintegration of the French army and a counter-revolution inside France, had committed to the campaign. The invasion was in effect a side-show for them: their real concern was with Russia and developments in Poland. Brunswick commanded an army of 42,000 Prussians, 29,000 Austrians, and 6,000 Hessians, a force which in normal circumstances would have been regarded as inadequate for a serious invasion of France. After months of delay, at last, on 19 July, he crossed the French frontier by the traditional route of invasion, penetrated between the two French armies of Sedan and Metz, and marched on the fortress of Longwy. Badly supplied, the Prussians pillaged the countryside and met with a hostility that should hardly have been unexpected. Slowly moving forward, dragging with them an immense baggage train, they reached Longwy on 20 August. Under a comparatively slight bombardment the inhabitants cried out for capitulation and the garrison was allowed to march out on condition of not serving during the remainder of the war. After staying six days at Longwy the Prussians moved on. Verdun was the next objective: it yielded, after an even slighter bombardment, on 2 September. The invasion seemed to be turning into a military promenade.

In Paris, the Legislative Assembly was dying daily as more and more deputies drifted back to their homes in the provinces. Political excitement had not ended with the attack on the Tuileries. The general opinion of the revolutionaries, and perhaps of most of the population of Paris, was that the tenth of August had saved France from an aristocratic plot, timed to coincide with the invasion. Orators and journals demanded the punishment of the guilty and the Assembly yielded to the popular demand by arresting large numbers of suspects, including many refractory priests. Riots, sporadic murders, and attacks on property were daily occurrences. The panic produced by the apparently inexorable advance of Brunswick was increased when La Fayette, having vainly tried to lead his army back to suppress the revolution in Paris, fled to the Austrians. With the fall of Longwy the road to the capital seemed open. The Legislative Assembly took no adequate measures to meet the danger, apart from deciding to raise an additional 30,000 men from the National Guard in Paris and the neighbouring departments for the defence of the country. By 20 September, 20,000 had been sent off to the frontier.

The situation of France and the general climate of opinion provided growing weather for a renewed popular panic, which has obvious similarities with the Great Fear of 1789 and the more artificially contrived *complot des prisons* later. Rumour had it that, when the Prussians were within reach of Paris, a 'fifth column' of aristocrats and priests would break out of the prisons to strike at peaceful citizens and murder the women and children of those who had marched to the frontiers to defend the *patrie*, at the same time letting loose the cut-throats and criminals of the jails to join in the massacre of patriots and the pillage of their property. When the news of the attack on Verdun reached Paris on Sunday, 2 September, the Commune issued a panic-stricken proclamation: 'To arms! The enemy is at the gates!' The tocsin was sounded and the drums of the National Guard called the citizens to the Sections. Whether the subsequent events were planned in advance, and if so by whom, will probably never be known. At two o'clock in the afternoon a convoy of suspects, being moved from the Mairie, insulted by shouts and wounded by blows on their way as was now normal, reached the Abbaye prison, where a small mob, becoming more menacing, demanded an immediate trial, lacking which it attacked the prisoners and massacred seventeen out of twenty-two. At about four o'clock another band broke into the prison of the Carmes, where there were more than two hundred priests. After some initial murders, a kind of mock tribunal was set up, which called the priests before it one by one and after a few questions turned them out to be assassinated with the simple weapons that were to hand and their bodies thrown into a well. Similar scenes took place at other prisons. At the Salpêtrière women who were branded as criminals were picked out for trial and thirty-five of them were hacked down. It may not be true that female victims were raped, or that obscene mutilations were performed on the body of the princesse de Lamballe, but the *massacreurs* were well plied with wine and there was a good deal of drunken sadism mixed with their patriotic ardour. The massacres continued sporadically from 2 September up to 7 September. As late as 10 September a party of fifty-three prisoners, sent from Orleans to be tried at Paris, was set on at Versailles by a mob, to which the escort joined themselves, and slaughtered. Although the events at Paris were the most dramatic and have attracted most attention, similar episodes occurred in the provinces on a smaller scale, which suggests that though the actual *massacreurs* were few in number they were only giving bolder and bloodier expression to a state of mind shared by many.

Of some 2,600 prisoners in Paris, it is estimated that between 1,100 and 1,400 were massacred. Among the victims were 225 priests, about 80 Swiss or members of the king's bodyguard, and between 49 and 87 other political prisoners. The remainder, between 67 and 72 per cent of the total, were ordinary common-law criminals. Throughout the period when the massacres were taking place the authorities remained in a state of almost complete passivity, at most making some weak efforts to limit the number of victims. The general public was either equally terrified of interfering with the butchery or else shared the sentiments that inspired it. Only the fear of a general outbreak of anarchy led the authorities belatedly to pluck up their courage. On 6 September the Commune of Paris issued a proclamation calling for a cessation of the massacres. The Brissotins, who had remained helpless spectators while the bloody harvest they had sown was being reaped, now began to repudiate their responsibility and represent the massacres as a manoeuvre to eliminate themselves. In this they were not entirely without justification, for on either 1 or 2 September Robespierre had denounced them to the Commune as accomplices of Brunswick. They could also regard the massacres as an attempt to influence the elections to the Convention which were proceeding concurrently.

Though the atmosphere of September 1792 was not that best calculated for the free expression of the will of the people, the Convention is commonly taken as the embodiment of revolutionary democracy. The accuracy of this interpretation depends, of course, on what one means by democracy. There were few voters. Many were excluded by law or force; fear or indifference kept others away from the electoral assemblies; the rural population had largely ceased, if indeed it had ever begun, to play an active part in politics. Altogether perhaps one-tenth of the primary electors went to the polls, and of those they chose to represent them at the secondary elections a quarter abstained. The Convention thus represented an effective vote of some 7.5 per cent of the whole electorate, and the votes even of these were not always freely cast. At Paris the Electoral Assembly transferred itself, on the proposal of Robespierre, who was himself the first to be elected, to the hall of the Jacobin Club, where the votes were given orally, in the presence of a tumultuous public. Marat, more closely identified than any other leading personage with the September massacres, was also elected. Brissot did not obtain a single vote in Paris. Elsewhere it was very different. In the provinces the Brissotins were all re-elected, along with a mass of provincial deputies who had no particular affiliations. If the revolution of the tenth of August had been intended to remove them from the political scene, it had failed. Brissot and his friends were to be given a second chance, and in much more favourable conditions, for when the Convention met the wave of terror was receding and the events of 2 September were to provide the justification for a counter-attack on Robespierre, Marat, and their supporters.

The general lightening of the political atmosphere was due to more than a sentimental reaction against the deeds of the terrorists. As the panic aroused by the Prussian advance had created the terrorist outburst, so a dramatic change in the situation on the frontiers was to eliminate, at least temporarily, the chief grounds for panic and with them the Terror. After the flight of La Fayette, the command of the armies on the north-east frontier had been given to Dumouriez. Still clinging to his plan for an invasion of the Austrian Netherlands, he began to take up his position on the Belgian frontier; but in face of Brunswick's advance he had to abandon this. He moved south and concentrated the French forces, calling up Kellerman to join him, in the hills behind the Argonne, taking the risk of practically denuding the northern frontier for this purpose. On 7 September Brunswick reached the Argonne, and following his customary policy of manoeuvring the enemy out of position, began to move round Dumouriez, expecting him to retreat, as on orthodox principles he should have done. Kellerman and the other French generals were all convinced of the necessity for withdrawal, but Dumouriez now had his hour of greatness. He drew his forces closer together on the semicircle of hills surrounding the little village of Valmy and there awaited the attack of Brunswick's army, which had moved in an arc round the French position and stood between it and Paris.

On the foggy morning of 20 September Brunswick's forces came unexpectedly under fire from Kellerman's guns. The value of Gribeauval's reform of the artillery and of Lavoisier's powder was now to be proved. Moreover, apart from two battalions of volunteers, the French consisted entirely of regiments of the line of the old army, with many men and officers who had fought in the American War, whereas the Prussian army, which had not fought a serious campaign since the time of Frederick the Great, had never been under fire. After a few local panics, the French troops held firm before the counter-cannonade of the Prussians. Firing went on till nightfall and neither army budged. Brunswick was now in a difficult position. While the Prussians cut the French army off from Paris, it stood between them and the supply base at Verdun, on which they depended for their foodstuffs. The weather throughout the campaign had been frightful, torrential storms made Brunswick's circuitous communications even more difficult, and dysentery was ravaging his troops. Though only a few hundred men had fallen on either side, he really had little choice but to withdraw. As he did so, Dumouriez might have launched an attack with considerable chance of destroying the Prussian army; but for him Austria was always the enemy and he still had his eyes fixed on Belgium. Brunswick was therefore allowed to retreat to the frontier unmolested while Dumouriez moved his armies to the North, to resume his plan for an attack on the Austrian Netherlands.

In Paris the victor of Valmy was the hero of the hour. Roland had not forgiven the general, who had been responsible for his dismissal earlier in the year, but Dumouriez had the support of Danton, now the strong man of the government. One of the most controversial figures in the history of the Revolution, Danton, son of a solicitor of Arcis in Champagne, was a mass of contradictions. Of good education and culture, able to purchase for 78,000 livres, mostly of borrowed money it is true, the office of an *avocat* to the king's council, in 1789 Danton set himself up as a mob orator and agitator at the left-wing Cordeliers Club. He

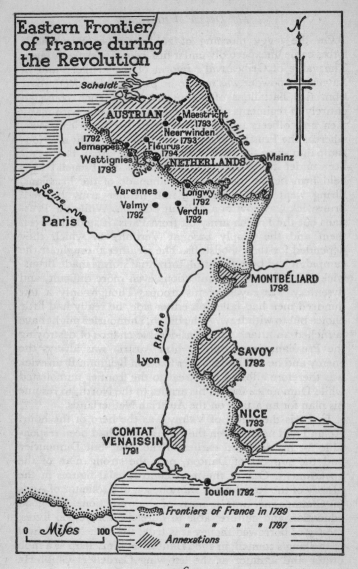

Eastern Frontier of France during the Revolution

Scheldt

N

AUSTRIAN

Maestricht
1793

Neerwinden
1793

Rhine

1792
Jemappes
Wattignies
1793

Fléurus
1794

NETHERLANDS

Give

Mainz

Seine

Varennes

Longwy
1792

Paris

Valmy
1792

Verdun
1792

MONTBÉLIARD
1793

Rhône

Lyon

SAVOY
1792

NICE
1793

COMTAT
VENAISSIN
1791

Toulon 1792

0   Miles   100

⟋⟍⟋⟍ Frontiers of France in 1789

····· "   "   "   "   1797

⫽⫽⫽⫽ Annexations

obtained, in 1791, a post under the Commune of Paris. His role in the various revolutionary *journées*, and especially the revolution of the tenth of August, was suspected, probably rightly, but he always remained sufficiently in the background to escape direct responsibility. During these years, while he was building up a reputation as a tribune of the people, Danton was living extravagantly and in spite of this managing to accumulate a considerable fortune. The evidence for his venality – he certainly obtained money from the court and possibly from other sources – is overwhelming, but what services, if any, those who paid him received in return, remains unexplained. Venality did not prevent him from acquiring the stature of a colossus among the petty intriguers and street-corner orators of the factions. He was, indeed, literally a huge man, whose inexhaustible energy and force of personality recalled the figure of Mirabeau. A great orator, Danton was one of the few revolutionaries who practically never wrote his speeches, which is the reason why, when we have so many complete speeches of his contemporaries, all that survives to remind us of the torrent of oratory that could overwhelm his opponents is a collection of fragments. The contradictions running right through Danton's character rob him of true greatness. He could stir up popular passions and organize revolutionary *journées*, yet, with too much magnanimity and too little hatred in him ever to be really a man of blood, he would endeavour to save the victims of the passions he had himself aroused. He attracted a group of corrupt adventurers round him, but it is almost impossible to doubt the sincerity of his patriotic invocations. He probably took bribes to betray the Revolution and his country, yet there is no evidence that he betrayed them. Easy-going, fond of his pleasures, lazy, the crisis of France in the autumn of 1792 stirred him to tireless activity. When Dumouriez came to Paris before the new offensive, Danton rallied the revolutionaries behind him, supported his efforts to discipline the volunteers, and obtained from Santerre, now commander of the National Guard at Paris, a part of his artillery for the campaign.

The invasion of the Netherlands is not to be interpreted as the mere result of the personal ambition of Dumouriez, nor as simply the renewal of the traditional anti-Austrian sentiments of the *ancien régime*. Equally, it was not just an expression of revolutionary ardour: there were more material interests at stake. With the aid of Belgian resources the French could hope to restore financial stability and obtain supplies for their armies. It must not be thought that the wars of loot began only with Napoleon, though it would equally be wrong to suggest that the revolutionaries thought only of the economic benefits that would come to them from liberating neighbouring territories. Patriotism reaches its height when it can combine ideal ends with material benefits. On the crest of a wave of revolutionary patriotism, therefore, in the autumn of 1792, the French armies flooded over the frontiers to north-east and south-west. Savoy and Nice were occupied in September. In October, Custine took Spires, Worms, Mainz, crossed the Rhine in pursuit of the Austrians, and occupied Frankfurt. In November, Dumouriez, with 40,000 men, routed the Austrians at Jemappes and entered Brussels in triumph, to the sound of bells ringing and through streets lined by Austrian deserters, for the most part Belgians incorporated in the Austrian army.

The Convention, carried away by these successes, proceeded to lay down the principles of revolutionary war in two decrees which had wide European repercussions. On 19 November it offered help to all peoples who wished to recover their liberty; and on 15 December decreed the abolition of feudal dues, tithes, and all corporations in occupied territories, and the establishment in them of popularly elected governments. Less idealistic aims appeared in other clauses of the same decree. All the property of the ruler and his agent or supporters, the treasury and other public offices and corporations, lay or religious, in occupied territory was to be taken under French protection; French national commissaires were to be appointed for the purpose of cooperating with the locally elected administrations on measures of common defence, of procuring clothing and supplies for the French armies, and meeting the expenses of the occupying forces. These decrees, and the speeches which accompanied them, were an open defiance to the powers of Europe and the first acts of the Convention were no more calculated to reassure them.

The Convention began its task by abolishing the monarchy. To symbolize the opening of a new era it henceforth dated its decrees from the year 1 of the Republic. With this, united action ended and open conflict began between the two small factions which the Convention had inherited from the Legislative Assembly. On one side were the Brissotins and Rolandists, to whom a number of new members joined themselves; on the other, the Jacobin deputation from Paris, which became known, from the seats it took high up at the back of the Assembly, as the Mountain. The mass of the deputies formed the Plain, or *Marais*, and were uncommitted to either faction, but their main allegiance at first naturally went to those like Brissot and the deputation from the Gironde whose names they knew, rather than to the Paris extremists whose reputation in most cases hardly extended beyond the capital.

Brissot and his friends had returned from their electoral campaign in the provinces conscious of victory and burning to avenge their defeat of August, as they rightly saw it, on those whom they regarded as the real leaders of that revolution, Robespierre, Marat, and Danton. Personalities, not policies, still dominated their tactics and determined their alliances and enmities. Danton, who after the election had given up his ministry in order to be able to take his place in the Convention, leaving Roland as the chief minister in so far as there was one, made approaches to them but was repulsed. 'I cannot associate the idea of a good man with that face,' said Mme Roland. However, the new deputies from the provinces did not yet appreciate the bitterness of the feuds that had developed in Paris. Attempts to persuade the Convention to put Robespierre and Marat on trial failed to win the support of the Plain. The Mountain transformed its position from one of defence to offence by a more subtle tactic. The Brissotin faction was faced with the nemesis of its earlier attacks on the monarchy in the form of a demand for the trial of the king. The discovery, at the Tuileries, of the secret *armoire de fer*, containing the royal correspondence with Austria, was the death-warrant of Louis XVI. After the revelation of the papers it contained, his trial could not be avoided. Robespierre saw clearly the dilemma in which the Brissotins were placed and pressed the issue remorselessly. If they opposed the trial, or voted for the innocence of the king, they could be denounced as royalists and traitors, as well as in effect tacitly repudiating and confessing the dishonesty of their earlier denunciations of Louis; if they voted for the king's death they sacrificed moderate support and were left isolated. Vergniaud and Brissot attempted to evade the fatal vote by pleading for a referendum, but Robespierre, who had often advocated a direct vote by the people when it suited his purpose, would have none of it now; the proposal was rejected. There was not a shadow of doubt in anyone's mind that Louis had been guilty of treachery, as indeed he had from the point of view of revolutionary France. In the decisive vote, 28 were absent, 321 voted for penalties other than death, 13 for death but with a respite, 26 for death but with a debate on postponement of execution, and 361 for death without qualification, an absolute majority of one. The king's trial had reduced the Brissotins and Rolandists to chaos, and proved how little they formed an organized party with a settled policy, for their votes were to be found scattered on all sides. In a subsequent debate on the proposal for a respite, which was rejected by 380 to 310, the opposition to sparing the king's life was led by Mme Roland's young paladin from the south, Barbaroux.

The fate of Louis XVI, it might be said, had been settled on the day when he signed the decree for war with Austria; by it he became the king of a nation that had reduced him to the status of a constitutional rubber stamp, the leader of a crusade against those whose only declared motive was to protect him from his own subjects and restore his power. King at the same time of the revolution and of the counter-revolution, whatever he did or did not do, the essential falsity of his position spelt doom. On 21 January 1793, Louis XVI was carried through roads lined with the National Guard and a silent populace to the Place de la Révolution, formerly Place Louis XV, and there guillotined. For the regicides there could now be no turning back.

At the moment there seemed little occasion for second thoughts. The offensive that had been launched by the victories of Dumouriez and Custine was carrying all before it and the Convention was intoxicated with success. It proclaimed the annexation of Savoy in November 1792. The Scheldt, closed except to the Dutch since the Treaty of Münster in 1648, was declared open to all shipping. In January 1793 Danton proclaimed the doctrine of natural frontiers, often, but incorrectly, attributed to Louis XIV, and thereby staked a claim to the Rhine frontier. These actions were bound to lead to an extension of the war, but the Convention did not wait for its enemies to take the initiative. The former calculation on English neutrality was now forgotten: the time had come for the Seven Years War to be avenged, as well as the more recent humiliation of 1787. Anglophobia in France was hardly less strong than hatred of the Austrians. For the purpose of maintaining English neutrality, as I have said, early in 1792 the young marquis de Chauvelin had been sent over to the court of St James as French ambassador. His first dispatches, probably dictated by Talleyrand and his Swiss adviser, du Roveray, were moderate and raised no hopes of an imminent revolution in England; but when Chauvelin was deprived of these experienced advisers and came to realize that such views only aroused suspicions at Paris of his loyalty to the Revolution, he changed his tune and produced more acceptable reports. The French Foreign Office was not relying on mere official information, however. It had sent over a small army of secret agents to spy on the English and on one another, whose reports drew a picture of a nation awaiting only the

call from France to burst the bonds of tyranny. The British
government itself was disturbed by the association of French
agents with the English Jacobins. It was not these activities,
however, but the deposition of Louis XVI, in whose name
Chauvelin's credentials ran, that led to the withdrawal of
official recognition from the ambassador, though unofficial
contact was maintained with one or two of the more respectable of the French agents. It was inevitable, when the news
of the execution of Louis XVI was received, that Chauvelin
and the French official mission should be ordered to quit
England. The breach of diplomatic relations with France
did not necessarily mean war, even though the decrees of 19
November and 15 December, and the opening of the
Scheldt were regarded as sufficiently provocative to justify
military and naval preparations.

On the French side there was also hesitation. The Brissotins, the Executive Council, with its weak but not stupid
foreign minister, the former journalist Lebrun, and even
some of the Mountain, including Robespierre, hesitated before the final step and saw the dangers, external and internal,
that a general war with all Europe would bring on the new
Republic. Such doubts, however, were reserved for their
secret thoughts and expressed in public, if at all, only with
great caution; for the revolutionary leaders were now at the
mercy of the patriotic ardour which they had been whipping
up for the past three years. Public opinion, including that of
the great majority of members of the Convention, had no
reservations or private doubts. When the comte de Kersaint, Breton noble and naval officer, and as such sharing
the traditional Anglophobia of the French navy, delivered a
resounding call for war with England on 1 January 1793, he
spoke for the Convention. Brissot, who had lived in England,
was Anglophile in his private sentiments, but here once
again we see how little the Brissotins formed a coherent
party, for Kersaint had been one of their most ardent supporters in the attack on the Mountain. Similarly, while
Brissot and some of his friends were trying to postpone war ·
with the Dutch, Dumouriez was pressing for the invasion of

the United Provinces. In the presence of general enthusiasm for war the revolutionary leaders found it easier to win popular applause by denouncing pacific tendencies as treachery to the Revolution than to attempt to moderate the bellicose ardour of their followers. Nor should the influence of the foreign revolutionary refugees, whose only hope of gaining power in their own countries lay in French assistance, be underestimated. On 1 February 1793 Brissot himself introduced the decree of the Convention declaring war against Great Britain and Holland. It was voted unanimously. In March hostilities were declared against Spain, and the French republic was soon at war with all Europe except Switzerland and Scandinavia.

France had still no effective government to conduct the war. A Committee of General Defence, including three representatives from each of the committees of the Convention, had been set up on the proposal of Brissot, but it had no executive powers and remained ineffective. The army, from which the volunteers had been flowing back home after Jemappes, was in no condition to conduct a major campaign. The Convention decreed the raising of 300,000 men but met with much opposition in its attempts to put the measure into effect. In these circumstances, the frustration of the hopes that had been raised by Jemappes rapidly followed the extension of the war. Early in March the French army besieging Maestricht was driven back in disorder, and Dumouriez, perhaps foreseeing further defeats, addressed a letter to the Convention attributing the reverse to the policy of the ministers and the tactless and tyrannical conduct of the French commissaires in Belgium. On 18 March the Austrian general, Coburg, defeated him at Neerwinden and he was compelled to evacuate Brussels. The scheme for a quick victory over Austria was in ruins.

The French general was left with the second and more secret part of his plan to attempt: this was to march his army on Paris and restore the Constitution of 1791 with the young Louis XVII as king. After a secret meeting with the Austrian general Mack, in which they reached an understanding, he was allowed to withdraw the French armies to the frontier unmolested. Representatives of the Convention, where suspicions of Dumouriez' intentions were growing, were sent to summon him to the bar of the house. They were arrested on his orders and handed over to the Austrians; but his efforts to persuade the army to march on Paris failed and on 5 April he too passed over, with most of his general staff, like La Fayette before him, to the Austrians.

Meanwhile, farther south, Custine had been driven back and forced to give up the left bank of the Rhine. Within France the first of the provincial revolts against the Revolution broke out when, in March, the Vendée rose in arms against the attempt to enforce conscription for the army. The accumulation of disasters renewed the panic mentality that had been responsible for the events of August and September 1792, and as on former occasions, popular unrest was fed by economic distress. The expense of the war intensified the torrent of inflation – at the moment when war was declared on Great Britain and Holland 800 million of new assignats had to be voted by the Convention to meet its initial cost – and inflation meant a new food crisis. Leaders were now beginning to appear in the streets of Paris who differed from earlier popular agitators in that their primary demand was for the remedying of the economic distresses of the populace and for economic and not political measures to bring this about. One of the most prominent of these was Jacques Roux, accused in 1790 of instigating a peasant rising, who had been elected as one of the constitutional clergy in Paris and had acquired influence through his violent speeches at the Cordeliers Club. Another of the *enragés*, as they were called, was a prosperous postal official named Varlet, who became a successful mob orator though he failed to obtain a hearing from the Convention or the Jacobins. How far these were men of violent temperament, anti-parliamentary by nature, who were prepared to exploit the sufferings of the people to build up a following for themselves and climb into power by way of rioting in the streets, and how far they genuinely believed in the economic views which they put forward and which differentiated them from the rest of the revolutionaries, whether advanced or moderate, it is difficult to say. To the members of the Convention, the *enragés*, because they advocated a revival of the economic controls of the *ancien régime*, seemed crypto-counter-revolutionaries; but whereas the Brissotins and the ministers offered nothing but open hostility to them, the Jacobin Mountain, with greater political realism, was prepared to use them against its political opponents so long as it seemed possible to do so.

In February 1793 food riots, led by Jacques Roux, failed to achieve anything. Another popular movement, in March, in which the *enragés* probably had secret support from the Mountain, was checked only after the destruction of Brissotin printing-presses. The treachery of Dumouriez, combined with military defeat, led to a revival of fears of foreign invasion and counter-revolution, and gave an increased impetus to unrest; but the Convention, which remained preoccupied with the faction fight between Brissotins and the Mountain, could only agree on increasing the severity of the repressive legislation against counter-revolutionaries. The punitive laws against refractory priests and émigrés were intensified; a Revolutionary Tribunal was set up to judge traitors; representatives on mission were sent out to strengthen the revolution in the provinces; a decree condemned to summary execution all rebels taken in the act. The numbers who were to perish by this last law are uncalculated and probably incalculable, but they were to exceed by far the victims of the Revolutionary Tribunal. On 21 March watch committees were set up in every commune: they were to become one of the principal instruments of the Terror. On 6 April, at the proposal of the Brissotin Isnard, a Committee of Public Safety was formed, entrusted with the duty of supervising the Executive Council and elected for a month at a time. The most important new feature was that it was given 100,000 livres for the payment of its agents and another 100,000 for secret expenses.

Most of the machinery of the revolutionary government

and the Terror was thus created in the spring of 1793, and it was the work of a Convention in which the Brissotins still retained considerable influence. This was evidently suffering, however, from the inadequacy of their efforts to cope with the national crisis. A change was needed not in machinery but in personnel. In the election of the first Committee of Public Safety the Convention marked its dislike of the faction fight that Brissotins and the Robespierrist Mountain continued to wage, by the choice of middle-men, like Danton and Barère, uncommitted to either faction. Danton was to devote the next two months to an attempt to mediate between the hostile factions, relying on the votes of the Plain. The Mountain, for its part, wanted no mediation and was prepared to repeat its tactics of the previous year, though the situation was now not so simple as it had been then. In August 1792 the aim had been to secure the dissolution of the Legislative Assembly; now they wanted to purge the Convention of their chief enemies, without destroying it, and with it themselves, altogether. Whether the Mountain, behind the scenes, organized a new popular movement at the end of May 1793, or whether it was the work of the lesser men of the Commune of Paris and the Sections, unwittingly playing the game of the Mountain, again cannot be said. Whatever its inspiration, on 28 May an insurrectionary committee drawn from the Sections was set up at the Archbishop's Palace. As in August 1792, a revolutionary commune was constituted and Hanriot, a former customs official and a swaggering braggadocio, usurped command of the National Guard.

On 2 June a huge mob, including many National Guard with their cannon, concentrated round the Tuileries where the Convention sat, and demanded the arrest of the factious members. This meant specifically the leading Brissotins, the two ministers associated with them, Lebrun and Clavière, and the members of a Commission of Twelve which had been formed to repress the Commune. However spontaneous the action of the mob may have been, it is hardly likely that this list of chief enemies of the Mountain could have been drawn up without inspiration from above. Among those attacked, only the Breton lawyer, Lanjuinais, a constitutional monarchist, with the Mountain shouting him down and crying for the deputation from the mob to be admitted, dared to denounce the illegal authority which had surrounded the Convention with armed men and cannon and was offering it a petition which he boldly described as, 'dragged through the mud of the streets of Paris'. When the butcher Legendre called to him, 'Come down or I'll fell you', it is said that Lanjuinais replied, 'First of all decree that I am an ox.' On the other hand, a number of the Brissotins weakly offered to resign their legislative functions. Only the young Marseillais, Barbaroux, the Antinoüs of Mme Roland, joined Lanjuinais in defying the armed hordes outside and their advocates within the Chamber. While the debate proceeded in the Convention, Hanriot and his forces ranged remorseless without and cut off all avenues of escape. It was finally Couthon, the devoted follower of Robespierre, which is not without significance, who demanded to be carried, for he was partly paralysed, to the tribune and there proposed that the Convention accept the demands of Hanriot and his forces and decree the arrests they were demanding. There was no roll call, but Hérault de Séchelles, who had taken over the presidential chair, declared the decree carried.

In the following days many deputies signed protests, which were later to be used to justify more arrests and to build up the legend of a great and menacing Girondin Party; but the more timid, in considerable numbers, left Paris, and the Jacobins of the Mountain, with the mob behind them, secured control of the Convention. Their situation was potentially dangerous; they had to prevent the popular movement which had given them control of the rump Convention from getting out of hand and overthrowing it. The solution was a simple one: they voted the demonstrators a payment of 40 sous a day in compensation for their lost days of labour and in return secured the dissolution of the insurrectional committee. To prove their impeccable principles, the Mountain presented the Convention with a democratic Constitution, drawn up by a committee of Jacobins, which was rapidly passed into law and as rapidly consigned to a cedar chest, to be kept moth-proof, inviolable, and inoperative until the end of the war.

As a result of the uprising of June, the political situation had been drastically changed. One side in the faction fight having been decisively defeated, there was no scope left for mediators in the Convention. Some of the middle-men, like Barère, rapidly aligned themselves with the victorious Mountain. Danton and his group, who had dominated the Committee of Public Safety for its first three months, now lost their places on it. When the Committee was re-elected in July it included Hérault de Séchelles, Jeanbon Saint-André, Saint-Just, Couthon, and Prieur of the Marne, from the Mountain, along with Barère and Robert Lindet, from the Plain, who had joined them. Robespierre entered the Committee in July, in August Carnot and Prieur of the Côte d'Or, and in September Billaud-Varenne and Collot d'Herbois. Apart from Hérault, who was rapidly eliminated, this completed the great Committee of Public Safety, which was to hold power for the most critical year of the Revolution from July 1793 to July 1794.

5. THE COMMITTEE OF PUBLIC SAFETY

WITH the new Committee of Public Safety, revolutionary France for the first time had an effective executive government and an Assembly from which the opposition had been eliminated. For the next twelve months the Convention was to be the faithful echo of the powerful Committee and the ministers its mere agents, poor creatures, the American ambassador described them, hardly daring to blow their own noses without permission. Such a concentration of power was unprecedented, but it would have been of little avail if it had not been in the hands of a group of men who were equal to the opportunity they had created. The great

Committee of Public Safety embodied the results of a ruthless struggle for survival of the fittest in the internecine warfare of revolutionary politics. The result was a government of perhaps the ablest and most determined men who have ever held power in France. The desperate situation of the country forced unity on them. Though there was to some extent a division of labour, the attempt of historians to discriminate among the members of the Committee between the 'politicians' who conducted the Terror and the 'administrators' who reorganized the army and the government and saved France has not survived the test of more detailed research: the glory and the terror were bound up together and the members of the Committee stand out too clearly as individuals in the round to be reduced to pasteboard silhouettes or identified by any conventional labels. The only way of dealing with them is to take them one by one.

We can dismiss rapidly Hérault de Séchelles, a strikingly handsome young noble of the robe who, with distinguished ancestry, wealth, and ambition, had thrown in his lot with the patriot party. The role he played on the occasion of the revolution of 2 June made him temporarily a leading figure in the Convention. He presided over the fête at the Champ de Mars to celebrate the acceptance of the Constitution of 1793, and cut a fine figure as he presented the chalice of lustral water that poured from the breasts of the Statue of Liberty on the altar to the deputies as they filed up one by one. Insouciant, gay, with aristocratic connexions and a mistress whose husband served in the army of the king of Sardinia, he was out of place among the hard, uncompromising men of the Mountain; he naturally lost his position on the Committee and in due course his head.

The remaining members were made of very different metal. Billaud-Varenne and Collot d'Herbois stand apart from the others. These were the real men of blood. Collot had been a not very successful actor and dramatist, whose histrionic talent served him well with a popular audience. He was the one member of the Committee who was a mob

orator and may have owed his position to the Committee's
need to keep in touch with the subaltern agitators of the
streets on whom their power in the last resort depended.
Billaud-Varenne, though commonly linked with Collot as a
mere terrorist, was an abler and more interesting figure than
is usually recognized. Son of a lawyer of La Rochelle, he
became a teacher in one of the schools of the Oratory,
where a colleague was Fouché, and like him entered revolutionary politics. He built up connexions with the Commune
and the Sections of Paris and supported in the Convention
the movement of 2 June. By no means a mere vulgar
agitator, he had produced books and pamphlets which
indicate serious thought on the problems of government
and was perhaps to be responsible for the great law of
Frimaire reorganizing local government in November 1793.

The two Prieurs are the members of the Committee whose
personalities emerge least from the pages of history. Prieur
of the Marne, a lawyer from Châlons-sur-Marne, spent
much of his year of office on mission to the armies and the
departments. The other Prieur, of the Côte d'Or, an engineer officer when the Revolution broke out, was a friend of
Carnot and played a useful part in the organization of the
supply of munitions of war. Lazare Carnot had before the
Revolution been a captain in the engineer corps. His failure
to prove noble descent, despite persevering efforts, robbed
him of both marriage with the girl he loved and further ad-
vancement in the army. He was to be the organizer of
victory. Almost equally important for the salvation of the
Republic, though history has neglected him, was Robert
Lindet, with special responsibility for food supplies. Forty
years later, in Balzac's *Les employés*, the old concierge at the
ministry compares the modern 'paper-scratchers' with the
hard-working officials he knew when he was young. But
that, he adds, was under Robert Lindet. Jeanbon Saint-
André, a Protestant from Montauban who after a career in
the merchant navy became a pastor, was to spend much of
his year in the Committee of Public Safety organizing the
navy at Brest. Barère de Vieuzac owned a small fief and

held legal office at Tarbes in the Pyrenees. Prosperous, eloquent, with ingratiating manners and literary tastes, he combined social and professional success. Elected to the Constituent Assembly in 1789, he reported its debates in the *Point du Jour*, moved steadily to the left with the current of revolutionary opinion, gained influence in the Convention as a facile orator and was to be the regular reporter to it of the views of the Committee of Public Safety, ornamenting its measures of proscription with flowers of rhetoric, 'Burke's Anacreon of the guillotine'. Couthon, the little, lame lawyer from Auvergne, gentle and idealistic, was devoted to Robespierre, whom he was to follow to the bitter end. On mission at Lyon, he moderated the violence of his colleagues; but, not a man of blood himself, he could make bloodthirsty speeches, and his reputation has lived by what he said rather than what he did. The other close associate of Robespierre was a very different figure, Saint-Just, a terrifying young man, only twenty-one when the Revolution broke out. 'His arrogance surpasses all bounds,' protested Carnot, and Camille Desmoulins. 'He carries his head like the Holy Sacrament.' The political essays and draft constitution he wrote during the Revolution are the ground plan of a Spartan republic. On mission to the armies he showed that he was a man of action. Pity and moderation were not in his vocabulary.

With such ruthless and able men as his colleagues, to treat the Committee of Public Safety as the dictatorship of Robespierre is patently absurd. Yet there is a sense in which the little lawyer from Arras was the one man who was essential. Precise and even elegant in dress, prim in manner, living decently and dying poor, an eminently respectable figure but capable of winning love as well as admiration, the part he played in the Revolution has been reduced to nonsense and himself to a meaningless horror by the systematic blackening of his reputation after Thermidor. Robespierre's rise to a position of pre-eminence among revolutionary politicians has been made inexplicable by the biased reporting which concealed his effectiveness as a speaker in the

Constituent Assembly. Though he spoke always as if he were
the voice of the people, he was no mere demagogue: he held
out almost single-handed against the war fever in the spring of
1792 and later was to face and defeat *enragés* and Hébertists.
'I have seen him,' wrote a fellow member of the Constituent
Assembly, 'resist the entire assembly and demand, as a man
aware of his own dignity, that the President should call it to
order.' His 'sea-green' incorruptibility may not be an attractive virtue, but it was not too common a quality and not
confined to mere freedom from pecuniary temptations.
Robespierre, it was truly observed, was a dangerous man
because he believed everything he said. He was compared to
the leader of a sect. He sought out the faithless like an inquisitor. He was a political Calvinist to whom principles
were everything and men nothing. It would be too much to
expect that as well as being virtuous he should also be
likeable; yet no man in the history of the Revolution had
more devoted friends and followers. He can be admired or
hated, excused or condemned, he should not be belittled.
When David, in 1832, went to see the aged Barère, on his
bed of sickness, to speak to him of a plan for portraying the
great men of the Revolution, the old revolutionary sat up
and with a commanding gesture declared, 'Do not forget
Robespierre! He was a man of pure integrity, a true
republican.'

The Committee of Public Safety had an apparently desperate task before it. Not only was France at war with most
of Europe, but Paris was at war with most of France, and for
this widespread civil war it is only fair to say that the Committee was itself in large measure responsible. The Mountain, in its conflict with the Brissotins, and above all in the
methods it had used to destroy them, had sowed the seeds of
civil strife and was now to reap the harvest. Yet if we ask
what the struggle with its opponents had been about, it is
hard to give a satisfactory answer. The leaders of the Mountain are difficult to distinguish in their social and political
ideas from the Brissotins. Both factions believed in the
sacred rights of property and the principle of economic free-

dom; both had abandoned their earlier support of constitutional monarchy, the Brissotins possibly with more alacrity than their opponents; both recognized the sovereignty of the people and neither regarded the people as including a propertyless proletariat; in their attitude to the religious question the Brissotins tended to exhibit more extreme anticlerical sentiments than the Mountain; both, in speeches and in their journals, had invoked popular violence; the Brissotins had taken the initiative in attempting to proscribe their enemies in the Convention. The difference between the two factions is to be looked for chiefly in their attitude to the problem of the turbulent populace of Paris and the agitators who could exploit its fears and passions. Two things were guaranteed to arouse these: military defeat and the economic pressure of high prices and shortage of supplies. In the spring and summer of 1792, and again in the spring of 1793, the Brissotins found themselves responsible for disaster to the armies. In economic matters they were too wedded to the principles of free trade to be able to take any steps to alleviate popular distress. The Mountain was free from governmental responsibility for the former and was prepared to compromise with its principles in dealing with the latter. A further source of strength to the Mountain was the contacts it had established with the leaders of the Paris mob. The Jacobins did not hesitate to call in the Sections and Commune of Paris to redress the balance in the Convention; but by accepting, even on grounds of expediency, the demands of the revolutionary Commune and aligning themselves with the mob, they were purchasing the support of Paris at the price of a break with the more conservative provinces. The Brissotins, by the operation of the same causes, found themselves looking for support to the provinces against Paris. They were therefore again put in a position to be out-manoeuvred by the Mountain and represented as federalists aiming to destroy the unity of France, and as allies of the royalists who had been attempting to raise provincial revolts since the beginning of the Revolution.

The most dangerous and long-lived of these revolts was

that in the west. Measures against the Church aroused resentment in Catholic Brittany, but what ultimately provoked the outbreak of large-scale civil war in the Vendée
was the attempt to apply conscription in the spring of 1793.
By June the Vendéan rebels were masters of a wide area in
the west and besieging Nantes. In Normandy there was a
minor rising which was easily repressed. At Marseille and
Bordeaux the representatives on mission were expelled by
force. At Lyon, where the silk industry was stagnating, the
National Guard revolted, threw the mayor of the city into
prison with many of his supporters and massacred some 200
of the local Jacobins. Some of the deputies proscribed on and
after the rising of 2 June, who had fled from Paris, joined
these uprisings; but most of them either went into hiding or
were captured and perished miserably. They had neither
provoked nor were they able to profit by the outbreak of
civil war.

Externally the situation continued to deteriorate. On the
north-eastern frontier foreign invasion again threatened
with the fall of Valenciennes. The port of Toulon revolted
and was handed over by the royalists to the English. The
factions in Paris were brought vividly to a sense of their
peril when Charlotte Corday stabbed Marat to death on 13
July 1793. His body with its wound was exhibited to the
public next day; and the same night, after a procession by
the light of torches, with muffled drums and firing of cannon,
was interred in the garden of the Cordeliers. No more fatal
event than Marat's murder could have occurred for the
moderates or for any who could be suspected of moderatism.
The imprisonment of all suspects was decreed and the
revolutionary committees in the communes of France became in effect the masters of life and death. Representatives
sent out on mission from the Convention, to enforce a *levée en
masse* of all unmarried men between eighteen and twenty-
five, repressed opposition, sometimes with moderation,
sometimes, as Carrier at Nantes, with massacre and bloodthirsty sadism. In Paris the Revolutionary Tribunal, which
had operated slowly hitherto, speeded up its production

under the impulsion of the public prosecutor, that devoted public servant Fouquier-Tinville. The guillotine cut a swathe through the ranks of counter-revolutionaries and revolutionaries alike. Marie-Antoinette, after a trial in which all the indecent slanders of her enemies of the old court were dragged up to discredit her, was executed in October, a tragic figure, sketched on her last journey, all her beauty gone, by the bitter pen of David. Brissot, Vergniaud, and twenty-nine of those arrested with them, their mouths silenced at their trial by a decree of the Convention, died, sacrificial victims on the altar of the republic they had striven to achieve. Roland, Condorcet, Clavière, Pétion, evaded execution by suicide. The Duke of Orleans, unworthy Philippe-Égalité, mounted the steps of the guillotine instead of the throne and died with more dignity than he had lived. Mme du Barry perished shrieking her head off, and Elizabeth, sister to the dead king, with religious devotion. Military leaders who had been defeated were guillotined to encourage the others. In Lavoisier was executed the former Farmer General; it was a pity that France's greatest scientist had to die at the same time. ' *Les dieux ont soif*,' cried Camille Desmoulins, and they cared little whose blood was poured out for their libation.

The victory of the Mountain and its allies of the left brought to power also those who were not satisfied with the compromise represented by the Civil Constitution of the Clergy, and enabled the anti-clericals to launch a violent campaign of dechristianization. A new republican calendar dated the year 1 from 22 September 1792 and introduced a ten-day week, which had the advantage of eliminating Sundays and substituting a rest-day every ten days for one every seven. Extremists took matters into their own hands, holding anti-religious processions in the streets and attacking churches and priests. In Notre-Dame the festival of liberty, personified by an actress suitably garbed and elevated on an artificial mountain in the choir, was celebrated. Among the continual deputations of patriots, intoxicated not only with revolutionary ardour, which helped to pass the time of the

Convention, may be singled out for distinguished mention a procession of one of the Paris Sections. National Guards with their drums were followed by a group of women dressed in white, to symbolize what is not said, and a double file of men clad in cassocks, chasubles, and copes, carrying with them the spoils of Saint-Germain-des-Prés, including all the utensils of superstitious practices, and escorting a black drapery beneath which was supposed to be the dead body of fanaticism. After the robed men had executed dances to the sound of the *Ça ira* and other revolutionary tunes, the demonstrators took their seats on the now un-populated right side of the Convention, while their orator delivered a speech which was received with transports of universal joy. Three days after this, on 23 November 1793, the Commune closed all the churches in Paris. What the Committee of Public Safety thought of these proceedings is not revealed; but while some members, like Collot, shared the sentiments of the dechristianizers, most of them saw po-litical dangers in thus alienating the great mass of the French people, which had not been greatly concerned at the confiscation of church property or even the establish-ment of the Constitutional Church, but would be likely to react more positively to an open war on religion. Robe-spierre, who preferred to have things done decently and even the Terror conducted with some appearance of law and order, was too good a Rousseauist in his religious ideas not to see behind dechristianization the sinister shade of atheism.

However, the left-wing extremists now had the bit be-tween their teeth and seemed on the point of bolting with the Revolution. The economic situation was playing into their hands. Since the beginning of the revolutionary war the assignat had been falling rapidly and by July 1793 had lost 77 per cent of its face value. The economic distress of the populace of Paris, which had been exploited by successive political factions for five years, presented a challenge and a threat to the Committee of Public Safety; all the more be-cause, perhaps somewhat disillusioned at the failure of a series of political revolutions to bring about any improvement, the people were now listening to agitators who demanded economic measures such as the punishment of monopolists and profiteers and the fixing of maximum prices. In the description of the spokesmen of this agitation, men like Jacques Roux and Varlet, as the *enragés*, the wild men of the Revolution, is reflected the horror with which the respectable middle-class citizens of the Convention, however extreme they were in their political views, regarded the prospect of any interference with the economic order. But the Mountain, having overthrown their opponents with the aid of the populace of Paris, had now to pay the price or be overthrown by an alliance of dechristianizers and *enragés* in their turn. Unlike Brissot and Roland, they were political realists and accepted the necessity of doing something to alleviate economic distress. They put French economy on a war basis, inaugurated a policy of requisitioning, and imposed a maximum on the prices of essential goods. Their measures improved the situation temporarily. By the end of 1793 the assignat had risen to 50 per cent of its face value.

The *enragés* were few in number, their propaganda was ideological and lacking in demagogic appeal, and their proto-socialist ideas ill-adapted to win the support of the small masters who formed the backbone of the revolutionary mobs. The Committee of Public Safety, having stolen the practical points in their programme, clapped them into prison as counter-revolutionaries. A very different threat was presented by the movement of the sans-culottes, all the more dangerous because it was so inchoate and incoherent. What the sans-culottes wanted is almost as difficult to say as what they were. Their name indicates that they did not wear knee-breeches, which is about as useless a class distinction as could be found. They constituted the militants of the Sections of Paris, the professional revolutionaries who spent their time at the Section meetings, orating and denouncing in an alcoholic haze. Their leaders, men like Hébert and Chaumette, were themselves professional revolutionaries on a higher level, interested mainly in power for themselves and the guillotine for their enemies. If they stood for anything it was for anti-clericalism, but only for this, one suspects, because the clergy were easily-identifiable victims against whom to whip up popular passions. They maintained their control of the Sections by packing them with a clientèle paid for attendance, or in the less sans-culottist districts with supporters from outside, and by strong-arm methods. Hébert's *Père Duchesne* flourished with the aid of a large government subsidy for its free distribution in the provinces and the army. It is now unreadable. If murder had to be advocated, at least it might have been done with the literary qualities of a Marat. All the *foutus* and *bougres* of Hébert are as stale and artificial as their author. It is difficult to find anyone else in the whole history of the Revolution as completely contemptible as the leaders of the sans-culottes. Perhaps in the end even their followers thought so, for when the time came for their elimination hardly a voice was raised in their defence. The threat of sans-culottist anarchy was removed in two stages. Towards the end of 1793 the Committee of Public Safety re-established the control of the central over local government.

For the first time since 1789 France had a real government. Along with determination at the centre was needed the machinery for regaining control of the provinces. This was provided by the law of 14 frimaire year 2 (4 December 1793), of which the chief author may have been Billaud-Varenne. All subordinate authorities and officials were put under the authority of the Committee of Public Safety, except for the police, which remained in principle the responsibility of the Committee of General Security. National agents, placed in control of the districts, were to report every ten days to the two supreme Committees. The movement that had commenced with a spontaneous outburst of communal liberties had thus ended, only four years later, with the creation of a far more ruthlessly centralized system of administration than ever the *ancien régime* had known.

With a strong impulse now coming from Paris, the military

fortunes of the Revolution, both within France and on the frontiers, improved. In October, Lyon fell to the republican army. Its defenders fled or were massacred and the total destruction of the city was decreed. Toulon, bombarded by the artillery of the young Corsican, Bonaparte, surrendered in December. The Vendéans, after a series of victories, failed to capture Granville in the Cherbourg peninsula and establish contact with the British fleet. Their armies, divided and lacking coherent leadership, became dispersed and were defeated, though the massacres and counter-massacres which marked this bloody and cruel civil war prohibited any lasting pacification for another seven years.

Despite the anarchic conditions in France, conscription had given the Committee of Public Safety an army of some 650,000 by July 1793. However badly equipped and clothed they were, this was a formidable body of men, inspired by revolutionary ardour, and far surpassing in numbers any armies that could be brought against it. In October the allies under Coburg were defeated at Wattignies by Jourdan; in Alsace, Hoche crossed the Vosges and drove back the enemy; Savoy was freed by Kellermann; the Spaniards were driven across the Pyrenees.

These victories strengthened the hand of the Committee of Public Safety in Paris. As well as the dangerous movement of the *enragés* and the dechristianizers, who had found a would-be leader in the demagogue Hébert, journalist of the professionally obscene *Père Duchesne*, opposition was reappearing from another quarter in the early months of 1794. The austere economic policies of the Committee of Public Safety were not to the liking of the crowd of political adventurers, government contractors, and financiers who had found patriotism a profitable speculation. The game of playing the markets and speculating for a rise or fall in the shares of companies, which had created mutually profitable alliances between the world of finance and that of government in the years before the Revolution, had not ceased with the triumph of virtue. Indeed, the fall of the assignat and the need for vast contracts to supply the revolutionary armies provided opportunities for speculation to reach unprecedented new heights. Foreign financiers, Belgian, Dutch, Swiss, Austrian, congregated in Paris, and found an ample supply of politicians, even in the pure atmosphere of the Mountain, who were open to the lure of wealth and women. It is difficult to believe that the speculators had any political principles, but some of them were associated with the Hébertists and dechristianizers on the left, and others with a new tendency which was appearing to the right of the Committee of Public Safety, demanding a relaxation of the terror.

Danton, more capable of wild bursts of energy than of persistent political action, had ceased to play a leading role in revolutionary politics after he left the first Committee of Public Safety. For months he had withdrawn with a new young wife to his home at Arcis-sur-Aube. If he were not entangled with corrupt financiers himself, he certainly had many friends who were, and when they came under attack in November 1793 from the Hébertists and their financial allies, he returned to Paris to their aid. To save those who were already in prison, though not necessarily to the exclusion of more disinterested motives, Danton put himself behind a campaign for the relaxation of the Terror. With the approval of Robespierre, the Dantonist Camille Desmoulins, one of the most brilliant if one of the least reliable of revolutionary journalists, launched, in the *Vieux Cordelier*, a devastating attack on the system of spies and informers which in the name of patriotism was turning France into a police state. The machinery of denunciation, arrests, and executions was indeed getting out of control: it was being used by all kinds of subaltern agents and petty agitators for their own private ends. The *Vieux Cordelier* and the campaign for clemency found so unexpectedly wide a public welcome that Robespierre became alarmed and withdrew his support. Collot d'Herbois and Billaud-Varenne reacted violently and the forces they could rally in Paris were still too powerful to be repudiated. Robespierre therefore drew back from his tentative alliance with Danton and temporized.

Meanwhile, on the other flank the Hébertists were still a potential threat to the régime. In March 1794 Robespierre decided to finish with them. At the same time, to carry the whole Committee with him, he had to abandon his half-hearted protection of the Dantonists. On 24 March, Hébert and his chief lieutenants were sent to the scaffold. The 'Revolutionary Army', a little private army of a few thousand sans-culottist heroes of the home front, which had been used for requisitioning food from the surrounding countryside, suppressing opposition by force, and as a side-line closing the churches and dechristianizing, was dissolved in Paris; its numerous provincial copies had already disappeared. Danton and his friends followed their enemies to the guillotine on 5 April. The complicity of both factions with alien financiers was used to represent their execution as the suppression of a 'foreign conspiracy'; the fact that many who perished had already been under arrest for months enabled the police to present it also as another 'prison plot'. In eliminating by a bold stroke to right and left both Dantonists and Hébertists, the Committee of Public Safety had won the most brilliant victory in the history of the Revolution, but it had also destroyed many of the men whose command of the mob had brought it to power.

Henceforth the Committee was to rule in an increasing void, though its efforts to create a favourable public opinion must not be underestimated. Apart from the official or semi-official press, the greatest and perhaps the most successful propaganda effort took the form of the grandiose processional pageants that were organized by David. To celebrate the anniversary of the revolution of the tenth of August and the promulgation of the Constitution, the Convention voted the sum of 1,200,000 livres for the fête of 10 August 1793. Delegates of the primary assemblies from all over France, members of the Convention, of the clubs, and a miscellaneous collection of the sovereign people, gathered at the place de la Bastille, and after speeches, songs, and salvoes, formed in procession with chariots and floats symbolizing the republican virtues, moving down the boulevards, with halts at triumphal arches or colossal plaster figures, till they reached the Altar of the Patrie in the Champ de Mars. Huge crowds watched or participated in the celebrations, which lasted from seven in the morning to eleven at night. Another famous occasion was the Fête of the Supreme Being, at which Robespierre set fire, with a torch handed to him by David, to a huge cardboard figure of Atheism, which went up in flames, exposing to view a rather smoky statue of Wisdom, after which the whole Convention, and delegates from the Sections, ascended an artificial mountain where appropriate ceremonies were performed.

Similar fêtes, though on a smaller and simpler scale, were held in the provinces, where the communes were dominated by small groups of ardent revolutionaries organized in Jacobin clubs and receiving guidance from Paris. The membership of the clubs was perhaps half a million at their height; but active membership was much smaller, and there were constant complaints of non-attendance at meetings. They fell under the influence of small cliques of militants, which obtained control of local affairs. Thus in Metz 61 Jacobins out of 148 held government office, and at Toulouse 103 out of 731. They exploited their offices and used popular violence to establish petty local tyrannies. Though the majority of the Jacobins were men of the middle classes, who stood for the smaller property owners against both the rich and the propertyless, the bond that united them was not class but faith. The Jacobin clubs had many of the characteristics of a political church, with rituals, tests of orthodoxy, public confessions, and purges. Their members thought of themselves as a body of the elect, marked out by the possession of virtue, or patriotism: they were the élite of the Revolution. Yet as they became increasingly mere cogs in the revolutionary machine, and from the point of view of efficiency rather incompetent ones, their ardour cooled and their spontaneity disappeared. This was what Saint-Just meant when he complained, 'La Révolution est glacée.'

Success, in fact, brought to the fore the basic contradictions in revolutionary ideology, for a clear demonstration of which we must examine the political evolution of the man who was the mind and the conscience of Jacobinism. Robespierre's strength, and ultimately perhaps his weakness, lay in his greater awareness of the significance of ideas in a period when ideas, if – as I have tried to show – they seldom determined practical decisions, played a large part in the formulation of political and social policies. To put it at the lowest, they provided the symbols over which and in the name of which the struggle was waged, and it was no Homeric battle over the dead body of a hero, for the ideas themselves were living forces which developed and even changed sides as the Revolution progressed. Robespierre himself was the true child of a century which had been so strongly concerned with ethical questions. The basic problem for him was the application of moral principles in government; and with the optimism of the pre-revolutionary world he believed it was not a difficult one. As Montesquieu said, immorality was the basis of despotism and virtue of the republic. To find the morality suppressed in the corrupt society of the *ancien régime*, it was only necessary to release the natural virtue of the people. Political virtue was thus equated with the sovereignty of the people. To restore their sovereignty to the people was to inaugurate the reign of virtue. With the victory of the Mountain it seemed that this had been achieved and all opposition should then have come to an end, for there could not be two separate and different expressions of a single, sovereign will. Since, on the contrary, opposition continued and even grew, Robespierre, was faced with the need for an agonized re-appraisal of his position. The explanation was soon obvious to him. We have built the temple of liberty, he said, with hands corrupted by the chains of despotism. Intriguers were still at work, perverting the naturally good will of the people. Practical considerations were added to theoretical ones. France was torn into fragments by internal strife. We need, he wrote, *une volonté une*. On what could it be based? At first, it seemed, on the people of Paris, 'the citadel of liberty'. But even here there was corruption. Intriguers were at work in the Convention, in the Sections, in the clubs other than the Jacobins. Robespierre was driven to believe that while the people in normal times rule by virtue, in times of revolution to virtue must be added terror. His programme was not merely one of repression, however. Opinion, he knew, was the basis of political power – had it not been the instrument of his own rise? – and it was not enough to repress hostile opinion on the platform, in the press, at the theatre: something must be put in its place. Hence good writings, speeches, pamphlets, journals, were to be encouraged and distributed widely. A national system of education, something which he had formerly opposed as dangerous to individual freedom, must be set up. Great pageants were to be organized for the purpose of propaganda. The ground plan of a totalitarian state, it seems, was being laid down, so far were Robespierre and the Jacobins being driven – by force of circumstances and the logic of their theory – from their earlier liberal views.

Yet to read their policies in unduly modern terms would be a mistake. Even at the height of the Terror, Robespierre remained, so far as he could, a defender of religious toleration. When a letter was received from the president of a commune asking what measures should be taken against women detected wearing crosses, he referred it to the *bureau de police* with the comment that the writer must either be a fool or a rogue. A circular of the Committee of Public Safety ordered the local authorities not to persecute Anabaptists and to allow those conscripted for the army to serve as pioneers or in the transport or else to purchase exemption. Such signs of moderation did not endear Robespierre to the extremists. The ultimate crisis, in theory as well as in fact, was to come for Robespierrist democracy when even the purged Convention, which he had called more than once the 'boulevard (i.e. the bulwark) of liberty', was to turn against him. The circle of virtue was narrowing. There are two peoples in France, he declared in May 1794: 'One is the mass of citizens, pure, hungry for justice, and loving liberty. It is this virtuous people which pours out its blood to establish liberty, which overcomes foreign enemies and shakes the thrones of tyrants. The other is that collection of factious intriguers, appearing everywhere, turning everything to abuse, seizing the tribune and often public office, who use the education which their advantages under the *ancien régime* gave them to deceive public opinion.' 'I see the world,' he cried despairingly in his last speech of all, 'peopled with dupes and knaves.' The will of the people, which expressed their sovereignty, had by now long ceased for him to be the actual will of an actual majority; it had become an ideal will incarnated in 'the few generous men who love virtue for its own sake'.

Having said all this, it must be added – and it is equally true – that practical circumstances dictated to theory. The rule of the Committee of Public Safety was essentially a war dictatorship. Under it, for the first time in modern history, appeared the phenomenon of a nation in arms. By 1794 France had over 850,000 men in its armies. Soldiers of the old regiments of the line, volunteers, and conscripts were gradually fused into a single fighting force. Authority and discipline were restored. The ability of the generals was tested by the pitiless crucible of war and failure was a death sentence. It was under the Committee of Public Safety that the generals who were to lead the armies of France in victory across Europe were discovered and tested – Jourdan, Hoche, Pichegru, Masséna, Moreau, Davout, Lefebvre, Sérurier, Augereau, Brune, Bonaparte – eight future marshals of Napoleon among them. Youth had its chance along with ability: the average age of the generals was thirty-three, of the Committee itself thirty-seven. Commissaires sent out from Paris kept the armies and their generals faithful to the Revolution; and as confidence increased it became possible for a general to risk at least a minor reverse without having to contemplate the guillotine. The new artillery and the tactics evolved by military theorists in the last years of the *ancien régime* served the revolutionary armies well. National factories for the manufacture of arms were extended.

Behind the scenes in France there had been those, in particular Danton, who saw in the repulsion of the enemy from the soil of France the possibility of opening peace negotiations and ending at the same time the war and the terror. The revolutionary ardour of the Committee was not to be held back thus. 'Who dares to speak of peace?' cried Barère, and answered, 'The aristocrats, the moderates, the rich, the conspirators, the pretended patriots.' Carnot deployed the French armies for a fresh advance on the Austrian Netherlands and after months of complicated manoeuvres Jourdan defeated Coburg at Fleurus on 26 June, advanced to Liège and Antwerp. Belgium fell again under French occupation.

At sea, the efforts of Jeanbon Saint-André to restore efficiency to the French navy after the loss of so many capable officers and the breakdown of discipline, were, through no fault of his own, less successful. The revolutionary effort at sea has been, until recently, underestimated. It was not unambitious. The pre-revolutionary plans of de Castries for the construction of ships were implemented and expanded. The naval war against Great Britain called for a treble armament – flotillas of small boats to guard the coastal trade, a fleet of ships of the line capable of engaging the British navy, and an invasion fleet to put into effect long-cherished plans for invasion. A remarkable effort of construction was in fact achieved, though it was to be frustrated, largely by the internal revolts. The royalist seizure and the British occupation of Toulon robbed France of one fleet. Even more serious were the effects of the revolt of the Vendée, which kept supplies of material and men away from the great naval bases of the Atlantic coast in a vital period. Jeanbon Saint-André had also to deal with the efforts of local revolutionary committees to undermine discipline in the ports and the fleet. In spite of all difficulties, one main object of the French navy, which was to break the British blockade and enable convoys of food ships from America to reach France, achieved some measure of success.

The greatest of the convoys, protected by the Brest fleet, at the price of heavy losses, in three long days' fighting culminating on 1 June 1794, against a British fleet under the command of Howe, was enabled to reach port safely.

Whether the arrival of the Brest convoy had any substantial effect on the food situation in France cannot be said. But from the point of view of the Committee of Public Safety nothing could have been more fatal than military or naval success. A régime which had been founded on defeat was not stabilized by victory. Moreover, the economic problem remained intense despite all the efforts of the Committee, and it was easier to offer a distressed population scapegoats to be immolated on the guillotine than a solution to its economic problems. The defeat of foreign enemies and the crushing of organized opposition inside France was therefore followed not by a diminution but by an intensification of the Terror. An analysis of the number of official executions shows that its incidence varied greatly in different parts of France and that it reached its height in the departments where civil war raged. To give even an approximation to the number of those who were killed in one way or another in the course of the Terror is impossible, but one estimate of the number of suspects put under arrest arrives at the figure of 300,000. Every suspect had friends and relations whose sympathies were bound up with his fate. The more there were arrested, the larger grew the silent hosts of fear and hatred surrounding the great Committee. As the Terror became more and more a mindless, reasonless machine, it fell increasingly and indiscriminately on all sections of the community. Of those who were guillotined after trial, 85 per cent belonged to the Third Estate, some 6·5 per cent to the clergy, and 8·5 per cent to the *noblesse*. The Committee of Public Safety, at the time and since, has, it is true, been saddled with the blame for police measures many of which are attributable to the one other Committee, that of General Security, which had survived and retained its autonomy. The latter regarded police as its special province and, composed of purer terrorists and perhaps mere terrorists, was responsible for a large proportion of the rank and file arrests and executions, though the great political trials, conducted by the two committees jointly, have left a deeper mark on the pages of history.

An unsuccessful attempt to assassinate Collot d'Herbois, and a merely suspected one on the life of Robespierre, produced sufficient terror in the breasts of the ruling faction to evoke the law of 22 prairial (10 June), introduced by Couthon, with Robespierre presiding over the Convention. This deprived the proceedings of the Revolutionary Tribunal of the last semblance of judicial trial and allowed no verdict but acquittal or death. The largest and most miscellaneous batches of prisoners were now dispatched to the Tribunal *en route* for the guillotine. From March 1793 to 10 June 1794, 1,251 persons had been executed at Paris; from 10 June to 27 July there were 1,376 victims. The members of the Convention, even those not threatened hitherto, began to fear for their own necks, and the whole country, including the small ruling faction and its adherents, stifled in a miasma of suspicion and fear.

So long as the Committee of Public Safety remained united its authority could not be shaken. The press, public opinion, and all the organs of administration were under relentless control. But the successes of the armies, completed in the victory of Fleurus, by relaxing fear of the foreign enemy undermined the unity of the Committee. The law of prairial aroused alarm in the Convention of the use that might be made of it by the Robespierrists. In the Committee of Public Safety violent disagreements arose between Carnot and Saint-Just over the conduct of the war, in which Robespierre supported Saint-Just, and Carnot had the backing of his fellow technicians, Robert Lindet and Prieur of the Côte d'Or. The Committee of General Security found its authority challenged by a new police committee composed of Robespierre, Couthon, and Saint-Just. Robespierre personally provoked the resentment of the strong anti-religious element in the Committee of General Security, as well as exposing himself to barely veiled ridicule, by founding his new religion of the Supreme Being and celebrating it in a great public festival. Although the Convention followed him, in his new sky-blue coat, in procession to the Champ de Mars, it was with its tongue in its cheek. However classical the education and ideas of the revolutionaries, a *pontifex maximus* did not enter into their pattern of a republic. While he had antagonized Carnot and the men of the Plain, who had followed the Mountain and taken their share of responsibility for the terror when it seemed the only way of establishing a government strong enough to save France, Robespierre had also aroused the fears of those who were terrorists by nature and perhaps for the pure love of terrorism. Deputies who had been in charge of the repression in the provinces, men like Carrier, Fréron, Fouché, Tallien, had been called back from their bloody work by the influence of Robespierre and knew that he would not spare them when the time came for him to act. They were joined in scarcely veiled opposition by the Committee of General Security and by Collot and Billaud, who had never been Robespierrists. Barère – one of nature's middle-men – struggled to the last to effect a reconciliation in the Committee of Public Safety, but it had become divided into factions which hated and distrusted each other too deeply for them to be able to continue to work together. The conflict could only be settled by the elimination of one side or the other.

Robespierre still had many cards in his hand. He had defeated those who had dared to oppose him in the Convention so often that it did not occur to him that his mastery of the majority could be shaken. The Commune of Paris was packed with his devoted followers, and its armed force, under Hanriot, would be loyal to him. He felt supremely confident and only bided his time to strike. For a month after the passing of the law of prairial he waited, isolating himself from all but his closest adherents and manifesting his displeasure by abstaining from attending the meetings of the Convention and the Committee of Public Safety. On 8 thermidor (26 July), the lowering storm broke. Robespierre came to the Convention and denounced his enemies in terms which were menacing enough to carry a threat of death to all his opponents and vague enough to include practically anyone. He demanded, in effect, a blank cheque on the guillotine to fill in as he pleased. The speech was a masterly one but for once oratory was not enough. The next day the conspirators, desperate men who knew that it was Robespierre's life or theirs, took the offensive. The moment Saint-Just and Robespierre tried to speak, their voices were drowned with cries of 'Down with the tyrant'. A Mirabeau or a Danton would have made himself heard; the Robespierrists included no orator of that calibre, and in any case Collot d'Herbois, in the chair, gave them no chance. Tallien struck the first blow. In turn, Billaud-Varenne, Barère, Vadier, Fréron, took up the attack. In a tumult the Convention voted the arrest of Robespierre and the small group that devotedly gathered round him, before they could rally support in the streets or their allies in the Commune could come to their aid.

The man who should have saved the situation, Hanriot, probably drunk as usual, got himself arrested, was then released, but failed to make any use of the forces he commanded. The Commune sounded the tocsin and gathered a mob of some 3,000, but perhaps because the imposition of a maximum on wages had discontented the people of Paris, perhaps because arrests and executions had robbed them of the leaders of the street-fighters who had carried the Mountain into power, it remained inactive. The Convention outlawed Robespierre with all who supported him, and recruited a force of some 6,000 men from the moderate Sections, under the command of Barras, a member of the Convention, *ci-devant* count and infantry officer, who thus laid the foundations of his political fortune. The situation still seemed in the balance. The arrested Robespierrists, who had been freed in one way or another, joined with the members of the Commune at the Hôtel de Ville; but the troops of the Commune who should have defended them had dispersed and they found themselves surrounded by hostile forces.

Paris, which had followed Robespierre for so long, and on the support of which he relied unquestioningly, had deserted him. All was lost, only death remained. He was shot through the jaw, almost certainly in an attempt to commit suicide. On 10 thermidor, Robespierre, his brother Augustin, Saint-Just, Couthon, Hanriot, and seventeen others were hurried to the guillotine. 'He had on the sky-blue coat he had got made for the Feast of the *Être Suprême* – O Reader, can thy hard heart hold out against that?' wrote Carlyle. The next day the Robespierrist commune was exterminated: seventy-one heads fell in the biggest single holocaust of the Revolution. The Thermidoreans had won their victory and in making an end to Robespierre and his faction had ended far more than they knew. They had ended the Revolution.

They had saved their own heads. Two days earlier and they might have saved also, unknowingly, the one great poet of their generation in France. On 7 thermidor André Chénier, in whose lyrics a purer classical genius shone than that age of pseudo-classicism knew, died, at thirty-two, on the guillotine as an enemy of the people. His elegy, *La Jeune Captive*, written in prison, is in every anthology. One might think that, in *Néère*, he had foretold it and his fate.

> *Mais telle qu'à sa mort, pour la dernière fois,*
> *Un beau cygne soupire, et de sa douce voix,*
> *De sa voix qui bientôt lui doit être ravie,*
> *Chante, avant de partir, ses adieux à la vie.*

6. AFTERMATH OF REVOLUTION

THE régime that succeeded to Robespierre and the great Committee of Public Safety had been brought to birth by a *coup d'état*, it was to live by *coups d'état* and to die by a *coup d'état*. The Thermidoreans were united only in their fear of Robespierre. There is little to admire in them: no motive higher than self-preservation inspired their desperate attack, no ideals justified their executions, no laurels crowned their victory. Men like Carnot, Robert Lindet, Prieur of the Côte d'Or, were the best of them, practical and limited men driven to ruthless action by fear of the dangerous courses into which the Robespierrists were once more leading the Revolution. Other Thermidoreans were men like Cambon, one of the few who had entered revolutionary politics from the world of commerce and who had appropriately obtained control of revolutionary finances; Vadier and his supporters of the Committee of General Security, hoping, with the Robespierrists eliminated, to seize control of the machinery of terror and use it to establish their own rule; Fouché, Billaud-Varenne, Collot d'Herbois, fearing the turning of their own weapon against themselves; Tallien, a petty official before the Revolution, sent as terrorist commissaire to Bordeaux, to have his heart melted by the beautiful Thérèse Cabarrus and to rescue her from the impending guillotine; Barras, who was to emerge as the strong man of the Directory; Fréron, son of the old literary opponent of Voltaire, god-child of King Stanislaus of Lorraine, Cordelier, journalist of the *Orateur du peuple* in which he had rivalled Marat in denunciation and appeals to violence, colleague of Barras in a bloody proconsulate at Toulon and Marseille, cruel and corrupt Conventionnel. Such were the first leaders of the Thermidorean reaction.

Thermidor was a counter-revolution but it was not effected at a single blow. The raw material of revolution, the turbulent and distressed populace of Paris, remained, but its political power had been undermined and for this the great Committee of Public Safety was perhaps itself responsible. In consolidating its authority the Committee had unwittingly destroyed the foundations on which that authority rested. The great Terror had swept up in its indiscriminate slaughter so many of the agitators of the street corners and clubs; there had been, in the long succession of *journées*, such a wastage of leaders of revolt, that the mob never again became a coherent force. Henceforth it was an army without officers, anarchic, irrelevant. The politicians of the Convention, who had used and then cast aside the men of the streets, could not supply their places. The general staff of terrorist warfare had guillotined its own non-commissioned officers and its army had disintegrated. After Thermidor, Fréron stepped in and turned the chief weapon of the Jacobins against themselves. With a little group of adherents, and with invocations to the shade of Marat, he gathered round him former Dantonists, *enragés*, and many others, fresh from the prisons of the Convention, with bitter memories to avenge, and directed them against those who were denounced as *la queue de Robespierre*. With such men he united, in an unnatural and temporary alliance, the *jeunesse dorée*, not very gilded perhaps, of minor officials, lawyers, bankers' clerks, and the like, young aspirants to as yet unachieved social position. Among the Thermidorean mobs were doubtless also many of those who had formerly constituted the street army of the Mountain and the Commune, men ready to rally to any cry, so long as it gave them an opportunity to range through the streets, hunting, beating, tearing to pieces whoever was designated as the quarry, and seeking any opportunity of looting that offered.

These former Cordeliers and ex-Hébertists, with far more experience in the actual control of the streets than the Robespierrist Jacobins ever had, organized street bands which abandoned the uniform of the carmagnole, the peasant blouse and loose trousers. The Muscadins of the Thermidorean reaction affected a very different style, dressing in coats with square shoulders, tight breeches, wearing blond wigs, carrying weighted cudgels, and chanting *le Réveil du peuple*. Based especially on the Palais Royal, whence had issued agitators in a very different cause only five years earlier, they chased known Jacobins through the streets and attacked their headquarters in the rue Saint Honoré, providing an excuse for the new rulers of France to close the club. A counter-terror appeared spontaneously in the provinces. In the Lyonnais, where the deeds of the Jacobins had not been forgotten, a self-styled Company of Jesus assassinated former terrorists and their women and threw the bodies in the Rhône. In a new prison massacre, but this time the prisoners were the Jacobins, there were ninety-nine victims. Convoys of arrested terrorists were way-laid and the prisoners put to death. The massacres spread to all the surrounding departments. At Nîmes, Marseille, Aix, Orange, and elsewhere in the south a White Terror raged, conducted by bands calling themselves the Companies of the Sun.

From the prisons of the Jacobin Terror the suspects poured out, saved by Thermidor from the guillotine and with their sequestrated property restored to them. The enemies of the Mountain re-emerged from concealment or prison to take their seats again in the Convention, where a strong right wing of some 150 members reappeared and temporarily found an unexpected leader in the reformed terrorist Tallien. The complexion of the two governing Committees changed as each monthly election brought in new figures. On 1 September, Barère, Billaud-Varenne, and Collot d'Herbois left the Committee of Public Safety. The Revolutionary Tribunal, reorganized after Thermidor, inherited, as its first great post-thermidorean trial, the case of the Nantais, dispatched in January 1794, when Carrier was on mission at Nantes, to the prisons of Paris. Originally numbering 132, deaths during the months in prison had reduced their number to ninety-four. Their trial turned into a continuous indictment of Carrier, who himself appeared as a witness for the defence. He alleged that while at Nantes he had been concerned exclusively with the organization of food supplies and even professed himself unconnected with the arrests. This did not save him. The Nantais were acquitted amid scenes of enthusiasm. The next day Carrier was denounced at the Convention as a 'cannibal', and he and his associates were sent to the Revolutionary Tribunal. A host of witnesses, freed from fear, appeared to testify against him. He at least ended bravely. After a hopeless attempt to deny the overwhelming evidence, he admitted his deeds, exculpated those who were tried with him as mere agents executing his orders, and was condemned to the guillotine. After Robespierre, he became the symbol of the

Terror and there was little need to blacken his reputation as Robespierre's had been blackened.

The reversal of the terrorist machine and the repudiation of Jacobin policies was not completed at one blow. Early hesitations were shown by the passing of a decree translating Marat to the Panthéon. The whole Convention escorted the honoured remains of the Friend of the People to the temple of the great men of the Republic in September 1794; they were expelled again, with less ceremony, in February 1795. The Public Prosecutor, Fouquier-Tinville, arrested soon after the ninth of thermidor on the denunciation of his old enemy Fréron, was not brought to trial till the following March. He defended himself on the ground that he had merely carried out the orders of the Committee of Public Safety as a faithful civil servant should, but in spite of this he and fourteen jurors of the Revolutionary Tribunal passed beneath the knife to which they had condemned so many others.

While the reaction was progressing, however, the causes of popular unrest had not been brought to an end. A distressed populace still existed to be called into action. On 1 April 1795, the day of 12 germinal, it broke out in rioting. That there were still politically motivated leaders is shown by the cry of the crowd which invaded the Convention: 'bread and the Constitution of 1793', but they were obscure and ineffective men. The day of germinal was little more than a large-scale riot, suppressed without difficulty when the National Guard from the western Sections of Paris was brought up. Its supporters in the Convention dared not declare themselves and the riot merely provided the new majority with an excuse for turning against the three most prominent terrorists left in their midst, Collot d'Herbois, Billaud-Varenne, and Barère. Their deportation to Guiana and the arrest of some twenty other deputies was decreed. Collot rapidly died there of yellow fever; Billaud-Varenne settled down as a farmer in the tropics with a devoted negro girl named Virginie and spent the rest of his life in an obscure and Rousseauist pastoral idyll; Barère, for the first time in his life, it was said, failing to sail with the wind, remained in France and lived to beg for jobs from Bonaparte, to be exiled during the Restoration, and to die a poor pensioner of Louis-Philippe.

The discontents which had provoked the riot of germinal were not diminished by its failure, and protests and minor demonstrations against food prices were of daily occurrence. If the Convention did nothing to improve the economic situation, it took more effective precautions of another kind. The law prohibiting the army from penetrating within a certain distance of Paris was suspended and troops were brought to the outskirts; officers of suspected Jacobin tendencies were purged, including a young Corsican, Bonaparte; the National Guard was reorganized, excluding the poorer citizens. Precautions were certainly needed, for agitation was spreading among the people of Paris, little revolutionary cells were forming, manifestos were being distributed calling on the people to rise. On the morning of 1 prairial (20 May 1795) the tocsin was sounded in the faubourg St Antoine and in the neighbouring Sections; crowds of women gathered, mobs were formed, arms seized, and the traditional march on the Convention began. As in germinal, however, there seems to have been no central body to organize and control the demonstration and no coordination with a party in the Convention to exploit it. Bread and the Constitution of 1793 was still the cry. The entry to the Convention, which, contrary to tradition, tried to defend itself, at the price of the life of one member whose head was more traditionally put on a pike, was forced. Despite the howling presence of the mob, Boissy d'Anglas, in the presidential chair, boldly refused to suspend the session. Only after some hours of disorder did the few members who sympathized with the demonstrators venture to put into the form of a motion their demands. Meanwhile the National Guard, now composed of opponents and no longer of allies of the revolutionary movement, had been called out, had seized strategic points in the city, and marched to the protection of the Convention. Towards midnight they drove out the mob at the point of the bayonet. The next day the insurgent Sections reassembled and again surrounded the Convention, but a pitched battle with its defenders was somehow avoided. On the third day detachments of the army entered Paris, disarmed the faubourg St Antoine, and the crisis of the Thermidorean régime was over. It only remained for the Convention to arrest and condemn, by a summary military court, the six deputies who had supported the insurgents. On the steps of the tribunal, hurried from condemnation to execution, they stabbed themselves; three died on the spot and the others were borne bleeding to the guillotine, one, who had died *en route*, already a corpse when he was thrust beneath the knife. The remaining members of the great terrorist Committees were arrested, only Carnot being saved by a cry, 'He was the organizer of victory.' In the Sections there was a general denunciation and disarmament of former Jacobins and sans-culottes. The companies of gunners attached to the National Guard were dissolved, which was to rob insurrection of one of its chief weapons.

While the personnel of the Terror was thus being disbanded and dispersed, its governmental machinery had been rapidly dismantled. The changes that were made, and the precautions that the Convention took to safeguard its authority, are not only important in themselves, they also reveal clearly the administrative arrangements that had made the great Terror and the dictatorship of the Committee of Public Safety possible. The first step was to change the Committee of Public Safety from being in effect a self-perpetuating oligarchy and the master of the Convention into its servant. It was henceforth to be renewable by one-fourth every month, and retiring members could not be immediately re-elected. Its functions were reduced to the control of foreign affairs and war and there was a general distribution of governmental authority among the Committees of the Convention. In the provinces the revolutionary committees of the communes, which had been among the chief agencies of the Terror, were suppressed and a new army of representatives on mission was sent out from the Convention to assist in orientating local government to the new line. In Paris, which had been the stronghold of the Committee of Public Safety, despite the temporary dislocation of the revolutionary forces, both at the top and at intermediate levels, there was still a fear that they might reassert themselves unless they were deprived of the means of doing so. A series of administrative measures was enacted, therefore, which effectively destroyed this possibility. The headquarters staff of the National Guard, put under the direct control of the Committees of the Convention, was to be changed every ten days. The Sections were to meet only once in every decade and the payment of 40 sous for attendance was suppressed. The revolutionary committees were reduced from forty-eight, one for each Section, to twelve, one for each *arrondissement*, and were renewable every three months. The dreaded Commune, which had been first the creator and then the instrument of the terrorist dictatorship, disappeared altogether with the suppression of the administrative unity of Paris. It was replaced by two commissions of officials, one for police, responsible to the Committee of General Security, which also had the right of calling in the armed forces, and the other for taxation. Paris had ceased to rule France, it had ceased even to rule itself.

The Thermidoreans thus demolished the structure by which the Mountain had dominated France. In the Convention all that remained of that once fearful height was a tottering and diminishing '*crête*'. The work of destruction had been almost too successful, for it was carried on, far beyond the intentions and expectations of the Thermidoreans, by strong winds of public opinion which were sweeping France and bringing with them hopes of a royalist restoration. The problem for the historian now is not why the monarchy fell but why it was not revived, and this is an easier question to answer. The brothers of Louis XVI, identified with foreign invasion and émigré hopes of revenge, had excluded themselves by their words and deeds. The little son of Louis XVI and Marie-Antoinette, the prisoner of the Temple, would have provided the ideal solution. A mere child but the legitimate king of France, his presence on the throne would reconcile the nation to its government and in his name, under a revived Constitution of 1791, the new rulers of France could exercise power without fear of a counter-revolution and therefore without terror. Boissy d'Anglas, whose role during the days of prairial had marked him out as the key man of the new order, was cautiously preparing the way for a return to constitutional monarchy, when, on 8 June 1795, the little boy, on whose life so many hopes for France rested, and who stood, had the ambitious young Corsican who was now expiating in disgrace his former association with the Mountain but known it, between him and an empire, died of tuberculosis, exacerbated or caused by his shocking ill-usage in prison. 'The death of the young king, Louis XVII,' wrote the moderate royalist Mallet du Pan, 'is at this moment the most fatal of events. It has consternated and discouraged the constitutional monarchists, and ensured the triumph of the republicans and the success of the new farrago of nonsense which they are going to decree under the name of a constitution.'

Worst of all, the death of the little Louis XVII meant that the comte de Provence was now Louis XVIII. He celebrated his accession by issuing a manifesto from Verona proclaiming merciless punishment of the regicides and the restoration in its entirety of the *ancien régime*, with the parlements restored to their old powers, the higher orders back in their privileged position, and Catholicism again the exclusive religion of the state. This was an open warning that the counter-revolution was prepared to make no concessions to the new France. It was also evidence that the émigrés were as out of touch with reality as ever. A restoration on these terms was only conceivable if the revolutionary régime could be overthrown by force, and the improbability of this was to be demonstrated once again in 1795. In February, Charette, the most prominent of the leaders of the Vendéan rebels, signed a pacification at La Jaunaye with the republican authorities, and by May the whole of the west had temporarily laid down its arms. When, in June, the long-awaited expedition of the émigrés, with belated British support, at last sailed to the promontory of Quiberon in southern Brittany, it was too late. Defeated by Hoche, those of the luckless royalists who could not escape in the British fleet were captured and butchered.

The Thermidoreans, after a year of hesitation and uncertainty, had now no choice but to attempt to consolidate the Republic by providing it with a new Constitution. Sieyes reappeared once again to offer a plan, which was, as usual, patently unworkable. The chief author of the Constitution of the year III was the leader of the moderates, Boissy d'Anglas. It was based on a dual fear of democracy and dictatorship. Universal suffrage was abolished and elections were to be indirect. A restricted franchise gave political power to the propertied classes. 'We should be governed,' declared Boissy d'Anglas, 'by the best, and the best are those best educated and most interested in upholding the laws. With very few exceptions you will only find such men among those who, possessing property, are attached to the country containing it and the laws which protect it.' To prevent any concentration of power such as had fallen into the hands of the Committee of Public Safety, the executive and legislative powers were separated and the latter was put into commission by being entrusted to a directory of five. Finally, to prevent the electorate from supposing that it could do as it pleased, priests and former émigrés were disenfranchised, along with all those under arrest or accusation, that is all former leading Jacobins, and a decree was passed compelling the electors to choose two-thirds of the members of the new legislative body from among the surviving members of the Convention. This Constitution was submitted to a plebiscite in which it obtained just over a million votes. There was only a pitiable 200,000 for the decree of two-thirds. As thirty-three of the Paris Sections rejected the decree almost unanimously, only the votes of the remaining fifteen Sections were counted.

The obvious determination of the rump Convention to

perpetuate its power provoked unrest in Paris, culminating in a rising on 13 vendémiaire (5 October 1795). Barras, who had been successful against the Jacobins in Thermidor, was again entrusted with the defence of the Convention, this time against moderates and royalists. He called to his aid the victor of Toulon, the young general Bonaparte, temporarily unemployed because of his association with the Mountain. Troops to the number of some 6,000 were brought up to protect the Convention, threatened by about 25,000 men from the Sections; but Bonaparte had also cannon and did not hesitate to use them. Before musket and cannon fire the Sections fled, leaving behind them two or three hundred killed and wounded: Parisian revolts, whether of the right or left, were evidently out of date. Vendémiaire delivered a sharp check to the royalist revival. It did more, it brought the army into politics: but the consequences of that were not yet to be appreciated.

With the Directory a new age in the history of France begins. A class of new men, with newly acquired wealth and office, was emerging as the ruling element in the state. They were, naturally, not the cultured upper bourgeoisie of the *ancien régime* – the Farmers General, higher judicial officers and administrators, and the like – but the purchasers of national property, war contractors, speculators, profiteers, and politicians. De-classed nobles mingled with jumped-up plebeians to form a society of *nouveaux riches* in which the vices of the court met and fused with those of the courtyard. Salons reappeared, gathered round the elegant mistresses of revolutionary politicians and generals – the lovely Mme Récamier, Josephine de Beauharnais, Mme Tallien, formerly Thérèse Cabarrus and yet to become Princesse de Chimay, but best known to history as *notre dame de Thermidor*. The brilliant daughter of Necker, Mme de Staël, less decorative but with a mind nourished on the conversation of the great intelligences and wits of the last years of the *ancien régime* in the salon of her mother, provided a centre for intellectual society.

The end of the Terror, with its popular and puritan

austerities, was also marked by a revolution in dress. The exaggerated fashions of *incroyables* and *merveilleuses* were the visible sign of the birth of a new society, with men in badly-cut coats, padded shoulders, high collars, immense cravats and admiral's hats, and its women half-naked in pseudo-classical robes, gathered up in the high-breasted directoire style and falling in long diaphanous folds to the Grecian sandals. An affected 'de-boned' speech, leaving out the consonants, was adopted by the *jeunesse dorée*.

Wealth was now quite fashionable again, for a wild inflation followed the abandonment of the economic controls of the Committee of Public Safety. In August 1795 the daily expenditure of the government amounted to 80 to 90 million and the receipts to between 6 and 8 million. The assignat of 100 francs fell to 15 sous. Markets were deserted, vagabondage and brigandage endemic, and misery widespread. The deputies protected themselves by calculating their salaries in myriagrammes of cheese. The armies could only live by pillage. The towns were saved from wholesale starvation by free distribution of food, requisitioned from the peasantry, who were not thereby the more reconciled to the new régime.

In these conditions it was natural that the ideas of the *enragés* should reappear in the form of the primitive kind of communism advocated by the petty official Babeuf and his small band of followers who called themselves the Equals. His attempted conspiracy, in May 1796, attracted a few hundred former terrorists, including well-to-do professional men, and was financed by former Jacobins who were sworn enemies of the Directory. Government spies were in the movement from the beginning and it was crushed with little effort.

The real menace to the Directory came from the other side. Royalists within France were plucking up their courage and emerging from hiding or passivity; many were trickling back into France across the frontiers. The British government, through its envoy in Switzerland, William Wickham, was pouring in secret agents and supplying them lavishly with money. When the partial elections of April 1797 came round, only eleven former deputies to the Convention were returned out of 216. The majority of the new members were constitutional monarchists. Despite the *débâcle* of Vendémiaire, if the royalists had been united and competently led, and the émigrés capable of offering a modicum of concessions, France was theirs. This was to ask too much. The elements in France which were potentially favourable were alienated by the programme of the émigrés. The peasants were little enough interested in republican politics, but they did not contemplate with equanimity the loss of the confiscated noble and church lands and the revival of seigneurial dues. The new governing class which had acquired wealth and jobs during the Revolution had no desire to sacrifice them. The constitutional monarchists found all their efforts to come to terms with the pure royalists rebuffed. In the army, more or less isolated from the changing opinions of the country, the republican sentiments of earlier years still survived.

Yet, with a majority in the legislative bodies, and with Carnot and Barthélemy sympathetic in the Directory itself, it seemed inevitable that the monarchists should assume control of France by constitutional means. Their success in taking over the reins would have meant peace, for in 1797 negotiations had been opened with the British at Lille, and had been dragging on throughout the summer. Peace and war hung in the balance, turning on which party gained control at Paris. The decisive factor was to be not the politicians but the generals, who had a professional interest in war. The two republican Directors, Reubell and La Reveillière-Lépeaux, were joined, after much hesitation, by Barras. In September 1797 the three decided to take action against their colleagues and the royalist majority in the chambers, fully aware that if they did not do so their cause was lost. There was no question now of arousing a popular movement to save the republic. As in Vendémiaire the army was the decisive factor and a mere constitutional provision that excluded armed forces from the neighbourhood of Paris was a feeble barrier against it. Bonaparte, on campaign in Italy, sent his rough lieutenant Augereau to maintain the stability of the Republic at home while he pursued its conquests abroad.

On the morning of 18 fructidor (4 September 1797) Paris woke up to find itself under military occupation. Barthélemy was arrested and Carnot fled. The legislative bodies were purged, the elections of forty-nine departments quashed, all opposition journals suppressed, and seventeen of the more prominent enemies of the triumvirate dispatched to the 'dry guillotine', French Guiana, where eight of them rapidly died. A few hundred priests were also sent to Guiana, and a similar number of other opponents of the régime were tried by military courts and shot. For a short period it was a new Terror, but one inspired not by republican ardour but by political calculation. The Republic had been saved and even the appearance of liberty lost. With the aid of the army the politicians of the Directory still held precariously to their power and kept the centre of the stage, but the tramp of marching men increasingly drowned their voices, and from the wings the figure of Bonaparte cast a deepening shadow.

The decisive step, it might have been thought, had been taken earlier, when the Revolution had bound up its fortunes with war. France committed itself to ultimate military government, it may be said, when for the third time, in 1795, after Prussia, Holland, and Spain had accepted French terms and Belgium had been incorporated in France, it continued an aggressive war against Austria, aimed chiefly at the conquest of northern Italy. The motives for the Italian campaign were very mixed ones, but not least financial. Exaggerated conceptions of the wealth of Lombardy and Tuscany, of Genoa and Venice, tempted the invader as in centuries past. The riches of Italy lay waiting to be liberated by the ragged but battle-tested armies of revolutionary France.

Bonaparte, who had won the confidence of the Directory when he saved it in Vendémiaire, was given command of the army of Italy. He put the ideas of the *ancien régime* strategist, Guibert, into practice with a genius for improvisation all his own. Sardinia was beaten to the ground in the spring of 1796 and granted peace at the price of Nice and Savoy and the dismantling of the defences of the Alpine passes. Heavy convoys of bullion and works of art arrived in Paris as the first-fruits of the conquest of Italy. Serious opposition to the French armies was to be expected when they came into contact with the Austrians, who were defeated at Arcola in November 1796 and Rivoli in January 1797. Peace preliminaries were signed at Leoben in April, and in October the treaty of Campo-Formio brought peace with profit. The emperor recognized the French annexation of the former Austrian Netherlands and the left bank of the Rhine, and the creation of a new Cisalpine Republic out of the conquests in northern Italy. In return the French, who had occupied the territory of the Venetian Republic, handed it over to Austria, having first looted it of everything of value they could find, including the great bronze horses of St Mark. The peace treaty, like the campaign, was the personal achievement of Bonaparte, who, having intervened decisively in the domestic politics of France when he sent Augereau to implement the *coup d'état* of Fructidor, was now also determining the foreign policy of the Republic.

Only Great Britain remained to be dealt with, peace negotiations, which had been conducted in a leisurely manner at Lille, having been abruptly broken off. The British naval victories of St Vincent over the Spaniards and Camperdown over the Dutch, in 1797, made the prospect of a successful invasion of England an unpromising one. Bonaparte advised the Directory against it, but showed little enthusiasm for the idea of concluding peace, which Great Britain might now be expected to accept on terms favourable to France. In this situation there emerged the plan of an expedition to Egypt. In May 1798 Bonaparte sailed from Toulon with 400 ships, 40,000 troops, and a considerable body of scientists, scholars, and officials, for it was intended to turn Egypt into a French colony, as well as using it as a base for the destruction of English commerce and a stepping-stone to the creation of a French empire in the East. After the French fleet, having successfully escorted the expedition to its destination, had been caught by Nelson at anchor in Aboukir Bay and destroyed, the French army was cut off. Few of the soldiers who were marching across scorching sands, trying to apply the policy of living off the country in a land where even the inhabitants found it difficult enough to live, were ever to see France again. The mirage of the wealth of the East faded in the deserted ruins of Alexandria and the wretched huts of Cairo. Egyptian opposition was easily crushed but the international repercussions of the invasion were unfavourable to France. It brought Turkey into the alliance with Russia and Great Britain, and Russia, her interests in the East threatened, for the first time took an effective part in the European war. The Second Coalition of 1799, uniting Britain, Russia, and Turkey, was then joined by Austria. Defeated in Italy and on the Rhine, with an army shut up in Egypt, France was threatened again with invasion.

The Directory, which had welcomed the Egyptian expedition as a means of removing an ambitious and dangerous general from the scene, found that it had brought a new continental war upon itself and one which it lacked the energy or ability to cope with successfully. The political situation in France was now changing once more. Reubell, the Director most associated with the war policy, but also the ablest of them, retired. He was replaced by Sieyes, that 'mole of the Revolution' as Robespierre called him, who had for long been intriguing in search of an opportunity to show once again, and perhaps this time with success, his genius as a maker of constitutions. He secured the removal of the other Directors, except Barras, whose energy seemed to have evaporated and who presented no danger, and replaced them with nonentities. This was clearly only a preliminary measure, but preliminary to what? Since Thermidor, France had been living under a régime of improvisations. A government lacking real support in the country had been reduced to a see-saw policy of playing off royalists against republicans, conservatives against Jacobins – these two distinctions are not the same. To draw up a fair verdict on a period which has never received the detailed study that has been devoted to the earlier years of the Revolution is impossible. The work of the Directory has perhaps been underrated and the achievements of the Consulate which followed correspondingly overrated. Considerable efforts were made to restore budgetary equilibrium and stability to the currency, with very limited success. Good harvests in 1796 and 1798 improved the supply of food. Industrial production remained lower than it had been in 1789, and to the loss of ocean commerce resulting from the maritime war with Great Britain was added the closing of the markets in the Levant after the invasion of Egypt.

In 1799 economic difficulties and the defeat of the armies brought about a last tentative resurgence of the Jacobin spirit. The Directory, by its measures to conscript men, requisition supplies, and raise forced loans, had to a certain extent provoked this revival. After the expulsion of the royalists by the *coup d'état* of fructidor in 1797, the Council of the Five Hundred acquired a republican majority which in the crisis of 1799 showed itself still capable of by now largely meaningless Jacobin gestures, using language like *la patrie en danger* and calling for a new Committee of Public Safety. On the other side, royalist revolts broke out in the south-west and in Brittany. These were easily put down, while Paris made no move in response to the agitation of the neo-Jacobins. Troops were now permanently stationed in the capital to repress any attempt at a popular rising, but of this there was no sign. The political passions of the so-recent past had little life remaining in them. All that France wanted was a chance of tranquillity, peace at home and abroad, and the latter at least seemed within reach. A successful campaign by Masséna in Switzerland pushed back the Russian army and removed the threat of foreign invasion. Bonaparte, who had returned hurriedly from Egypt with his principal lieutenants to save the country, when he landed at Fréjus on 9 October found that France had unfortunately already been saved. The invincible conqueror, who had just, or so it was thought, founded a new empire in the East, was not received with any the less enthusiasm.

The immediate crisis being over, the apparent need for urgent measures had vanished, but Sieyes was not ready to abandon his schemes so easily. In the course of ten years he had fetched half a circuit about the political world and reached his political antipodes. Whereas in 1789 he had stood for the unlimited sovereignty of the legislature, his aim now was to expand and consolidate the authority of the executive. This meant a further *coup d'état* at the expense of the legislative bodies, which could only be effected by calling on the cooperation of a popular general, who could be none other than Bonaparte. Did Sieyes believe that, having served his purpose, a general, especially a Bonaparte, would then retire quietly into the background? It is possible: he was vain enough to believe anything. Bonaparte, to whom all the factions now looked anxiously, though he had nothing but contempt for Sieyes, saw the advantage of a temporary alliance with him. Talleyrand acted as the intermediary between them. Fouché, uninvited, gave his support. To depict Bonaparte as advancing, vice and crime in either hand, to the overthrow of the Republic would be poetic licence, but not inexcusable. The number of those actually implicated in the conspiracy of 1799 was small, but in a sense the whole nation was Bonaparte's accomplice, for propaganda in the journals had worked up a fear of terrorist plots, behind which the real conspiracy lay concealed.

An alleged terrorist conspiracy provided an excuse to move the legislative councils to St Cloud outside Paris. This transfer was carried through on 9 November 1799. The next day, the 18 brumaire, when the Council of the Five Hundred met, there were violent speeches against Bonaparte, despite the efforts of his brother, Lucien, who was in the chair. Bonaparte, who entered to harangue the Five Hundred, lost his head and denounced them wildly. They replied with cries for a vote of outlawry. He fled outside and called on the guards to support him. While the soldiers hesitated Lucien emerged and saved the situation by a dramatic appeal to them to rescue their general from the daggers of assassins. This lie did the trick. The Five Hundred were driven out by the troops and France's first essay in parliamentary government had come to an end.

7. BALANCE-SHEET OF THE EIGHTEENTH CENTURY

THE age that began with the death of a king ended with the virtual death of a republic. Such beginnings and such endings draw arbitrary lines across the pages of history. They are artificial interruptions in the grand unfolding theme of national life. Yet if history is, in the words of Carlyle, the essence of innumerable biographies, there are – among those whose lives, added together, make up the grand total – the millions who count in the statistical averages and generalizations, and the few who, because of their positions or personalities, cast a measurable individual weight into the balance. That Louis XIV and Napoleon Bonaparte fall into the latter category cannot be doubted. The disappearance from the scene of the former, and the rise to power of the latter, were events momentous enough to write *finis* to one age and *incipit* to another.

Between the grand monarch and the emperor there is, in France, no figure of comparable political magnitude, none of those men who can define an age and stamp the mark of their personalities on it. The French eighteenth century is not a period of great, dominating political figures. Yet if no one man counted overmuch, more men – and women – counted for something than possibly at any other time. The great mass forces of the modern world had not yet been born, while the individual – at the end of the century sometimes even the obscure individual – had at last emerged from the anonymity of the Middle Ages. If it was not a century of greatness, for the student of *l'homme sensuel moyen* there is no more fruitful field. The eighteenth century was also something more: it was, and above all in France, the nursery of the modern world. Ideas and social forces, the seeds of which were doubtless sown much earlier, can be

seen now pushing above the surface, not in the neatly arranged rows of the careful gardener but in the haphazard
tangle of nature. Yet they *can* be seen and distinguished: the
field is no longer a seed-bed but it is not yet a jungle, and a
pattern is discernible. The simple interpretations imposed
on eighteenth-century France by historians writing under
the influence of later social and political ideologies may have
to be abandoned, but the history that is beginning to emerge
from more detailed studies, if it is more complex is still coherent, it is not a chaos of unrelated facts.

The basic pattern of the age was inherited from the immediate past. French society and government bear the im-
press of the personality of Louis XIV throughout the century which witnessed his decline and death. If Louis XV
and Louis XVI failed and were to be hissed off the stage, it
was in part because they were mere understudies, and not
very good ones at that, trying to fill the role of the greatest
actor of majesty that France had known. Only Napoleon,
and he only for a short period, could successfully play the
part that had been created by the grand monarch. Failing
a great king, a great minister, supported by the king, could
have given France the government that she needed; but the
intrigues of a court were no breeding ground for greatness,
and after Fleury the whole system of government was calculated to prevent the king from finding the minister France
needed; or if he found him, from giving him the necessary
authority. This does not mean that the ministers of the
eighteenth century deserve all the condemnation that has
been lavished on them by historians who only admire success. There were among them many able and honest men
who could provide efficient administration: what they
could not provide was a united government and a con-
sistent policy. And when eventually, for lack of a policy, the
absolute monarchy collapsed, the revolutionary régime
which followed seemed to be attempting to push the weakness of the *ancien régime* to its logical conclusion by turning
anarchy into a form of government. In a sense, therefore,
the dominant factor throughout was a negative one: the

void left at the centre of the machine of state by the death of Louis XIV.

It was for the very reason of lack of central control that French society was able to develop so rapidly and freely and at the same time in such contradictory directions. First, when the king had become the prisoner of a court, instead of the court being the mere decorative background for the king, the way was open for aristocracy to re-emerge from the political insignificance into which it had been thrust in the shadow of the bureaucratic colossus erected by Louis XIV, to recapture the highest offices of state and in the end perish in a bid to gain control of the state itself. That many of the old nobility of Louis XV and Louis XVI were the sons or grandsons of those who had been, a generation or two earlier, the new nobles of Louisquatorzian officialdom is of little import. They intermarried with the old *noblesse*, their new names were lost in old titles, and they inherited more of the spirit of the Fronde than of the upstart administrators of Louis XIV. The *noblesse de l'épée* drew closer to that *noblesse de robe*, which in its parlements had for centuries past upheld the authority of the crown against a turbulent *noblesse* of the sword, but now itself aspired to usurp the authority of which it had formerly been the docile guardian. The parlements renewed on a more permanent basis the alliance with the aristocracy that they had momentarily consummated during the Fronde. The Church, reduced to subservience to the Crown by the Concordat of Francis I and kept in obedience by the Gallican liberties, its wealth and its higher offices put in the hands of the king to be given as rewards or taken away as punishments for the loyalty or disloyalty of the great houses of France, in the eighteenth century looked rather to its allies and relations of the aristocracy than to the Crown. The higher Church posts had either by long use become practically hereditary in great families, or else were distributed, as the prize of court intrigues, not to maintain the authority of the Crown, but to bolster up ministerial or aristocratic factions. Thus by 1788 the *noblesse* of the sword, robe, and church, which throughout the century had waged parallel campaigns against royal authority, had come so close together that they could unite in a single aristocratic revolt.

Yet their combined forces, dominant at Versailles, and with their centres of power in every cathedral, abbey, parlement, great château, or petty manor-house scattered through provincial capitals and countryside, though they were able to reduce the royal administration to impotence, were themselves to reveal only their weakness when they were challenged by another force which they had never associated, which indeed had never associated itself, with a claim to power. Looking backwards, the theme of eighteenth-century history in France is the rise of the Third Estate, but how many could have guessed this before 1789? Do we yet fully know what it means, for who were the Third Estate? We can give them another name and call them, if we will, the bourgeoisie, but this helps us no more, for what was the bourgeoisie? All that was not *noblesse* or people, we may reply. It may be suggested that the Third Estate consisted largely of officials, professional men, rentiers, and non-noble landowners; but for any more detailed or reliable estimate we shall have to wait until the social history of the period has been written.

However it was constituted, the problem remains why the Third Estate came to have the power to overthrow the combined aristocracies of France. In the course of narrating the history of this great overthrow, the explanation has perhaps emerged incidentally, for clearly it was not the bourgeoisie, whoever they may have been, who rioted in the market places, sacked the manor-houses and burnt the manorial rolls, dragged cannon to the Bastille, marched to Versailles, or mutinied in the army and fleet. The men who did these things, and constituted the rank and file of the peasant revolts and the great revolutionary *journées*, were peasants, craftsmen, artisans, small shopkeepers, soldiers. It was by making use of their discontents that the Third Estate was able to overcome the resistance of the privileged orders and divert the Revolution to its own ends. Once this fact is realized a restatement of the problem becomes possible. The grievances of the people in town and country need not be recapitulated, nor the breakdown of social discipline which at least in part followed from the aristocratic revolt. The real problem is how a class of officials, lawyers, financiers, rentiers, landowners, was able to acquire the leadership of a popular movement constituted mainly of peasants and craftsmen. What did such leaders and followers have in common? To ask the question is to go a long way towards answering it. What they had in common was evidently not economic interests, though each group had its own interest which, to the best of its ability and in so far as it understood that interest, it pursued. What they had in common was an enemy, primarily the *noblesse*, but along with it the superior clergy, *noblesse* of the robe, higher officials, and some sections of the wealthy such as the Farmers General: in other words, all those who might be described as belonging to the privileged classes.

Privilege was the enemy, equality the aim, though it must be remembered that the equality desired by the Third Estate was an equality not of property but of status. This was the inspiring motive of a social grouping which possessed talents, education, and at least moderate wealth, and yet was denied the position and status to which it thought these things entitled it. The peasants also found their primary objective in the assault on privilege and played their part in the events of 1789 under this banner. The better-off peasantry, having achieved their principal aims, and the remainder lacking the cohesion or consciousness for more than sporadic unrest, they dropped out of political life. The Revolution was henceforth mainly an urban phenomenon, kept alive in the towns, and above all in Paris, by the unrest of a populace which suffered increasingly from the pressure of high prices and shortage of supplies. The undermining of authority, the breakdown of police control, and the disintegration of the army led to a situation in which even a comparatively small popular demonstration could intimidate the Assembly. The political factions of the left naturally took advantage of the weapon they found to their hand and used it to overthrow their opponents; but the alliance of the Mountain with the masses was fortuitous and effected only a temporary diversion of the main stream of the revolution of the Third Estate. The populace gained little from it, except possibly during the period when the war economy of the Committee of Public Safety for a time halted inflation, and then only at the price of the Terror.

When the new revolutionary army was sufficiently professionalized and disciplined to be used in the streets of Paris the political role of the people was at an end. But as the politicians of the Third Estate, having made use of the populace, had found themselves at the mercy of their own instrument, so the oligarchy which emerged after Thermidor and leant on the army found its policies determined by the generals, until one rose above all the others and became the autocrat of France. Then, and only then, did the logic of Bourbon absolutism finally triumph over the liberal ideals of the Constituent Assembly, and divine-right monarchy find, with Bonaparte, its historical sequel in the sovereignty of force.

Yet, though the later régimes of the revolutionary decade were to leave their mark on France, it was under the Constituent Assembly that the real harvest of the eighteenth century had been gathered in. Its work was lasting because it was built on foundations which had been solidly laid and because it was the culmination of a social revolution which, underneath the formal, juridical structure of society, had been quietly proceeding for centuries. We can call it the triumph of the bourgeoisie if by this term we mean the venal officers, lawyers, professional men, proprietors, with a few financiers and merchants, who invested their money, for the most part, in land or *rentes*, after venal offices were no longer available. The Revolution gave them the opportunity to obtain some of the lands and more of the offices of the privileged classes and to complete the process of rising to become the ruling class in France. They were not, by and large, a commercial or industrial class; their wealth was only to a minor degree derived from trade or industry, and it did not go back to fertilize the economic life of the nation. In their way of life they were the heirs of the obsolescent *noblesse,* and if they were bourgeois their aim was to be *bourgois vivant noblement.* The pattern of life which they copied and gradually made their own was that of the eighteenth century, the graces of which they were to perpetuate, to the best of their ability, into a modern world. Their eyes remained turned to the past in which their ideal had been set.

The victors had no wish to go beyond the social and political victory they had won, nor had they any intention of sharing their gains with the petty shopkeepers, craftsmen, and journeymen, and all the *menu peuple* of the towns who had fought their battle for them. Equally, in the countryside, the better-off peasant proprietors were satisfied with what they had gained, indifferent to the grievances of the share-cropping *métayers,* and hostile to the barely conscious demands of the landless labourers. Out of the Revolution, therefore, there emerged a new and even stronger system of vested interests than had preceded it. Perhaps human capacity for change is limited: at any rate, the Revolution seemed to have effected changes so great that for a time they inhibited further progress. It did not inaugurate but brought to an end a great age of social transformation. The paradox of French history is that a revolutionary settlement was to provide the basis for a profoundly conservative pattern of society.

Yet it would be a narrow view to portray the Revolution as concerned only with material interests: the eighteenth century was an age of intellectual and moral as well as social development. Humanitarian and utilitarian reforms that had existed only on paper, or at best had received only scattered and partial expression before 1789, were given fuller effect in the legislation of the revolutionary assemblies. In one field, admittedly, the eighteenth century had sown dragon's teeth: clericalism and anti-clericalism were to bedevil French politics into the twentieth century. The phenomenon of anti-clericalism is, however, far from being understood: to attribute its outburst among the revolutionary masses merely to the influence of the *philosophes* is unsatisfactory, but if its tap-roots went – as they well may have done – deep into the obscure recesses of the popular mind, from what sources they drew nourishment, and driven by what inner urge it pushed its way to the surface, remain unsolved and perhaps insoluble problems. We can only add this to the sum total of all that the Enlightenment bequeathed to the Revolution and so to modern France, of which, intellectually and morally, as well as socially, the pattern had been already set when, on the eighteenth of brumaire, Bonaparte made himself First Consul. Undeniably, the Enlightenment set up ideals that the revolutionaries could aspire towards more often than they could achieve, yet what they did achieve would give the French eighteenth century greatness if nothing else did.

CHRONOLOGICAL TABLE

1643	Accession of LOUIS XIV
1648–53	The Fronde
1651	Formal ending of minority of Louis XIV
1661	Beginning of Louis XIV's personal rule
1685	Revocation of edict of Nantes
1697	Bayle's *Dictionnaire*
1701	War of Spanish Succession begins
1713–15	Peace of Utrecht
1713	Bull Unigenitus
1715	Death of Louis XIV. Accession of LOUIS XV
1715–23	Regency of Philip of Orleans
1716	Establishment of Bank by Law
1717	Creation of Mississipi Company
	Triple Alliance of France, England, and Holland
	Watteau paints *L'Embarquement pour Cythère*
1718	Quadruple Alliance of France, England, Holland, Austria
	Conspiracy of Cellamare
	Abandonment of *Polysynodie*
1718–19	Law acquires the General Farm of the taxes
1720	Collapse of Law's system
1721	Montesquieu's *Lettres persanes*
1722	Dubois becomes *premier ministre*
1723	Deaths of Dubois and Orleans
	Bourbon as *premier ministre*
1724–31	Club de l'Entresol
1725	Marriage of Louis XV and Marie Leczinska
1726	Disgrace of Bourbon
	Fleury becomes chief minister (without the name)
	Stabilization of livre
1731	Treaty of Vienna
	Marivaux's *La Vie de Marianne* (completed 1748)
	Prévost's *Manon Lescaut*
	Convulsionnaires of Saint-Médard
1733	Outbreak of the War of the Polish Succession
1734	Voltaire's *Lettres anglaises*
1735	Fleury signs peace preliminaries with Austria
1737	Disgrace of Chauvelin
1738	Treaty of Vienna: Duchy of Lorraine attributed to Stanislaus and on his death to France

1739	Outbreak of war between England and Spain
1740	Death of Emperor Charles VI
	Rise of Belle-Isle
1741	Franco-Prussian alliance. France enters the War of the Austrian Succession
1742	Loss of influence of Belle-Isle
1743	Death of Fleury
1744	Illness of Louis XV at Metz
	Strike of silk workers at Lyon
1745	Mme de Pompadour becomes titular mistress of Louis XV
	Fontenoy: victory of Marshal de Saxe
	Dismissal of Orry
1748	Treaty of Aix-la-Chapelle ends the War of the Austrian Succession
	Montesquieu's *De l'esprit des lois*
1749	Buffon's *Histoire Naturelle* (completed 1788)
	Machault's tax of the *vingtième*
1751	First volume of the *Encyclopédie*
	Failure of Machault's attempt at financial reform
1754	Recall of Dupleix from India
	Condillac's *Traité des sensations*
1755	British attacks on French ships
1756	Agreement of Westminster between Prussia and Great Britain
	France and Austria conclude Treaty of Versailles
	Outbreak of Seven Years War
1757	Defeat of Soubise by Frederick II at Rossbach
	Attack on Louis XV by Damiens
1758	French armies evacuate Hanover
	Voltaire's *Candide*
	Helvétius's *De l'esprit*
	Choiseul appointed Secretary for Foreign Affairs
1759	Minden: French defeat
	Loss of Quebec, Guadeloupe, Martinique, etc.
	French naval defeats of Lagos and Quiberon
1760	Rousseau's *Nouvelle Héloïse*
1761	Family Compact between France and Spain
1762	Execution of Calas
	Rousseau's *Contrat social* and *Émile*
1763	Peace of Paris
1764	Death of Mme de Pompadour
	Dissolution of Society of Jesus in France

Chronological Table

1765   Execution of La Barre

1766   Lorraine incorporated in France

1768   French purchase of Corsica from Genoa

1770   Marriage of the dauphin and Marie-Antoinette
          Fall of Choiseul

1770–4 Ministry of Maupeou and Terray

1771   Exile of parlements

1774   Death of Louis XV. Accession of LOUIS XVI
          Fall of Maupeou and Terray
          Maurepas acquires chief influence in government
          Recall of parlements

1774–6 Turgot as Controller-General

1776   Turgot's six edicts
          Fall of Turgot

1777–81 Necker in charge of finances

1778   France enters War of American Independence

1781   Necker's *Compte rendu*
          Dismissal of Necker
          Capitulation of Yorktown

1782   Defeat of de Grasse at naval battle of Saintes

1783   Treaty of Versailles ends War of American Independence
          Calonne becomes Controller-General

1784   Beaumarchais' *Mariage de Figaro*

1785   Affair of the diamond necklace

1786   Vergennes' commercial treaty with Great Britain

1787   Death of Vergennes
          February: Meeting of the Notables
                  Fall of Calonne
          May: Appointment of Loménie de Brienne as *principal
                  ministre*
                  Dissolution of Notables
                  Edict of toleration of Protestants
          August: Exile of parlement of Paris
          September: Anglo-Prussian intervention in Dutch Re-
                  public
                  Recall of parlement

1788   May: Suspension of parlement and creation of Plenary
                  Court by Lamoignon
           June: Revolt at Grenoble
                  Resignation of Brienne and Lamoignon
           August: Convocation of States-General
                  Return of Necker to office

1788 September: Recall of parlements
     December: Royal council approves decree doubling
         Third Estate
1789 January: Revolt at Rennes
     February: Sieyes' *Qu'est-ce que le Tiers État?*
          Bread and grain riots in spring and early
          summer
     April: Réveillon riots at Paris
     May: Meeting of STATES-GENERAL (Constituent)
     June 17: Third Estate adopts title of <u>National Assembly</u>
     June 20: Tennis-court oath
     June 23: Royal Session
     June 27: King orders first two orders to join third
     July 14: Fall of the Bastille
         Recall of Necker
     July-August: Grand Peur
     August 4–11: Decrees abolishing feudal rights and privi-
         leges
     October 5–6: October Days
     October 21: Decree on martial law
     November, December: Secularization of Church lands
          and issue of assignats decreed
     December: Law on local government
1790 July: Civil Constitution of the clergy
     August: Mutiny at Nancy
     September: Resignation of Necker
     November: Burke's *Reflections on the Revolution in France*
1791 April: Death of Mirabeau
        Papal Bull condemns oath of Civil Constitution
     June 21: Flight to Varennes
     July 17: Meeting at Champ de Mars dispersed by Na-
         tional Guard
         Formation of Feuillants Club
     August 27: Declaration of Pilnitz
         Negro revolt in St Domingo
     September: Annexation of Avignon and Venaissin
         Constitution of 1791 voted
         Dissolution of Constituent Assembly
     October: Meeting of <u>LEGISLATIVE ASSEMBLY</u>
     November: Pétion elected Mayor of Paris
1792 March: Formation of Brissotin ministry
     April 20: France declares war on Austria

1792   June 12: Letter of Roland to Louis XVI
        June 13: Dismissal of Roland, Servan, and Clavière
        June 20: Popular demonstrations in Paris
        July 11: 'La Patrie en danger'
                 Manifesto of Duke of Brunswick
        July 25: The Sections declared permanent
        August 10: Attack on Tuileries
        August 19: Flight of La Fayette
        August 20: Fall of Longwy
        September 2: Fall of Verdun
        September 2–6: September massacres
        September 20: Valmy: retreat of Brunswick
        September 21: Meeting of CONVENTION
        September 22: Abolition of monarchy
        September: French occupation of Savoy and Nice
        October: Custine crosses the Rhine
        November: French victory at Jemappes, occupation of
                  Belgium
                  Annexation of Savoy
        November 19: Decree of Convention offering help to all
                     peoples wishing to recover their liberty
        December 15: Decree on treatment of occupied territories
        December: Trial of Louis XVI
1793   January 21: Execution of Louis XVI
        February 1: French declaration of war on Great Britain
        February, March: Food riots led by Jacques Roux and
                         Varlet
        March: French declaration of war on Spain
               Revolt of the Vendée
               Revolutionary Tribunal set up
               Dumouriez defeated, evacuates Netherlands
        April: Treason of Dumouriez
               Establishment of Committee of Public Safety
        May: First law of the maximum
             Revolt of Lyon
        May 31: Rising in Paris
        June 2: Arrest of Brissotins
        June 24: Constitution of 1793 voted
        July 13: Assassination of Marat
                 Robespierre enters Committee of Public Safety
                 Suppression of remaining seigneurial rights
                 without compensation

1793 August: Toulon delivered to English
    Levée en masse declared
  September: Law against suspects
      General maximum established
  October: Lyon revolt repressed
     Execution of Marie-Antoinette
     Execution of 'Girondins'
     Dechristianization campaign
  December: Toulon retaken by revolutionaries
  December 4: Law on local government of 14 frimaire
      Defeat of Vendéans

1794 March 24: Execution of Hébertists
  April 5: Execution of Dantonists
  June 1: Naval battle off Brest
  June 8: Fête of the Supreme Being
  June 10: Law of 22 prairial reorganizing Revolutionary
    Tribunal
  June 26: French victory at Fleurus: reconquest of Bel-
    gium
  July 27–8: 9 thermidor – Fall of Robespierre
  September 1: Billaud, Barère, and Collot leave Commit-
    tee of Public Safety
  November: Jacobin Club closed
  December: Trial and execution of Carrier
      Abolition of maximum

1795 February: Pacification of La Jaunaye
  April 1: Day of 12 germinal
  April: Deportation of Billaud, Collot, Barère decreed
    Peace of Basle between France and Prussia
  May: Peace with Holland
  May 20: Day of 1 prairial
  June: Death of Louis XVII
  July: Quiberon: defeat of émigrés
    Peace between Spain and France
  August: Constitution of Year III voted
    Law of the two-thirds
  October 5: Revolt of 13 vendémiaire
     Dissolution of Convention
  November: Rule of DIRECTORY begins

1796 May: Conspiracy of Babeuf
    French victory at Lodi
  November: French victory at Arcola

1797   January: French victory at Rivoli
        April: Preliminaries of Leoben
                Partial elections return constitutional monarchists
        May: Bonaparte occupies Venice
        September 4: *Coup d'état* of 18 fructidor
        October: Treaty of Campo-Formio
1798   May: Departure of French expedition to Egypt
        July: French victory at Battle of the Pyramids
        August: Aboukir Bay: Nelson destroys French fleet
1799   March: War of the Second Coalition
        May: Sieyes enters Directory
        June 18: Day of 30 prairial
                La Revellière and Merlin expelled from Directory
        March–July: Austrian and Russian successes
        August: French defeat at Novi
        September–October: Russian army defeated in Switzerland
        October: Return of Bonaparte to France
        November 9-10: *Coup d'état* of 18 brumaire

FURTHER READING

To provide a full bibliography, or even a list of all the books, articles, and some unpublished material used in writing this history is not practicable. Ample bibliographies, up to the date of their publication, may be found in

Lavisse, *Histoire de France:* vol. 8, pt ii, H. Carré, *Louis XVI, 1715–1774* (1911); vol. 9, pt i, Carré, Sagnac, and Lavisse, *Louis XVI, 1774–1789* (1912)

Lavisse, *Histoire de France contemporaine:* vol. i, P. Sagnac, *La Révolution (1789–1792)* (1920); vol. ii, G. Pariset, *La Révolution (1792–1800)* (1920)

Halphen et Sagnac (eds.), *Peuples et civilisations:* vol. 11, P. Muret, *La Prépondérance anglaise (1715–1763)* (1937); vol. 12, P. Sagnac *La Fin de l'ancien régime et la révolution américaine (1763–1789)* (1941); vol. 13, G. Lefebvre, *La Révolution française* (1951)

Clio: Introduction aux études historiques, E. Préclin et V.-L. Tapié, *Le XVIIIᵉ siècle* (2 vols., 1952)

Clio: L. Villat, *La Révolution et l'Empire,* vol. 1, *Les Assemblées révolutionnaires, 1789–1799* (1936)

Thémis: Histoire des Institutions, by J. Ellul, vol. 2 (1956)

A useful bibliography of the eighteenth century, including works on France, is *A Select List of Works on Europe and Europe Overseas 1715–1815,* edited by J. S. Bromley and A. Goodwin (1956). The list of books which follows should be regarded as no more than a guide to further reading.

Among general histories, the Lavisse volumes and the *Peuples et Civilisations* series, both already cited, are of value. The Larousse *Histoire de France* (1954), edited by Marcel Reinhard (vol. 11: R. Mousnier, *La France de Louis XV,* and M. Reinhard, *La Crise révolutionnaire*), is a very readable, sound summary, magnificently illustrated. Ph. Sagnac's *La Formation de la Société française moderne* (2 vols., 1946), which surveys French social development from 1661 to 1789, provides an introduction to many important aspects of the period, but is too general in treatment, often because the fundamental research has still not been done, to provide a satisfactory synthesis.

The Ancien Régime

Original sources for the French *ancien régime* offer an embarrassing richness. The memoirs, of which there are hundreds in print, have to be treated with caution. Apart from their inherent faults as historical sources, many are later fabrications not even written by the authors to whom they are attributed. Thus the famous *Souvenirs* of Mme de Créqui, which passed through over a dozen editions, represent a bookseller's venture of the eighteen-thirties, Mme de Créqui, who knew the Versailles of Louis XIV and met the Emperor Napoleon at the Tuileries, being an admirable figure on whom to hang an anecdotal history of the whole century. The history of eighteenth-century France is still littered with the debris of such apocryphal or unreliable memoirs. Among those that are genuine must be named, first and foremost, the memoirs of Saint-Simon. In addition to the monumental and essential edition in 41 volumes by Boislisle (1879–1928), there are various volumes of selections, some in translation. D'Argenson's *Journal* (9 vols., 1859–67, also available in translation, 1909) represents the views of a disappointed minister, the *Journal* of Barbier (ed. in 4 vols., 1847–56 and in 8 vols., 1885) those of a gossiping lawyer, on the reign of Louis XV. Between them they have done a good deal to distort its history. The most reliable history of the court of Louis XV is the *Mémoires du duc de Luynes sur la cour de Louis XV (1735–1758)* (17 vols., 1860–5). Another interesting view of high society is presented in the *Mémoires du comte Dufort de Cheverney* (ed. R. de Crèvecoeur, 2 vols., 1909). The story of the *secret du roi* has been completed by the publication of the *Correspondance secrète du comte de Broglie avec Louis XV (1756–1784)* (ed. by D. Ozanam and M. Antoine, 2 vols., 1956–61). The literary world is reflected in the *Correspondance littéraire, philosophique et critique de Grimm, Diderot, etc.* (16 vols., ed. M. Tourneux, 1877–82). The people and daily life of Paris appear in L. S. Mercier's *Tableau de Paris* (many editions), with an abridgement in English, *The Waiting City: Paris, 1782–88* (trans. G. H. Simpson, 1933). An interesting account of a peasant household is Rétif de la Bretonne's *La Vie de mon Père* (ed. M. Boisson, 1924), for the author, though he achieved fame by the description of less simple manners, was himself the son of a peasant. The parish *cahiers* of 1789 throw much light on conditions in the countryside, though it must be remembered that these, like Rétif de la Bretonne, generally reflect the views of the better-off class of peasant farmers called *laboureurs*. An interesting selection of the observations of foreign visitors is given in C. Maxwell's *The English Traveller in France, 1698–1815* (1932). Among the sources quoted in this collection is the naïve and fascinating *Diary of a Scotch Gardener at the French Court at*

Further Reading

the End of the Eighteenth Century, by T. Blaikie (ed. F. Birrell, 1931).

The classic study of the *ancien régime* in relation to the Revolution is de Tocqueville's *L'Ancien Régime et la Révolution* (many reprints and also in translation). Taine's *L'Ancien Régime* is a brilliant piece of writing but lacks the depth and intellectual honesty that has enabled de Tocqueville's book to retain its value. F. Funck-Brentano's *L'ancien régime* (1926, translated as *The Old Regime in France,* 1929) is an amusing, lively anecdotal apology for France before the Revolution. P. Gaxotte's *Le Siècle de Louis XV* (revised ed., 1933, translated as *Louis the Fifteenth and his times,* 1934), which aims at rehabilitating the memory of Louis XV, may serve as a corrective to the many equally superficial works which have denigrated him. The *Dictionnaire des institutions de la France aux XVIIe et XVIIIe siècles* (1923) by M. Marion is an invaluable work of reference.

For many aspects or periods the historian will have to turn to books written in the nineteenth century, which he will neglect at his peril. I propose here, generally, to confine myself to more recent and more easily available works. Apart from the valuable notes and appendices to Boislisle's edition of Saint-Simon, the most complete account of the Regency is Dom Leclercq's *Histoire de la Régence* (3 vols., 1921). An introductory book is H. M. Hyde, *John Law* (1948). There is no satisfactory biography of Fleury, but on his foreign policy we have two sound studies, P. Vaucher's *Robert Walpole et la politique de Fleury, 1731–1742* (1925) and A. M. Wilson, *French Foreign Policy during the Administration of Cardinal Fleury* (1936). Among P. de Nolhac's many pleasant if slight works on the French court and eighteenth-century art, the most useful for the historian is *Louis XV et Madame de Pompadour* (1928). Nancy Mitford's *Madame de Pompadour* (1954) is eminently readable and sound. J. G. Flammermont's *Le Chancelier Maupeou et les parlements* (2nd ed., 1885) is scholarly and detailed but, writing at a time when the propaganda of the parlements was still taken at its face value, the author failed to appreciate the achievement of Maupeou and Terray, which still awaits its historian. The best book on Turgot, which also throws much light on the problems of local and central government, is D. Dakin, *Turgot and the Ancien Régime in France* (1939). On the affair of the diamond necklace there are, of course, innumerable books; the best, though it inevitably leaves some problems unsolved, is still Funck-Brentano's *L'Affaire du collier* (5th ed., rev., 1903, also in translation). An account of French foreign policy in the Dutch crisis of 1784–7 is given by A. Cobban in

Further Reading

Ambassadors and Secret Agents: the Diplomacy of the first Earl of Malmesbury at The Hague (1954), which also throws light on the defects of French diplomacy in the eighteenth century.

The more recent work on the *ancien régime* has tended to deal with special subjects rather than periods or episodes. There is no study of the system of government as a whole. The machinery of central government, rather than the way in which it worked, is described in P. Viollet, *Le Roi et ses ministres pendant les derniers siècles de la monarchie* (1912). A summary of the machinery for collecting indirect taxes is provided by G. J. Matthews in *Royal General Farms in eighteenth-century France* (1958). Funck-Brentano corrects some mistaken ideas in *Les Lettres de cachet* (1926). H. Carré's *La Fin des parlements, 1788–1790* (1912) provides a short general description of the parlements as well as narrating the history of their final phase. F. Ford in *Robe and Sword* (1953) concentrates his attention mainly on the social composition of the *noblesse de robe* and its connexions with the *noblesse de l'epée*; and R. Forster's *The Nobility of Toulouse in the Eighteenth Century* (1960) shows that at least in one area there was a shrewd, hard-working, commercially-minded provincial *noblesse*. Flammermont's *Remontrances du parlement de Paris au XVIIIe siècle* (3 vols., 1888–98) is an essential source. A useful survey of the political ideas of the parlements is made by R. Bickart in *Les Parlements et la notion de souveraineté nationale au XVIIIe siècle* (1932). The only general study of the intendants is P. N. Ardascheff, *Les Intendants de province sous Louis XVI* (trans. from Russian, 1909) which, however, needs much correction. Among many local studies the most recent, as well as the most important, is H. Fréville, *L'Intendance de Bretagne, 1689–1790* (3 vols., 1953). On French finances we have the first volume of M. Marion's *Histoire financière de la France depuis 1715* (6 vols., 1914–31), to which should be added the same author's *Machault d'Arnouville* (1892).

General outlines of international relations are given by G. Zeller in *Les Temps modernes, ii. De Louis XIV à 1789* (*Histoire des Relations internationales*, ed. P. Renouvin, vol. III, 1955), and P. Rain, *La Diplomatie française d'Henri IV à Vergennes* (1945). Useful general surveys of French colonial history are H. Blet, *Histoire de la colonisation française* (2 vols., 1946), and H. J. Priestley, *France Overseas through the Old Régime* (1939). The history of French Canada is treated by G. M. Wrong, *The Rise and Fall of New France* (1928). On Dupleix there is A. Martineau, *Dupleix, sa vie et son œuvre* (1931), and H. H. Dodwell, *Dupleix and Clive* (1920).

Further Reading

For the study of economic developments the general survey by H. Sée, *Histoire économique de la France* (vol. i, ed. R. Schnerb, 1948), is a useful introduction. An excellent outline of the social structure of France before the Revolution is given by Sée in his *La France économique et sociale au XVIIIe siècle* (1925, trans. as *Economic and social conditions in France during the eighteenth century*, 1927). H. Carré in *La Noblesse de France et l'opinion publique au XVIIIe siècle* (1920) describes the various divisions of the *noblesse*. The older books of A. Babeau, *La ville sous l'ancien régime* (2nd ed., 1884), *Le Village sous l'ancien régime* (5th ed., 1915), etc., provide much interesting, if scrappy, information which it is difficult to obtain easily elsewhere. On the army the most useful work is L. Mention, *L'Armée d'ancien régime* (1900). The effect of the shortage of suitable timber on French naval power is shown in P. W. Bamford's *Forests and French Sea Power, 1660–1789* (1956).

On the conditions of the peasantry important works, though they cover a broader period, are H. Sée's *Les Classes rurales en Bretagne du XVIe siècle à la révolution* (1906) and Marc Bloch's *Les Caractères originaux de l'histoire rurale française* (new ed., 1952), with a second volume of supplementary material published in 1956 by M. Dauvergne. G. Lefebvre's monumental *Les Paysans du Nord pendant la Révolution* (1924) contributes much to the understanding of the conditions of the peasantry before as well as during the Revolution. An interesting examination of the attempts to introduce more advanced methods of agriculture into France is A. J. Borde, *The Influence of England on the French Agronomes, 1750–1789* (1952).

Turning to industry, A. Remond's study of the Jacobite exile who became a leading French industrialist, *John Holker, 1719–1786* (1944), M. Rouff, *Les Mines de charbon en France au XVIIIe siècle, 1744–1791* (1922), and G. Martin, *Nantes au XVIIIe siècle, l'ère des négriers, 1714–1774* (1931), may be mentioned among other specialized studies of such topics. An important contribution to the economic history of the period is C. E. Labrousse, *Esquisse du mouvement des prix et des revenus en France au XVIIIe siècle* (1934), which prepared the way for his fundamental analysis of economic conditions, *La Crise de l'économie française à la fin de l'Ancien Régime et au début de la Révolution* (1944). On the economic thought of the physiocratic school we have G. Weulersse, *Le Mouvement physiocratique en France de 1756 à 1770* (2 vols., 1910) and *La Physiocratie sous les ministères de Turgot et de Necker, 1774–1781* (1950).

Behind the economic developments were technical advances, of which a remarkably full outline is given by R. Mousnier in the

Further Reading

Histoire générale des civilisations: Le XVIIIᵉ siècle, by R. Mousnier and E. Labrousse (1953). On the same subject is S. T. McCloy, *French Inventions of the 18th Century* (1952). The life and multifarious activities of the greatest French scientist of the century, Lavoisier, who also made many contributions to technical advance, are described in D. McKie's *Antoine Lavoisier* (1952), and among important works on the history of science P. Brunet's *L'Introduction des théories de Newton en France au XVIIIᵉ siècle* (1931) is notable.

In the field of religion, the Jansenists have been treated by A. Gazier, *Histoire générale du mouvement janséniste depuis ses origines jusqu'à nos jours* (2 vols., 1922), which is favourable to them, and E. Préclin, *Les Jansénistes du XVIIIᵉ siècle et la Constitution civile du clergé* (1928). The Protestants of France, whose existence is often forgotten, are dealt with by J. Dedieu in his *Histoire politique des protestants français, vol. ii: 1715–1794* (1925). The influence of the new climate of opinion on the Roman Catholic Church is shown in R. R. Palmer, *Catholics and Unbelievers in eighteenth-century France* (1939). A revealing study of the most famous act of persecution of pre-revolutionary France is David D. Bien's *The Calas Affair* (1958).

A general survey of eighteenth-century French thought is Kingsley Martin, *French Liberal Thought in the Eighteenth Century* (2nd ed., 1954). *The Philosophy of the Enlightenment* (trans. 1951), by E. Cassirer, is subtle, but to my mind misleading. Carl Becker's *The Heavenly City of the French Philosophers* (1932) is a brilliant essay but also carries one line of interpretation of a many-sided movement too far. It is severely, but in my opinion justly, criticized in a series of studies edited by R. O. Rockwood, *Carl Becker's Heavenly City Revisited* (1958). A recent interpretation of the Enlightenment, which differs fundamentally from that of Becker, is A. Cobban's *In Search of Humanity: the Role of the Enlightenment in Modern History* (1960). The essential introduction to the thought of the eighteenth century is the masterly work of Paul Hazard, *La Crise de la conscience européenne, 1680–1715* (3 vols. 1934), which has been translated. Probably the best book on the Encyclopedists is R. Hubert's *Les Sciences sociales dans l'Encyclopédie* (1923). A useful selection is *L'Encyclopédie of Diderot and d'Alembert: Selected Articles* (1954) by J. Lough. A. M. Wilson's *Diderot: the Testing Years* (1957) is the first volume of what is likely to be the authoritative life of the famous Encyclopedist, who is in some ways the most stimulating and provocative thinker of eighteenth-century France. The older books on French opinion in the eighteenth century by Aubertin, Roustan, and Roquain have largely been superseded and are not reliable guides. A general survey is D. Mornet, *La Pensée française au dix-huitième siècle* (1926), and a much more detailed study is provided by the same author in his *Origines intellectuelles de la révolution française* (1933). An interesting study of the spread of the new ideas is I. O. Wade's *The Clandestine Organisation and Diffusion of Philosophic Ideas in France from 1700 to 1750* (1938).

The history of French literature in the eighteenth century is hardly distinguishable from that of French thought. Perhaps for this reason a satisfactory general history of literature as such is hard to come by. F. C. Green's *Minuet* (1935) is an attractive *rapprochement* of some English and French themes. There is no space for a list of books on individual writers. E. Carcassonne, *Montesquieu et le problème de la Constitution française au XVIIIᵉ siècle* (1927) is a thorough discussion of the influence of Montesquieu, especially on the parlements. The basic work on Voltaire is still G. le B. Desnoiresterres' *Voltaire et la société au XVIIIᵉ siècle* (2nd ed., 8 vols., 1871–6), to which may be added A. Bellessort's brilliant *Essai sur Voltaire* (14th ed., 1933). The most important study of Rousseau's political thought in relation to its origins is R. Derathé's *J.-J. Rousseau et la science politique de son temps* (1950). Similar in its basic interpretation of Rousseau is A. Cobban's *Rousseau and the Modern State* (1934).

On architecture there is R. Blomfield, *History of French Architecture, 1661–1774* (2 vols., 1921), and L. Hautecoeur, *Histoire de l'Architecture classique en France* (tomes III and IV, 1943–5); on painting, L. Gillet, *La Peinture de Poussin à David* (2nd ed., 1935), and R. Schneider, *L'Art français: XVIIIᵉ siècle* (1926). A detailed compendium of the spread of French artistic influence through Europe is provided in L. Réau's *L'Europe française au siècle des lumières* (1938).

The Revolution

It would doubtless be an exaggeration to say that the amount of original material in print on the revolutionary decade in France is equal to that available for the whole of the rest of modern history put together, but to any historian of the revolutionary period it must seem no more than a pardonable exaggeration. A few of the better known original sources alone can be mentioned here. The many volumes of *cahiers* which have been edited are essential for the study of social conditions in France on the eve of the Revolution. Arthur Young's *Travels in France in 1787, 1788 and 1789*, available in many editions, the best being that of the French translation by H. Sée (3 vols., 1930), is invaluable, though the views of Arthur

Further Reading

Young need a good deal of correction. The flood of memoirs continues in the revolutionary period. Among the more important are E. Dumont's *Souvenirs sur Mirabeau* (ed. J. Bénétruy, 1950), the *Correspondance inédite, 1789, 1790, 1791* of the marquis de Ferrières (ed. H. Carré, 1932), and the *Mémoires de Madame Roland* (ed. C. Perroud, 2 vols., 1905).

An extensive sample of revolutionary journalism is provided in G. Walter's *La Révolution française vue par ses journaux* (1948). There are also extracts from the journals in L. G. Wickham Legg's *Select Documents illustrative of the history of the French Revolution. The Constituent Assembly* (2 vols., 1905). There is a modern edition of Camille Desmoulin's famous *Le Vieux Cordelier* (ed. H. Calvet, 1936). *L'Ancien Moniteur* (30 vols., 1850–4) is a reprint of the journal which, by the skill of its editors in following the official line as faction after faction rose to power or fell, survived throughout the period and can be regarded as reflecting the governmental view at each stage. It should be noted that up to 3 February 1790 this reprint is a later compilation. *The Principal Speeches of the Statesmen and Orators of the French Revolution, 1789–1795,* edited by H. Morse Stephens (2 vols., 1892) has unfortunately long been out of print and is difficult to obtain. An interesting collection of contemporary verdicts on Robespierre is made by L. Jacob in *Robespierre vu par ses contemporains* (1928). The most convenient selections of laws and decrees are J. M. Thompson's *French Revolution Documents 1789–94* (1933, reprinted) and *L'Œuvre législative de la Révolution* by L. Cahen and R. Guyot (1913).

A definitive edition of the writings, speeches, and correspondence of Robespierre is in progress and there are editions of the writings, letters, and speeches of many other prominent revolutionaries. The famous pamphlet of Sieyes, *Qu'est-ce que le tiers état,* has had no reprint since 1888, which is regrettable for it is essential to the understanding of the political ideas of the revolutionaries.

The study of the historiography of the Revolution has become a subject in itself, but cannot be dealt with here. The histories of Mignet (1824) and Thiers (1823–7) still have something to tell the student of the Revolution. Carlyle's *French Revolution* (1837) is in a class by itself. Michelet's history (1847–53 and many subsequent editions) is closer to Carlyle than to modern scholarship. Louis Blanc's twelve-volume history (1848–62) brought in new themes inspired by his socialistic ideas. De Tocqueville's masterpiece has been cited above. Taine's history (1882–7) is a brilliant polemic. Aulard's *Histoire politique de la révolution française (1789–1804)* (1901, translated in 4 vols., 1910) is the first general history based on the results of modern scholarship, but, as its title suggests, is mainly political in approach. Jaurès' *Histoire socialiste*, vols. i–iv (1901–4), is valuable, not only because it inaugurated the study of the Revolution as a struggle of social classes, but also for its interpretation of some of the major episodes. This line of research was continued by A. Mathiez, whose *La Révolution française* (3 vols., 1925–7, translated in 1928), which ends in thermidor 1794, is still one of the best general histories of France in these years. A masterly history of the whole revolutionary age is Georges Lefebvre's *La Révolution française* (3rd ed., 1951), cited above. The best account by an English historian is J. M. Thompson, *The French Revolution* (1943), and a valuable short introduction, embodying the results of modern research and concentrating particularly on the opening stages of the Revolution, is that by A. Goodwin, *The French Revolution, 1789–1794* (1953). There is much important material in the shorter studies of Aulard, Mathiez, and Lefebvre. The histories by Madelin and Gaxotte are readable but of little serious value.

Turning to more detailed monographs on the history of the Revolution, the finest account of the outbreak of the Revolution is G. Lefebvre's *Quatre-vingt-neuf* (1939), translated as *The Coming of the French Revolution* (1947). The most thoroughly worked out, though not convincing, exposition of the conspiracy thesis of the origins of the revolution is A. Cochin's *Les Sociétés de pensée et la Révolution en Bretagne, 1788–1789* (2 vols., 1926). Relevant to the aristocratic revolution are Carré's *La Fin des Parlements*, cited above, P. Renouvin, *Les Assemblées provinciales de 1787* (1921), and J. Egret, *La Révolution des notables: Mounier et les monarchiens* (1950). *La Grande Peur de 1789* by Lefebvre (1932) is a model of historical detection. The legend that the members of the Jacobin clubs were drawn from the lowest strata of the population was dissipated by C. C. Brinton's *The Jacobins* (1930). D. Greer in *The Incidence of the Terror during the French Revolution* (1935) and *The Incidence of the Emigration during the French Revolution* (1951) analysed the social composition of the victims of the Terror and of the émigrés. A stimulating and perverse Trotskyite interpretation of the social struggles of the Revolution, in which Robespierre appears as the supreme counter-revolutionary, is D. Guérin, *La Lutte des classes sous la première république* (3rd ed., 2 vols., 1946). The revolution of 10 August 1792 is described in Mathiez, *Le Dix Août* (1931). P. Caron's *Les Massacres de septembre* (1935) is a work of minute and detailed research. Taine's picture of the revolutionary mob is successfully criticized

Further Reading

by G. Rudé in *The Crowd in the French Revolution* (1959). A major reinterpretation of revolutionary politics, which demolishes the legend of a great Girondin party, is M. J. Sydenham's *The Girondins* (1961). The episode of *Les Sansculottes parisiens en l'an II* (1958) is described in massive detail by A. Soboul; and R. Cobb deals, in many articles and a forthcoming book, with the little, local *armées révolutionnaires*. The only comprehensive study of the composition and achievements of the great Committee of Public Safety is R. R. Palmer's *Twelve who Ruled* (1941). On the thermidorians we have Mathiez, *La Réaction thermidorienne* (1929), and Lefebvre, *Les Thermidoriens* (1937); and for the Directory *Le Directoire* (ed. J. Godechot, 1934) by Mathiez and *Le Directoire* (1946) by Lefebvre. A. Vandal's *L'Avènement de Bonaparte* (2 vols., 1907-8) is brilliantly written; it may overpaint the scene and exaggerate the defects of the directorial régime, but until much more work has been done on this phase of revolutionary history no judgement of the faults and merits of the Directory can be much more than a guess.

The best short survey of the constitutional history of the Revolution is the introduction to *Les Constitutions et les principales lois politiques de la France* by Duguit and Monnier (many editions). In recent editions the introduction has unfortunately been omitted. A valuable survey of revolutionary institutions is the *Histoire des institutions de la France sous la Révolution et l'Empire* (1951) by J. Godechot, to whom we also owe *Les Commissaires aux armées sous le Directoire* (1937).

The standard work on international relations is A. Sorel, *L'Europe et la Révolution française* (8 vols., 1885-1904), though Sorel's work is susceptible of many major corrections and additions. A shorter account is P. Rain's *La Diplomatie française de Mirabeau à Bonaparte* (1950). A. Fugier's *La Révolution française et l'Empire napoléonien* (1954) is rather slight on the revolutionary period. A significant reinterpretation of the outbreak of the revolutionary war is made by G. Michon in *Robespierre et la guerre, 1791-2* (1937). R. Guyot's *Le Directoire et la paix de l'Europe* (1911) is a major contribution to diplomatic history. Closely linked with foreign relations is the story of the Vendée, on which the literature is vast but partisan. E. Gabory, *L'Angleterre et la Vendée* (2 vols., 1930-1), has the virtue of using the extensive English as well as French sources. The effect of the Vendée on French naval power is revealed by N. Hampson in *La Marine de l'an II* (1959), which gives more credit than is customary to the Committee of Public Safety for its efforts to build up the French fleets, though showing also the reasons for its comparative lack of success.

A useful introduction to the economic policy of the revolutionaries, with extensive bibliographical references, is provided by the first chapters of S. H. Clough, *France: a History of National Economics, 1789–1939* (1939). The importance of bankers and financiers in revolutionary politics emerges in J. Bouchary, *Les Manieurs d'argent à Paris à la fin du XVIIIᵉ siècle* (3 vols., 1939–43). On the finances of the government we have Marion's *Histoire financière de la France*, cited above, and S. G. Harris, *The Assignats* (1930). The significance of the struggle initiated by the *enragés* was revealed by Mathiez in *La Vie chère et le mouvement social sous la Terreur* (1929). Lefebvre's *Paysans du Nord*, cited above, and his *Questions agraires au temps de la Terreur* (1932) throw much light on the problems of the countryside. Interesting technical material on agriculture is to be found in O. Festy, *L'Agriculture pendant la Révolution française* (1947).

The relations of the revolutionaries with the Papacy and the question of Avignon are described in A. Mathiez, *Rome et la Constituante* (1910). Recent Catholic historians of the religious policy of the revolutionaries are A. Latreille in *L'Église catholique et la Révolution* (1946–50), rather hostile to the Revolution, and J. Leflon in *La Crise révolutionnaire, 1789–1848* (1949), remarkably free from bias.

Among a host of biographies only a few can be selected for mention. J. M. Thompson's *Leaders of the French Revolution* (1929) contains a series of short but penetrating sketches. G. C. van Deusen, *Sieyes: his life and his nationalism* (1932) is concerned mainly with Sieyes' ideas. The standard work on the Mirabeau family is L. and C. de Loménie, *Les Mirabeau* (5 vols., 1878–90). Other biographies are O. J. R. Welch, *Mirabeau* (1951), L. Barthou, *Danton* (1932), L. R. Gottschalk, *Marat* (1927), L. Madelin, *Fouché* (2 vols., 1900). The best and most detailed life of Robespierre is by J. M. Thompson (2 vols., 1939). M. Reinhard has written the authoritative life of Carnot (1950–2), and L. Gershoy of Barère (1962).

On literature and art may be mentioned P. Trahard, *La Sensibilité révolutionnaire, 1791–1794* (1936), D. L. Dowd, *Pageant-Master of the Republic: Jacques-Louis David and the French Revolution* (1948), and L. Hautecoeur, *L'Art sous la Révolution et l'Empire* (1953).

INDEX

Abbaye, prison of, 202
Aboukir Bay, battle of, 256
Academy of Sciences, 14
Adélaide, Mme, 99
agriculture, methods of, 49
Aguesseau, d', 33
aides, 60
Aiguillon, duc d' (d. 1780), 93, 95, 97, 99
Aiguillon, duc d' (son of preceding), 158
Aix-la-Chapelle, Treaty of, 72
Alberoni, 27
d'Alembert, 101
Alexandre, 195
Amelot de Chaillou, 33, 70
American Independence, War of, 116, 120-3, 126
Ami du Peuple, l', 195
Anabaptists, 234
Angervilliers, d', 33
Angiviller, d', 115
anti-clericalism, 172, 225-6, 265-6
Antilles, see West Indies, French,
Anzin, mines of, 45
architecture, 40-2
Arcola, battle of, 255
Argens, d', 101
Argenson, comte d', 61, 70, 80
Argenson, marquis d', 52, 71-2, 85
Armed Neutrality, 121
armoire de fer, 210
army, French, 30, 91, 108-9, 192, 213, 229, 235
artillery, 91, 108, 235
Artois, comte d', 126, 128, 146, 150-1, 188
Assembly, National, 144, 158-9, 162-3, 166-7, 180
    Legislative, 184-6, 192, 195, 198-9
    of Notables, 127-9, 134
assignats, 172, 193, 229-30, 252
Aubusson tapestries, 54
Augereau, 35, 254
Augustus II of Saxony, 34
Augustus III of Saxony, 34-5
Austria, 34-5, 69, 72, 75, 200, 205, 254-5
Austria, declaration of war on, 192

Austrian alliance, 75-8, 91, 94, 113, 189
Austrian Netherlands, 75, 122, 189, 192, 204, 205, 213, 236
Austrian Succession, War of, 69-72
Autun, bishop of, see Talleyrand
Avignon, 174, 187, 194

Babeuf, 252
Bailly, 145, 153, 183, 197
banalités, 155
Barbaroux, 210, 217
Barbier de Seville, le, 116
Barère, 216, 218, 220-2, 236, 240, 244-6
Barnave, 153, 168, 183-4
Barras, 240, 242, 253, 256
Barry, Mme du, 77, 94, 97, 99, 113, 225
Barthélemy, 253
Bastille, 110, 149-50, 168
Bavaria, elector of, 69
Bayle, 83-4
Beauharnais, Josephine, see Bonaparte, Josephine
Beaumarchais, 115-16
Beaumont, Christophe de, 64
Beauvais tapestries, 54
Beauvillier, duc de, 21
Belle-Isle, comte de, 50, 68-70, 72, 80
Berg-op-zoom, capture of, 72
Bernard, Samuel, 37
Bernis, abbé de, 52, 77, 80
Bertier de Sauvigny, 152-3
Berwick, Duke of, 35
Billaud-Varenne, 89, 218-20, 228, 230, 240, 242, 244-5
billets de confession, 64
Bodin, 10, 29
Boissy d'Anglas, 246, 249
Bolingbroke, 84
Bonaparte, Josephine, 251
Bonaparte, Lucien, 258
Bonaparte, Napoleon, 26, 108, 121, 229, 235, 246, 251, 254-60
Bordeaux, 40-2, 48, 58, 62, 133, 224, 242
Boscawen, 74
Bossuet, 15
Boucher, 55

285

Bouillé, marquis de, 177, 182
Boulainvillier, 85
Bourbon, duc de, 25, 28–9, 32
Braddock, General, 74
Brest, 237
Breteuil, 110, 118–19, 127–9, 147, 150–1, 188
Breton club, 158, 177
Brienne, Loménie de, 128–33
Brissot, 185–7, 189–96, 204, 209–10, 212–13, 225, 227
Brissotins, 186, 189–99, 203–4, 209–10, 212, 216, 222–3
Brittany, 93, 133, 136, 159, 224, 257
Broglie, comte de, 76, 97–8
Broglie, maréchal de, 147, 150
brumaire, 18ᵉ, 258
Brune, 235
Brunswick, Duke of, 79, 192, 196, 200–1, 204–5
Brussels, 208
Buffon, 86
Bull Unigenitus, 63–4
Burgoyne, duc de, 20, 21
Burgoyne, General, 120
Burke, Edmund, 180, 188
Byng, Admiral, 78

Cabarrus, Thérèse, 242, 251
Cagliostro, 119
cahiers, 141–2, 155–6, 176
Calas, 63, 86
calendar, republican, 225
Calonne, 111, 126–9, 132, 188
Cambon, 242
Camisards, revolt of, 15, 62, 86
Camperdown, battle of, 255
Campan, Mme, 114
Campo-Formio, treaty of, 255
Canada, Anglo-French conflict in, 74
    French colony in, 39, 73
    loss of, 79–81, 90
canal du Midi, 14, 40
Candide, 102
Cape Breton Island, 39
capitaineries, 156
capitation, 58, 99
Carmes, prison of, 202
Carnot, 218, 220–1, 236, 238–9, 242, 247, 253
Caron, *see* Beaumarchais
Carrier, 224, 239, 244
Cartesianism, 83
Castries, marquis de, 129, 236
Catherine II, 97, 121, 188
Cellamare, conspiracy of, 27
censorship, 84, 86
Champ de Mars, massacre of, 183–4
Champs Élysées, 42
Chancellor, 31

Chardin, 115
Charette, 249
charity, 49
Charles VI, 68–9
Châteauroux, duchesse de, 50–1, 68, 71
Châteauvieux, regiment of, 177
Chaumette, 227
Chauvelin, garde des sceaux, 33, 35–6, 50–1, 69, 76
Chauvelin, marquis de, 191, 211–12
Chénier, André, 241
Cherbourg, 118, 127
Chevreuse, duc de, 21
Choiseul, 76, 80–1, 88, 90–5, 108, 113
Choiseulists, 106, 113, 118
Choiseul-Praslin, 81, 90
Church, French, 62–5, 86–90, 109–10
Church lands, nationalization of, 154, 172–3
cinq grosses fermes, 46, 57
Cisalpine Republic, 255
classicism, 179
Clavière, 191, 216, 225
Clergy, 64–5, 89–110, 143, 145
    Assembly of, 109, 132
    Civil Constitution of, 173–4, 225
    non-juring, 186
    taxation of, 61–2
Clermont, 42
Clive, 79
Clootz, Anacharsis, 177
Closter-seven, Convention of, 79
Club de l'Entresol, 84
Clubs, revolutionary, *see* Jacobin Club
    Cordeliers Club
coal-mining, 44–5
Coburg, 213, 229, 236
Colbert, 12, 14–15, 33, 42–3, 46, 56
Collot d'Herbois, 218–20, 226, 230, 238, 240, 242, 244–8
colonies, French, 39, 73–4, 79–81, 91–2
commerce, bureau de, 40
commercial treaty of 1786, 111
commission des reguliers, 110
Committee of General Defence, 213
Committee of General Security, 228, 237–9, 242, 248
Committee of Public Safety, 215, 218–19, 226–31, 235, 237–9, 247–8
Commune of Paris, 198, 203, 216, 223, 240, 248
Compagnie des Indes, 39–40, 73–4, 92
Company of the West, 24
compte-rendu, 124–5, 133
Condé, 150–1
Condillac, 86, 102
Condorcet, 102, 135, 225
Conseil de commerce, 31
Conseil de conscience, 31
Conseil des dépêches, 31

Index

Conseil des finances, 23, 31
Conseil d'en haut, 30–1, 52, 125
Conseil des partis, 31
Constitution of 1791, 184–5
  Jacobin, 218
  of year III, 250
Conti, prince de, 25, 76
Contrat social, 163
Contrôle général, 47, 60, 107, 125, 127, 129
Convention, 198–9, 203–4, 208–9, 211–18, 226, 231–2, 234, 240, 245–8
Corday, Charlotte, 224
Cordeliers Club, 177, 205, 214, 224
corn trade, 105–6
Cornwallis, 121
corporations, 42–3, 46, 176
Corsica, 92, 187
corvée, 47, 93, 107
Council of the Five Hundred, 257–8
counter-revolution, 163, 188
Couperin, 54
Couthon, 217, 218, 221, 238
Crébillon, 53, 55
criminal law, *see* laws, reform of
Croÿ, duc de, 52
Crozat, 37
Cumberland, Duke of, 79
currency, stabilization of, 39
Custine, 191, 208, 211, 214
customs, internal, 46, 57–60, 176
customs posts, attack on, 148

Damiens, 80
Danton, 168, 177, 197, 200, 205, 207, 209, 211, 216, 218, 230–1, 236
Darien Company, 25
Dauphiné, 133
  États of, 133
David, 179–80, 222, 225, 231–2
Davoust, 235
dechristianization, 225–6, 229
Declaration of Rights, 163–5, 175
Deffand, Mme du, 128
deism, 85
democratic movements, 122, 189
Denain, battle of, 17
departments, formation of, 169–71
Descartes, 82, 85, 101
Desmoulins, Camille, 177, 179, 221, 225, 230
dévot party, 61, 65, 71, 99, 106
Diamond necklace, affair of, 98, 118–20
Dictionnaire historique et critique, 84
Diderot, 85–6, 114–15
Dijon, 48, 133
dîme royale, 24
Directory, 251–9
Discours préliminaire, 101
divorce, law of, 175
dixième, 58

don gratuit, 60, 132
Dubois, cardinal, 27, 32
Dumont, Étienne, 181, 185
Dumouriez, 191–2, 204–5, 207–8, 211–15
Dunkirk, 40
Dupleix, 73–4
Dupont de Nemours, 111
Duport, Adrien, 136
Dutch Patriots, 122–3
Dutch Republic, *see* United Provinces

École militaire, 91, 108
Edict of Nantes, revocation of, 15
Égaux, conspiracy of the, 252
Egypt, invasion of, 255–6
elections, of 1789, 142–3
  of Convention, 203–4
  of 1795, 250
  of 1797, 253
Elizabeth, Mme, 182, 225
Elizabeth Farnese, 27
emigration, 151
émigrés, 188, 248–50
enclosures, 154–5, 176
Encyclopédie, 86, 101
England, plans for invasion of, 71, 97–8, 121
enragés, 214, 227
Éon, chevalier d', 97–8
Esprit des lois, de l', 53, 86
Estrées, d', 79
États généraux, 22, 131, 133–5, 138, 143–5
Evelyn, John, 9

Fabre d'Églantine, 177
Falkland Islands, dispute over, 95
famine, 48, 139–41
Farmers general, 24, 38, 46, 60, 105, 126
fashions, 19, 114–15, 252
fédérés, 196
Fénelon, 20, 21, 29, 84
Ferrières, marquis de, 184
Fersen, comte de, 117–18, 182
Fête, of 20 June 1790, 168–9
  of the Supreme Being, 231–2
Feuillants Club, 184–5
Figaro, 20, 116
finances, royal, 14, 22–4, 37, 56–62, 91, 95, 123–5, 127, 171
financiers, 23–5, 28, 37–8, 61, 106, 126–8
fisheries, 39, 91
Flesselles, de, 149
Fleurus, battle of, 236, 238
Fleury, cardinal, 28–9, 32–6, 50–2, 60, 68, 70, 84, 90
Florida, 81, 121
Fontenelle, 53, 101
Fontenoy, battle of, 72
Fort Duquesne, 80
Fort Frontenac, 80

Fouché, 89, 220, 239, 242, 258
Foullon, 152–3
Fouquet, 10, 68
Fouquier-Tinville, 225, 245
Fournier l'Américain, 195
Fourth of August, night of, 158–9
Fragonard, 115, 180
Francis of Lorraine, 36, 113
Frankfurt, occupation of, 208
Franklin, Benjamin, 120, 168
Frederick II, 69–72, 75, 77–9
freemasons, 135
Fréjus, Bishop of, *see* Fleury
Fréron, 239–40, 242–3, 245
Fronde, 10
fructidor, 18*ᵉ*, 254–5

Gabelle, 58–60
Gabriel, A.-J., 40, 42
Gallican liberties, 63
Gallicanism, 63–4
Garde des Sceaux, 31–2
Gardes françaises, 149–50
germinal, 12*ᵉ*, 245
Gibraltar, siege of, 121
Gil Blas, 20
gilds, 42–5
Gironde, deputation of, 186, 191, 209
Girondin party, 217
Givet, 192
Gluck, 115
Gobelins tapestry, 15, 44, 54
Gorée, 79, 122
Gournay, 103–4
Grand e Peur, 157–8
Granville, 229
Grasse, de, 121
Great Britain, declaration of war against, 213
    free trade treaty with, 11
    relations with, 27, 34, 71–2, 111, 211–13, 253
Grenada, 80–1
Grenoble, 48, 58, 133
Grétry, 160
Greuze, 115
Gribeauval, 91, 108, 205
Guadeloupe, 73, 80
Guiana, French, 92, 254
Guibert, 254
Guillotin, Dr, 176

Hanover, invasion of, 79
Hanriot, 216–17, 239, 241
Hastenbeck, battle of, 79
Hébert, 195, 227–9, 231
Hébertists, 230–1
Hérault de Séchelles, 217–19
Histoire naturelle, 86
Hobbes, 9

Hoche, 229, 235, 250
Holker, John, 44
Holland, *see* United Provinces
Homme machine, l', 85
Hood, Admiral, 121
Howe, Admiral, 236
Huguenots, 15, 62–3, 86, 106, 109, 174
Humanitarianism, 111–12

Illuminés, 119
incroyables, 252
India, Anglo-French struggle in, 74, 79
India, French, 39, 73–4, 79, 81
India, French East India Company, *see* Compagnie des Indes
industry, 42–6, 49
inheritance, laws of, 175
intendants, 12, 41, 131, 141
Invalides, 149
Isnard, 190, 215
Italian campaign, 254–5

Jacobin Club, 158, 177–80, 184, 190, 197, 203, 232
Jacobins, 178–9, 194, 243–4, 256–7
Jacquard, 45
Jansenists, 9, 18, 36, 63–5, 67, 86, 88
Jeanbon Saint-André, 218, 220, 236
Jemappes, battle of, 208, 213
Jesuits, 18, 61, 63–4, 88–90, 101
Jews, 109, 174
Jourdan, 229, 235–6
Jourdan Coupe-tête, 194
jurandes, 107
Jurieu, 83–4
justice retenue, 30

Kaunitz, 75, 77
Keeper of the Seals, *see* Garde des Sceaux
Kellerman, 204–5, 229
Kersaint, comte de, 212

La Barre, chevalier de, 87
La Bouexière, 38
La Bruyère, 20
La Chalotais, 93
La Fayette, 120–1, 135, 153, 161–2, 182, 184, 192, 197, 201, 204, 214
Lagos, battle of, 80
La Jaunaye, pacification of, 249
La Luzerne, 129
Lamballe, princesse de, 117, 202
La Mettrie, 85
Lamoignon, 129, 131, 133
La Motte, comtesse de, 119–20
La Motte de Vayer, 83
Lanjuinais, 217
La Reveillière-Lépeaux, 253
La Rochefoucauld-Liancourt, 135
La Rochelle, 40
Laufeldt, battle of, 72

Launay, de, 149
Lavalette, père, 88
Lavater, 119
Lavoisier, 49, 101, 105, 205, 225
La Vrillière, 106
Law, John; Law's System, 23–6, 37–8, 40, 68
Laws, reform of the, 175–6
Lazowski, 195
Lebrun, 97
Le Brun, Vigée, 115, 179
Lebrun-Tondu, 212, 216
Le Chapelier, law, 176
Lefebvre, 235
Legendre, 195, 216
Le Havre, 40
Le Labourer, 20
Le Normant d'Étioles, 53
Leoben, Preliminaries of, 255
Leopold II, 188
Le Sage, 19–20
lettres de cachet, 30, 87, 96, 110
Lettres persanes, 29, 53, 84
Lettres philosophiques, 85, 101
Leuthen, battle of, 79
Levassor, Michel, 21
levée en masse, 224
Lévis, duc de, 117
Lille, 192
    negotiations at, 253, 255
Limoges, 104
Limousin, 103–4
Lindet, Robert, 218, 220, 238, 242
Lisbon, earthquake of, 55
lit de justice, 67
local government, laws of, 153, 169–71, 228
Locke, John, 82–3, 86, 130
Loménie de Brienne, *see* Brienne
Longwy, fall of, 200–1
Lorient, 25–6, 40
Lorraine, 35–6, 92, 142
Louis XIV, 9–22, 26, 29, 32, 38, 51, 56, 63, 67–8, 71, 82, 84, 259–61
Louis XV, 18, 21, 27–30, 32, 50–4, 61, 68, 70–2, 76–9, 89, 92–6, 98–9, 112–13
Louis XVI, 99–100, 105, 112–13, 138, 145, 150, 161–2, 186, 195–6, 210–11, 260
Louis XVII, 213, 248–9
Louis XVIII, *see* Provence, comte de
Louisberg, 80
Louisiana, 24, 37, 39, 48, 73, 81
Lyon, 43, 45, 58, 221, 224, 229

Mably, 168
Machault d'Arnouville, 61–2, 80, 88, 129
Mack, 213
Madagascar, 92
Maestricht, siege of, 213

Mailly, Mme de, 51
Maine, duc de, 17
mainmorte, 110, 156
Maintenon, Mme de, 18–19
Maison du roi, ministre de la, 32
Malesherbes, 106, 109, 130
Mallet du Pan, 249
Manon Lescaut, 20, 25
manufactures, *see* industry
manufactures royales, 44
Marat, 167, 182, 195, 200, 203–4, 209, 224, 228, 243, 245
marc d'argent, 167
Maria Theresa, 68, 70, 72, 75, 78, 94, 98, 113, 117–18
Mariage de Figaro, le, 116
Marie-Antoinette, 94, 98, 110, 113–20, 125, 147, 172, 181–2, 188–9, 194, 225
Marie Leczinska, 28
Marigny, 55
Marivaux, 55–6
Marly, 145
marque de cuir, 60
marriage, laws of, 175
Marseille, 40, 48, 194, 224, 242
Martinique, 73, 80, 88
Masséna, 235, 257
Maupeou, 94–6, 99–100, 104, 107, 131, 141
Maupertuis, 101
Maurepas, 33, 70, 78, 99–100, 103–4, 107, 109, 123, 125
Maurice de Saxe, *see* Saxe, Maurice de
maximum on prices, 227
Mazarin, 10, 12, 32, 34, 79
Meissonier, 55
Mercy-Argenteau, comte de, 117
merveilleuses, 252
Meslier, 85
Mesmer, 119
métayers, 154
Metz, 71, 150, 182, 192, 200, 232
militia, 108
Minden, battle of, 79
Minorca, 78, 121
Miquelon, island of, 121
Mirabeau, bailli de, 103
Mirabeau, comte de, 133, 136, 174, 180–2, 191
Miromesnil, 107
Mississipi, le, 25–6
Mœurs, Les, 85
Montaigne, 82–3
Montcalm, 80
Montespan, marquise de, 17
Montesquieu, 26, 29, 53, 84, 86, 129, 166
Montmorin, 128, 129
Montpellier, 62
Montreal, 73
monts de piété, 110

Moreau, 235
Mountain, the, 209, 212, 215–18, 222–3, 227
Muscadins, 243
music, 54, 115

Nancy, 36, 42
   mutiny at, 177
Nantais, trial of the, 244
Nantes, 29, 224
   massacres at, 224
   revocation of edict of, *see* Edict of
Narbonne, comte de, 190–2
National Guard, 153, 157–8, 161, 184, 194, 196, 198–9, 201, 207, 216, 224 245–7
Nattier, 115
natural frontiers, 211
navy, French, 91, 109, 236–7
Necker, 110–11, 123–9, 132–3, 136, 142–8, 150, 177
Necker, Mme, 123
Neerwinden, battle of, 213
New Orleans, 25–6
Newton, 82, 101
Nice, 208, 255
Nîmes, 41
Noailles, archbishop of Paris, 63–4
Noailles, duc de, maréchal, 23, 50–1, 85
Noailles, Mme de, 117
Noailles, vicomte de, 158
noblesse, 10, 12, 21–2, 61, 108–9, 132, 143, 145
Nootka Sound, dispute, 187
Notables, Assembly of, 127–9, 134

October Days, 161–2
octrois, 58
Orange, Prince of, *see* Stadtholder
Orateur du Peuple, l', 242
Oratorians, 89, 220
Orleanist faction, 132, 135, 148, 185
Orleans, 58
Orléans, duc d', 132, 135, 148, 150, 161, 185, 225
Orleans, Philip of, Regent, 17–19, 21–3, 28
Orry, 33, 44, 47, 60–1, 70
Ottoman Empire, relations with, 36, 39 125–6

Pacte de famille, 81, 91, 95, 187
pacte de famine, 100, 105, 141
painting, 19, 29, 55, 115, 179–80
Palais Royal, 21, 135, 148, 243
Panthéon, 179, 245
Paoli, 92
Papacy, 174
Paris, 41, 47–8, 58, 110–11, 147–50, 160

Paris, Commune, *see* Commune of Pisar
   municipality of, 153
   Peace of, 81
Pâris, deacon, 64
Pâris-Duverney, Pâris brothers, 34, 38, 53, 61, 69, 79, 126
parlements, 18, 31, 36, 61–7, 80, 86–90, 94–7, 100, 105–7, 118, 120, 129–36, 138, 146, 164
Pascal, 63, 82
Patriots, Dutch, 122–3
Pau, 133, 141
péages, 155
peasantry, 49, 141–2, 154–8, 252, 263
Père Duchesne, le, 195, 228–9
Perrault, 19
Pétion, 197, 225
Petit Trianon, 114, 116–17
Philip V, of Spain, 16, 27, 51
Philippe Égalité, *see* Orléans, duc, d'
Phillipsburg, capture of, 35
philosophes, 87, 123, 173
Physiocrats, 92, 103–4
Pichegru, 235
Pilnitz, Manifesto of, 188
Pitt, the elder, 78
Pitt, the younger, 111, 188
plague, 48
Pluche, abbé, 101
Poissin, Jean Antoinette, *see* Pompadour, Mme de
Poitiers, 42
Poland, 34–6, 75, 97, 188
Polignac, Cardinal de, 64
Polignacs, the, 117, 126, 151
Polish Succession, War of, 35–6
Polish throne, candidature for, 75
Polysynodie, 21–2, 27
Pompadour, Mme de, 53–6, 61–2, 77, 79–80, 92–4, 116
ponts et chaussées, corps des, 47
population, 48–50, 139, 154
portion congrue, 65, 110
Port-Royal, 9, 63
posts, 106
Pragmatic Sanction, 36
Prague, capture of, 69
   retreat from, 70
prairial, 1e, 246
prairial, law of, 22, 238
premier ministre, 32, 51, 90
pre-romanticism, 114
Prévost, abbé, 20
Prie, Mme de, 28–9
Prieur of the Côte d'Or, 218, 220, 238, 242
Prieur of the Marne, 218, 220
Protestants, *see* Huguenots
Provence, comte de, 118, 249
provincial assemblies, 127, 132
Prussia, 69, 75, 123, 188, 206, 254

Quebec, 73, 80
Quesnay, Dr, 103
Quesnel, 63
Qu'est-ce que le Tiers État?, 136, 165
question, 110, 175
Quiberon, battle of, 80
    expedition of, 250
Quincampoix, rue, 25

Rabelais, 82
Racine, 20
Rameau, 54
Ramsay, le chevalier, 21, 84
Raynal, 169
Rayneval, 123
Réaumur, 101
Récamier, Mme, 251
Regency, 17–27
Regency, Council of, 17–18, 22
Regent, *see* Orleans, Philip of
Reims, 44
Rennes, 38, 41, 48, 93, 133
republicanism, 183, 186
Reubell, 253, 256
Réveillon riots, 148
reversal of Alliances, 78
Revolutionary Tribunal, 215, 224, 238, 244
Revolutionary War, 186–92, 200–1, 204–9, 213–14, 224, 235–6, 254–7
Rhine frontier, 211
Richelieu, cardinal de, 10, 32, 34, 62, 79
Richelieu, duc de, 50, 79
Richer, Edmond, 65
richerism, 65, 88
Rigaud, 29
Rivoli, battle of, 255
roads, 46–7
Robert, Hubert, 179
Robespierre, Augustin, 241
Robespierre, Maximilien, 137, 167–8, 179, 183–4, 190, 197–8, 200, 204, 209–10, 212, 218, 221–2, 226, 230–5, 238–41, 256
Rochambeau, 121
rococo, 55
Rodney, 121
Rohan, cardinal de, 64, 98, 118–20
Roland, 191, 194–5, 196, 199, 205, 209, 225
Roland, Mme, 191, 194–5, 197, 209, 217
Rosicrucians, 119
Rossbach, battle of, 79
Rossignol, 195
Rotundo, 196
Rouen, 42, 58, 182
Rouillé, 76
Rousseau, Jean-Jacques, 20, 55, 114–15, 163, 169
Rouveray, de, 211

Roux, Jacques, 214, 227
Royal Session, 145–6

St-Antoine, faubourg de, 149, 198, 246–7
St Domingo, 74, 193
Saint-Germain, comte de, 107–9
Saint-Germain, faubourg de, 41
Saint-Honoré, faubourg de, 41
Saint-Huruge, marquis de, 195
Saint-Just, 218, 221, 232, 238–41
Saint-Malo, 39–40
Saint-Pierre, abbé de, 84, 102
Saint-Pierre, island of, 121
Saint-Simon, duc de, 11, 15–16, 21–2, 33
Saint-Vincent, 80–1
St Vincent, battle of, 255
Saintes, battle of, 121
Salpétrière, prison of, 120, 202
saltpetre, manufacture of, 106
sans-culottes, 227–8
Santa Lucia, 80, 121
Santerre, 195, 198, 207
Saratoga, capitulation of, 117
Sardinia, 35, 71, 255
Sartine, 109
Savoy, 208, 211, 229, 255
Saxe, Maurice de, 71–2, 108
Saxon party, 72, 76
Saxony, 78
Scheldt, opening of, 211–12
science, 101–2
Second Coalition, 256
secret du roi, 76, 97–8, 121
Secretaries of State, 32, 51, 70, 77
Sections of Paris, 197–8, 216, 223, 227–8, 247–8
Ségur, comte de (son of following), 122
Ségur, marquis de, 128–9
seigneurial dues, 43, 155–6
Senegal, 24, 79, 81, 122
separation of powers, 166
September massacres, 117, 157, 202–3
Serrurier, 235
Seven Years War, 40, 55, 74, 79–81
Sèvres, china manufacture, 44, 54
Sieyes, 135–6, 144, 165, 167, 250, 256, 258
Silesia, 69–70, 72, 75, 78–9
silk manufacture, 43, 45, 224
slavery, slave trade, 39, 175
Société des amis des Noirs, 175
Société de Trente, 135–6
Soissons, camp at, 197
Soubise, prince de, 79, 98
South Sea Bubble, 25
sovereignty of the people, 84, 165–7, 233
Spain, alliance with, *see pacte de famille*
Spain, relations with, 26–7, 34, 81, 120–1, 187
Spectacle de la nature, 101
spinning jennies, 45

Spires, 208
Stadtholder, 122
Staël, Mme de, 190, 251
Stanhope, 27
Stanislaus Leczinski, 28, 34–6, 42, 92
Stanislaus Poniatowski, 97
States-General, *see États généraux*
Suffren, bailli de, 121
Swiss Guard, 149, 199, 202

Taille, 58, 105
Talleyrand, 135, 172, 191, 211, 258
Tallien, 239–40, 242, 244
taxation, 24, 56–60
Teissier, 38
Tencin, cardinal de, 50, 52
Tencin, Mme de, 50
tennis-court oath, 145, 180
Tenth of August, revolution of, 198–200
Tercier, 76
Terray, abbé, 94–7, 99, 104–5, 124–5
Terror, the, 215–16, 224–6, 237–8
theatre, 55, 114–15, 174
Thermidor, Ninth of, 240–1
Thermidoreans, 241–2
Tiers État, 134–6, 138, 141, 143–8, 157, 162–3, 165, 264
Tobago, 81, 121
toiles peintes, 44
toleration, edict of, 109
Torcy, 17
torture, *see question*
Toulon, 224, 229, 236
Toulouse, 14, 86, 128, 133, 232
Toulouse, archbishop of, *see* Brienne, Loménie de
Toulouse, comte de, 17
Tournai, battle of, 193
Toussaint, 85
towns, 48
Townshend, 34
trade, overseas, 23–4, 37, 39–40
Traité des sensations, 86
Traité des systèmes, 102
Triple Alliance of 1717, 27
Tuileries, 21, 42, 162, 183, 196, 199, 210, 216
Turgot, 103–9, 111, 123–4
Turkey, *see* Ottoman Empire

Unemployment, 139–40
Union of Orders, 144–7
United Provinces, 71–2, 111, 121–3, 213
utilitarianism, 89–8

Utrecht, Treaty of, 17, 39

Vadier, 240, 242
vagabondage, 49, 140
Valenciennes, 224
Valmy, 204–5
Valois, club des, 177
Vanloo, Carlo, 55
Varennes, flight to, 182–3
Varlet, 214, 227
Vatican, *see* Papacy
Vauban, 24
Vaucanson, 145
Vaux-le-Vicomte, 10
Venaissin, 174, 187
venality, 13, 24, 30, 171–2
Vendée, 159
Vendée, revolt of, 214, 224, 229, 236, 249
vendémiaire, 13e, 251
Verdun, fall of, 200
Vergennes, 98, 107, 111, 120, 123, 128, 176
Vergniaud, 186, 196, 210, 225
Verona, manifesto of, 249
Versailles, 11–12, 21, 58, 160–1, 202
Versailles, Treaty of (1756), 77
   (1783), 121
veto, royal, 166
Vie de Marianne, 56
Vienna, Treaty of, 34
Vieux Cordelier, le, 230
Villars, 17, 35
Vincennes, 21
vingtième, 61–2, 97
Vintimille, Mme de, 51
Voltaire, 9, 11, 53, 55, 83, 85, 87–8, 96, 101–2, 173, 242

Walpole, Robert, 34–5, 69–70
Watteau, 19
Wattignies, battle of, 229
West Indies, French, 39–40, 73–4, 80–1, 121
Westminster, Convention of, 75, 77
Westphalia, Treaty of, 79
White Terror, 244
Wickham, William, 252
Windham, 188
Wolfe, General, 80
Wordsworth, 169
Worms, 208

Yorktown, capitulation of, 121
Young, Arthur, 40, 47, 60, 154, 187

MORE ABOUT PENGUINS
AND PELICANS

Penguinews, which appears every month, contains details of all the new books issued by Penguins as they are published. From time to time it is supplemented by *Penguins in Print*, which is a complete list of all titles available. (There are some five thousand of these.)

A specimen copy of *Penguinews* will be sent to you free on request. For a year's issues (including the complete lists) please send 50p if you live in the British Isles, or 75p if you live elsewhere. Just write to Dept EP, Penguin Books Ltd, Harmondsworth, Middlesex, enclosing a cheque or postal order, and your name will be added to the mailing list.

In the U.S.A.: For a complete list of books available from Penguin in the United States write to Dept CS, Penguin Books Inc., 7110 Ambassador Road, Baltimore, Maryland 21207.

In Canada: For a complete list of books available from Penguin in Canada write to Penguin Books Canada Ltd, 41 Steelcase Road West, Markham, Ontario.

A HISTORY OF MODERN FRANCE
VOLUME 2: 1799-1871

The second volume of Professor Cobban's *History of Modern France* begins with the refashioning of French laws and institutions under Napoleon Bonaparte in 1799 and ends with the Commune of Paris in 1871. While there is an ample supply of 'facts', Professor Cobban devotes most attention to the great turning points of the period; he does not aim to force agreement with his own interpretation but rather to stimulate the reader to ask his own questions and formulate his own judgements.

A HISTORY OF MODERN FRANCE
VOLUME 3: 1871-1962

This volume covers the period from the Franco-Prussian war to de Gaulle.

In this book, Professor Cobban steers the reader skilfully through the political and social problems besetting modern France. His balanced and stimulating account of the three republics is invaluable to anyone interested in the development and present position of a great European nation.